RELIGION AND CULTURE IN NATIVE AMERICA

SUZANNE CRAWFORD O'BRIEN
Pacific Lutheran University

With INÉS TALAMANTEZ

D1210781

ROWMAN & LITTLEFIELD
Lanham • Boulder • New York • London

Executive Editor: Natalie Mandziuk
Editorial Assistant: Deni Remsberg
Higher Education Channel Manager: Jonathan Raeder

Credits and acknowledgments for material borrowed from other sources, and reproduced with permission, appear on the appropriate pages within the text.

Published by Rowman & Littlefield
An imprint of The Rowman & Littlefield Publishing Group, Inc.
4501 Forbes Boulevard, Suite 200, Lanham, Maryland 20706
www.rowman.com

6 Tinworth Street, London SE11 5AL, United Kingdom

British Library Cataloguing in Publication Information Available

Library of Congress Cataloging-in-Publication Data

Names: Crawford O'Brien, Suzanne J., author. | Talamantez, Inés, author.
Title: Religion and Culture in Native America / Suzanne Crawford O'Brien, Pacific Lutheran University ; with Inés Talamantez.
Description: Lanham : Rowman & Littlefield, [2020] | Includes bibliographical references and index.
Identifiers: LCCN 2019045558 (print) | LCCN 2019045559 (ebook) | ISBN 9781538104743 (cloth) | ISBN 9781538104750 (paperback) | ISBN 9781538104767 (epub)
Subjects: LCSH: Indians of North America—Rites and ceremonies. | Indians of North America—Religion. | Indians of North America—Social life and customs.
Classification: LCC E98.R3 C7553 2020 (print) | LCC E98.R3 (ebook) | DDC 299.7—dc23
LC record available at https://lccn.loc.gov/2019045558
LC ebook record available at https://lccn.loc.gov/2019045559

♾™ The paper used in this publication meets the minimum requirements of American National Standard for Information Sciences—Permanence of Paper for Printed Library Materials, ANSI/NISO Z39.48-1992.

This book is dedicated to the memory of Professor Inés Talamantez, my teacher, mentor, dear friend, and coconspirator. This book would not exist if not for her and her passionate commitment to this work. Sadly, Inés passed away just as this book was going to press. She will be deeply missed.

Professor Inés Talamantez and Suzanne Crawford O'Brien, June 2003.
(Photo by Michael O'Brien)

CONTENTS

Acknowledgments

I MUST BEGIN BY OFFERING DEEP GRATITUDE to my mentor and friend Inés Talamantez. Without her, I would not be doing the work I am doing, and this book would never have been written. Thank you for so many years of heartfelt lessons, long drives, late-night songs, laughter, and friendship. Gratitude is also due to the many colleagues who gave generously of their time to read drafts of this book, offering corrections, suggestions, and new ideas: Natalie Avalos, Seth Dowland, Dennis Kelley, Michelle Jacob, Matt Mais, Angela McComb Sanchez, and Kevin O'Brien. Any remaining errors or oversights are of course mine alone. Thanks as well to the students in my Native American Religious Traditions class at Pacific Lutheran University, who heard from early drafts, and whose questions and curiosity helped to guide the writing and revising of this project. Sincere gratitude to the artists and photographers who gave permission for us to reprint their work in this volume: Christi Belcourt, Scott D. Hall, Christopher Griner, Ossie Michelin, Kent Monkman, Linda Roy, and Ryan Vizzions. And a particular thanks to my dear friend, mapmaker, and GIS goddess extraordinaire, Elizabeth O'Dea Springborn, who graciously created the maps that accompany each of the chapters in this book. Thanks to my parents, Jeanne and Timothy Crawford, whose empathy, faith in me, and generous gifts of food and childcare make all things possible. Finally and always, it's impossible to adequately express gratitude enough for the two souls closest to my heart, Michael and Declan. Your love, your patience, and your faith forever astound and surprise me in the best of ways. You always bring the light, helping me see what really matters. (And Declan: *Yes*, the next time I write a book, it will be a middle-grade fantasy replete with trolls and talking rodents. I promise.)

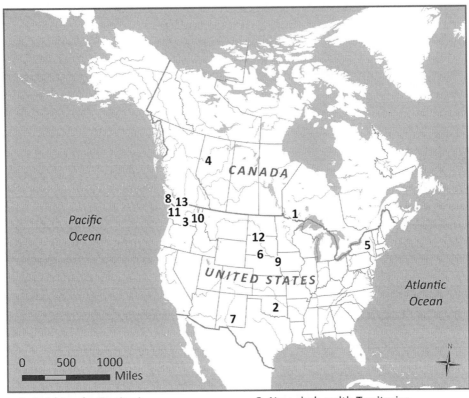

1 Anishinaabe Territories
2 Citizen Potawatomi Nation
3 Columbia River Tribes
4 Dane Zaa Nation (Beaver)
5 Haudenosaunee (Iroquois) Territory
6 Lakota Territories
7 Mescalero Apache Tribe

8 Nuu-chah-nulth Territories
9 Omaha Tribe
10 Schitsu'umsh (Coeur D'Alene) Tribe
11 Skokomish Nation
12 Standing Rock Sioux Tribe
13 Stó:lō First Nation

Map 1.1. Map of North America locating the tribal communities, nations, and cultural groups mentioned in this chapter. Basemap data made with Natural Earth. (Liz O'Dea Springborn)

Practical Reverence, Radical Reciprocity   1
Indigenous Theories of Religion

When the Creator was preparing to bring humans onto the earth, Creator called a grand council of all the animal people, plant people, and everything else. In those days, the animals and plants were more like people because they could talk. He asked each one to give a gift to the humans—a gift to help them survive, since humans were pitiful and would die without help. The first to come forward was Salmon. He gave the humans his body for food. The second to give a gift was Water. She promised to be the home to the salmon. After that, everyone else gave the humans a gift, but it was special that the first to give their gifts were Salmon and Water. When the humans finally arrived, the Creator took away the animals' power of speech and gave it to the humans. He told the humans that since the animals could no longer speak for themselves, it was a human responsibility to speak for the animals. To this day, Salmon and Water are always served first at tribal feasts to remember the story and honor the First Foods.

                         Columbia River Inter-Tribal Fish Commission, Creation Story

NOW, THERE ARE A LOT OF THINGS going on with this story, and if you're paying attention, it'll give you a lot to think about. What's this about *animal* and *plant people*? (Aren't human beings the only people?) And what about those humans! They're described as *pitiful*, dependent upon the generosity and kindness of other species—down to the gift of their very lives. (Aren't humans supposed to be the ultimate pinnacle creation? The ones who run the show?) And what's this talk of *responsibility*? (Don't we get to *subdue* the earth?) And how are human beings supposed to speak for animals anyway? For fish? (How in the world would we know what to say?)

This story demands that we rethink some very fundamental ideas about who we are and why we're here: and that's what religious traditions are all about.

Of course, we also shouldn't think that one story is going to do the job.

After all, writing this book meant facing a fundamental conundrum: how to tell the story of religious and cultural life in Native North America when there is no one story. There are in fact millions of stories, each drawing on lived experience, family memory, and deeply held cultural beliefs.

In the 2015 census, 6.6 million people, 2 percent of the U. S. population, identified as American Indian or Alaska Native, and 1.5 million people as Native Hawaiian or Pacific Islander. As of 2018, there were 573 federally recognized tribes in the United States. In Canada, 1.8 million people claim Indigenous ancestry (5.6 percent of the population), and there are more than 600 First Nations tribes or bands, and 3,100 Indian reserves. Each of these communities has its own history, tradition, worldview, language and dialect, and each has its own understanding of what it means to be Indigenous, how to honor the sacred, and how to go about doing the work of being an ethical person in the world. For some, this means reclaiming the traditions of their ancestors. For others, it means creating their own individual blend of popular culture, Christianity, intertribal ceremonies, and family traditions. What it means to be Native American and how individuals and communities work this out is no simple thing. Given such diversity, trying to craft an introduction to Native American cultures and traditions is indeed a daunting task.

Redefining Religion

Despite this challenge, it is our hope that this book points students, teachers, and interested readers toward work by Native scholars and their allies that explores and celebrates the resurgence and diversity of Indigenous cultures in Native North America. We also hope to push the boundaries of what is thought of as "religion." Indigenous spirituality is found in oral traditions and ceremonies, but it is also found in YouTube videos, political protests, health clinics, creative arts, and community gardens.

Religion is a complicated term. In European and Euroamerican parlance, the term has historically been based on a series of binaries: something is religious or secular, sacred or profane, clean or unclean, natural or supernatural. The word *religion* also usually implies a codified list of rules and theological ideas, a priestly class, a temple, a system of sacrifice or payment. It assumes, in other words, a whole host of things that simply did not exist in most Native North American cultures and communities prior to colonialism.

As is often noted, there is no word equivalent to *religion* in Indigenous languages. Mary Lou Fox (Anishinaabe) puts it this way:

> If you ask me to differentiate between organized religion and religion of Indian people, we really don't have a religion per se, but really it's a way of life and we call it *anishnaabe bimaadiziwin*. It's just the way you live and it's something that's really twenty-four hours a day. It's your thinking and it's not like just on Sunday that you go to church or that you pray at a certain time. But really they say that every act should be an act of thanksgiving and praise. (Smith, 25)

From this perspective, the sacred quality of life is not just experienced in a cathedral or a church service: it happens in a fishing boat, in a dialysis center, in a classroom, in an artist's studio.

Thus, this book might surprise readers who are looking for a more classical approach to the study of religion, one dictated by the categories considered standard in scholarly textbooks. This book does talk about visions, encounters with spiritual beings, and sacred ceremonies. And, its primary concern is with the lived concerns of Native people and how they are informed by their philosophical traditions and spiritual principles. This is what religious studies scholars sometimes call "religion on the ground."

For instance, Michael Zogry has pointed out another complicating factor in standard notions of "religion." The assumption has been that

> everyone in the world—monotheists and "idolators" alike—has some kind of religion, and their ceremonies share many characteristics. . . . Peoples are alike more than they are different in their attitudes toward religion. . . . In a nutshell, this is the classic recipe for world religions textbooks. . . . If all religions shared certain qualities, then distillation of those qualities might reveal a universal underlying religion. (Zogry, 9–10)

As Zogry argues, this search for a universal underlying religion was historically shaped by the goals of European imperialism: just as a single monarch might rule the globe, a single religion or universal truth (and singular interpretation of that truth) might enforce that rule. The problem with this universalism is that it ends up erasing the ways in which Indigenous worldviews stand in opposition to settler colonialism—the ways in which they are simply different—and the possible new ways of seeing the world that they might offer. (The term *settler colonialism* refers to the process of displacing Indigenous peoples by an invasive settler society, as well as the culture of those settlers and their descendants, which works to occlude the ongoing presence of Indigenous peoples and refute their territorial claims.) In this context, Indigenous traditions are reduced to a more primitive form of some universal truth—the culmination of which is presumably found in European and Euroamerican Christianity—instead of taken on their own terms.

Our hope is that this book contributes to the recognition of *Indigenous* theories of religious and spiritual traditions. Rather than trying to fit Indigenous experience within Western categories and perspectives, this book considers the categories of concern put forth by Native communities themselves. Some of the questions that drove us were these: When one begins with cultures and communities as the foundation of knowledge, what do we see? What are the modes of rhetoric through which Indigenous knowledge about sacred power is conveyed? How are young people taught to observe, to hear, to pay attention? What are Native theories of healing? What does it mean to them to be healthy and live in balanced relationships with the natural world? As Inés Talamantez says, these ways of knowing may not be what academics are used to calling "theory," but that is what they are. They are cultural manifestations of concerns for body, mind, and spirit. As Talamantez contends, there *is* such a thing as Indigenous theory, and these communities and cultures do not need academics to tell them why they live the way they do: they are the experts on what it means to live ethically, to be compassionate, to understand concepts of power—and these understandings differ by family, by tribal community, and by region. When something emerges from a particular place, it is *autochthonous*. And these are autochthonous theories, growing from a people's relationship with place. These are ocean theories. Desert theories. Mountain theories. Forest theories. The goal of any contemporary scholar working with and alongside tribal communities must therefore be this: to find *their* theories, perhaps to bring them into conversation with other theoretical notions, but never to simply impose those outside categories upon them.

So, while we begin this book with common themes found throughout Native North America, we also begin with an important caveat: Indigenous communities each see the world through their own lens, informed by distinct and local relationships forged with places, ecosystems, and the other-than-human persons that share their territories. At the same time, amid this remarkable diversity, there are core values, shared experiences, and ways of seeing the world that continue to shape the contours of Native North America.

Learning How to Listen

One of the first lessons many Native children learn is how to listen: to sit quietly with their elders, and to *pay attention*. Don't ask questions right away. Watch carefully, and then think about what you've been given. For educators, there is an important pedagogical lesson here, and one that informs this book. The story that begins this chapter issues a call to speak for the animal people, and the salmon in particular, and this requires a very special kind of listening: How do you hear those who don't speak with a human voice?

Many Indigenous spiritual practices are intended to facilitate this different kind of listening. Internal silence is cultivated through the work that enables spiritual listening: fasting, prayer, and isolation. Seeking visions is an important part of many (but not all) Native spiritual traditions. Undertaken in isolation, an individual might go without food, water, or comfort in the hopes of hearing something, learning something, or perhaps having a transformational experience. This sounds like a pretty lonely thing to do. But in reality, such experiences are far from solitary. Anthropologist Robin Ridington has worked in partnership with the Dane-zaa (Beaver) people of British Columbia and Alberta for decades, and he explains:

> Although it is ultimately personal and begun in isolation, the quest is fundamentally conversational and social. Power comes from a person's conversation with the supernatural. It comes from an encounter with sentient beings with whom humans share the breath of life. . . . Power comes to people who listen carefully to the storied world around them. It comes when the story of a person's life joins the circle

of conversation. Power comes when a person realizes a story that already exists. Power comes when he or she adds a new episode to that story. It comes when the story of a person's life becomes that of life as a whole. . . . Power comes through conversation with natural and spiritual beings who appear as people. It is negotiated as a social relationship. (Ridington, 471)

Conversation with this storied world happens in many ways. In vision quests, yes, but also in the act of cultivating plants, of working with materials to weave a basket or to make medicinal tea. Conversation with the living world happens in listening to stories that have been embedded in the landscape. When you see the place where Coyote was taught a particularly painful lesson, the land speaks, and the conversation continues.

Skokomish elder and religious leader *subiyay* (Gerald Bruce Miller) encouraged people to listen to the teachings of the plant people. He recalled:

My aunt Emily, was who I asked if she'd show me how to make a basket. Before I was ten years old. And she says, I'm not gonna show you anything until you gather me some material. And at that time you actually only had to go across from the little house she lived in and down by the marsh to gather material. Now none grows there at all. That's how much the environment changed in the course of my adolescent years to my adult years. Some plants and things disappeared from the region. Period! We lost an interest in what the plant people had to say to us. We lost an interest in what the environment has to say to us. It's beginning to awaken now. We see the rainforest vanishing before our eyes. We see the water that reflected the path of life become so polluted we can't even swim in it. The environment has been trying to tell us. The air has been trying to tell us. The water has been trying to tell us. *Listen to us*. (*Teachings of the Tree People*)

Listening to the natural world isn't easy. For Robin Wall Kimmerer (Potawatomi), listening happens at the intersection of spirituality and science. A botanist, Kimmerer challenges her students to consider Indigenous teachings about the personhood of plants and animals, teaching that Native elders "remind us of the capacity of others as our teachers, as holders of knowledge, as guides. Imagine walking through a richly inhabited world of Birch people, Bear people, Rock people, beings we think of and therefore speak of as persons worthy of our respect, of inclusion in a peopled world" (Kimmerer, 58). When she considers the enormous challenges we face—climate change, water pollution, species extinction—Kimmerer reminds us that we are not alone. The Creator has given us teachers. "Plants know how to repair a place—heal the land, build up soil. Our job is to listen to them, follow their lead, and help" (Kimmerer, 333).

Lawrence Gross (Anishinaabe) reflects on Indigenous lessons about how to listen in his work as well. He puts it this way:

First, silence helps open one's heart and mind to the world. Second, once the heart and mind are open to the world, one can make the next step and become a very keen observer of the world as well, able to discern and appreciate the inconsistencies and incongruities of life. For the Anishinaabe, observing the world helps make them good listeners. They can hear the stories the natural world has to tell. Finally, being good listeners helps them relate those stories by being good storytellers. (Gross 2007, 70–71)

Gratitude and Reciprocity

Respectful listening is a first step on a path toward more ethical relationships: When we listen, we learn compassion and gratitude and begin to understand real reciprocity. Indigenous stories and ceremonies call on us to stop seeing the earth as a collection of resources to be extracted, used, and discarded. Instead, they show us a living world filled with gifts from the Creator. In the face of such abundant unmerited generosity, the response must be gratitude. These traditions also make clear that gratitude is not simply an expression of thanks, but essential for survival.

Two origin stories, told on opposite ends of North America, each teach of the dangers of forgetting gratitude. The first is a southern Coast Salish story, told by *subiyay* (Gerald Bruce Miller). The Coast Salish are a large cultural and linguistic group occupying the broader Fraser River and Puget Sound region, with communities as far south as the Oregon coast and as far north as British Columbia. There are over ninety different Coast Salish tribes and nations and fourteen different dialects, with a corresponding diversity of traditions and practices. For some of these communities, this story is considered one of their most important.

"The Origin of the Bone Game"

Long ago, when humans and animals were still able to talk to one another, they were given rules by the Creator. The animals were the first people. They were given the rules for learning how to survive in this land—for learning how to go through the hardships, joys, and frustrations of life. Through their sagas came the teachings for the human beings who were created later. The animals were given laws to protect them from the four seeds of destruction: greed, lust, hate and jealousy. . . . When human beings were created, they were told to observe the animals and to learn, through watching them, their laws and behavior and the repercussions they would face if these laws were broken. If humans obeyed the laws, the weather would stay warm all the year round, the food plants would grow in abundance, and there would be no sickness anywhere in the land. Everyone would grow and thrive.

But as time went on, the humans began to forget the promises they had made to the Creator. They forgot the Huckleberry Feast, the Salmon Feast, the First Elk Ceremony, and the Cedar Ceremony. Because food was abundant, they forgot to give thanks for each day's bounty. Then they began to desire each other's mates. They began to covet another tribe's territory. They began to copy each other's way of dressing. These things caused much jealousy and anger among the tribes. Soon anger flared into hate and the tribes began to war.

The Creator was angry at the breaking of laws, and cast hardship upon the land. He poisoned the salt water, dried up the fresh water, and stopped the life-giving rain.

The food began to disappear. But still the people fought one another. Soon they began to starve, because there was no more food.

The humans were defenseless creatures, for they had been given no special talents. They had no claws, no fur, no beaks with which to defend themselves. They were at the mercy of the animal people, who found them easy prey. One by one, the tribes became extinct.

You could see the people's bones scattered about the prairie. Other tribes became so small there were only a few members left. Soon the people began to eat one another. The strong preyed on the weak, and fear ravaged the land. One day, parents might be cuddling a child, the next day devouring it. Or the child might be stronger, and might prey on its elders just to survive.

There came a time when there were just a few elders left who remembered the days when the laws were obeyed and everyone lived in harmony. These elders called the animals and the people together to work out a truce. They said, "Let's go to the mountain. There is one called the Creator who made all of us. Let us go and call for aid. . . ."

The Creator told them a game would be played, and explained the rules: "Scores will be kept with the bones of trees. They will be marked in two pairs. . . . The losers will be food for the winners until the end of time."

Immediately all the animals joined on the same side. They alone had spirit songs. On the other side were the human beings, who had nothing. They situated themselves to play. . . .

Soon the animals were pointing to one tribe of humans and saying, "These humans are going to be our food until the end of time."

The humans began to grow desperate. . . . All that the humans could see were the animals bearing down upon them, choosing their food until the end of time. The humans huddled together and prayed to the Great Spirit for help. They vowed to keep alive the Huckleberry Ceremony, the Salmon Ceremony, the First Elk Ceremony, and the Cedar Ceremony. They vowed to keep alive the laws against the four seeds of destruction. They prayed until their prayer was heard. The Creator answered by giving them songs, granting them the right to sing the songs of the animals. (Ryan, Smyth, and Hilbert, 37–43)

With the help of those songs, humanity won. But it was *close!* The story accounts for the origin of the bone game (also known as the *stick game* or *slahal*), which is still played throughout the Pacific Northwest. The people still sing those spirit songs, remembering the enormous cost of forgetting to give thanks, for forgetting gratitude.

Across the continent, in Haudenosaunee (Iroquois) territory, the Great Tree of Peace was long ago planted to commemorate another hard-won truce among warring peoples. This truce resulted in the establishment of the well-known Iroquois Confederacy—an alliance of Iroquoian-speaking tribes in the northeastern United States that include the Mohawk, Onondaga, Oneida, Cayuga, Seneca, and Tuscarora. As in the previous story, the people forgot to live in gratitude. Jealous and

Photo 1.1.   Bone game at the Swinomish smokehouse. The January 22, 1946, Treaty Day Celebration at the Swinomish Reservation at La Conner, Washington, featured the gambling game known as *slahal*, or the bone game. Two teams of players sit in lines facing one another, with one player holding the pair of bones and the others singing and beating time with sticks and a drum. This photograph shows one line of players. Abel D. Joe of Swinomish sits to the left of a group of tall scoring sticks placed in the ground. He sings while holding one of the game bones in his open hand. (MOHAI, Seattle Post-Intelligencer Collection, PI 23871)

greedy, they fought among themselves, and one war led to another, until it seemed peace could never be reached. It was only with the establishment of the Great Law of Peace, embodied in the Great Tree of Peace, that warfare ended. But for peace to continue, the people had to remember gratitude, to teach it to their children, and remember it anew every day. The elders knew that wouldn't be easy. So they composed the Thanksgiving Address, a lengthy oration, still spoken at the beginning of significant public events, that continues to serve as a powerful reminder of the importance of gratitude. The prayer begins: "Today we have gathered and we see that the cycles of life continue. We have been given the duty to live in balance and harmony with each other and all living things. So now, we bring our minds together as one as we give greetings and thanks to each other as people."

Then, in turn, the people thank their Mother the Earth, the Waters, the Fish, the Plants, the Food Plants, the Medicine Herbs, the Animals, the Trees, the Birds, the Four Winds, the Grandfather Thunderers, the Sun, Grandmother Moon, the Stars, the Enlightened Teachers who have taught the people over previous generations,

Photo 1.2.   Suquamish game pieces made from decorated deer bones, Washington, 1947. These carved deer shin bones are used in the bone game. These are the two female bones of two sets. The male bones have a circle of blackened sinew about their middle, but it is the female bone that is guessed for. Property of Sam Snider, Suquamish. (University of Washington Libraries, Special Collections, NA 817)

and the Creator. After each meditation, which expounds on the importance of these sacred persons in the world, the gathered community affirms, "Now our minds are one." This address, which might take anywhere from ten minutes to an hour to complete, requires everyone to pause, to reflect on their place in an interconnected cosmos, and their dependency upon the gifts of the Creator. United in gratitude, only then do they continue with community business.[1]

The World as Gift

In his work with the Schitsu'umsh (Coeur d'Alene), anthropologist Rodney Frey writes about the stories of the First People: Amotqn (Creator), Coyote, and Crane. These First People traveled the world, endowing it with the gifts that would later sustain human beings. These stories help the people remember that every berry picked, every root dug, every water potato unearthed, every deer successfully hunted, every salmon pulled from the river is a gift freely given out of generosity and kindness. As Frey writes, "To be Schitsu'umsh is to view Lake Coeur d'Alene and Grassy Mountain in terms of their spiritual and familial significance, and to share unselfishly and not abuse the gifts that emanate from that landscape" (Frey, 19). Awareness of the gift inspires a sense of kinship, a call to generosity, gratitude made manifest.

Kimmerer likewise challenges us to consider the radical notion of gratitude at the heart of Indigenous traditions. Seeing the world as gift rather than commodity, she argues, "changes everything." Disconnected from place and the hands that create them, commodities are reduced to a product for sale. But a gift "creates ongoing relationship." A gift inspires gratitude; it calls us to take good care, to cherish, and to dream up a way to return the favor. As she writes, "If all the world is a commodity, how poor we grow. When all the world is a gift in motion, how wealthy we become" (Kimmerer, 31). The lesson of the gift is a transformative one because gratitude breathes life into a desire to give back. Here is one of the essential teachings of Indigenous spirituality: that we are called to give back. As Kimmerer writes, "One of our responsibilities as human people is to find ways to enter into reciprocity with the more-than-human world." But how do we give back? This seems a terrific challenge, given the demands of our daily lives. Kimmerer answers: "We can do it through gratitude, through ceremony, through land stewardship, science, art, and in everyday acts of practical reverence" (Kimmerer, 190). Giving back happens in the daily work of caring for a place and cherishing its gifts. It happens in a life of compassion. This cherishing is enlivened by our present moment, when climate change, consumerism, and pollution threaten the very ground on which we stand. But Kimmerer offers something here as well:

> It is not enough to weep over our lost landscapes; we have to put our hands in the earth to make ourselves whole again. Even a wounded world is feeding us. Even a wounded world holds us, giving us moments of wonder and joy. I choose joy over despair. Not because I have my head in the sand, but because joy is what the earth gives me daily, and I must return the gift. (Kimmerer, 326)

Everything Is Alive, Everything Is Connected

This call for hope is tied to the final central theme we wanted to highlight in this introduction: the lesson that everything is alive, and everything is connected. Gratitude and reciprocity assume a *relationship* within which those sensibilities are expressed. And a relationship requires a some*one*, not merely a some*thing*. Indigenous traditions teach that we live in a sentient, interrelated world, a world made up of relatives, of plant and animal *people* who are animated (all by the same spirit), aware (each in their own way), communicating (each in their own fashion), and endowed with a purpose (particular to their place in creation). Rather than a hierarchical worldview where human beings are assumed to be the most important, Indigenous philosophies describe an interconnected web where all beings are endowed with the same spirit, and no species can claim ontological dominance. Each element of creation is a thread in the web: remove one, and the web collapses.

To illustrate this point, consider the Omaha idea of *wa'konda*, as described by Alice Fletcher and Francis LaFlesche:

> An invisible and continuous life permeates all things, seen and unseen. This life manifests itself in two ways. First, by causing to move: all motion, all actions of mind or body, are because of this invisible life. Second, by causing permanency of

structure and form, as in the rock, the physical features of the landscape, mountains, plains, streams, rivers, lakes, the animals, and man. This invisible life is similar to the will power of which man is conscious within himself, a power by which things are brought to pass. Through this mysterious life and power all things are related to one another and to man; the seen to the unseen, the dead to the living, a fragment of anything to its entirety. This invisible life and power is called *wakon'da*. (adapted from Alice Fletcher and Francis La Flesche 1911, 134; quoted in Ridington, 480)

A similar idea can be found in the northern Coast Salish Stoh:lo idea of *shxwelí* as explained by elder Rosaleen George:

A plant or animal is not just a resource to be exploited, but like an ancestor. There's a connection there, and that connection is known as *shxwelí*. . . . *Shxwelí* is what's referred to as the spirit or the life force, and everything has that spirit and everything's connected through that. "*Shxwelí* is inside us here." And Rosaleen put her hand in front of her and she said, "*shxwelí* is in your parents." She raised her hand higher and said, "then your grandparents, your great-grandparents, it's in your great-great-grandparents. It's in the rocks, it's in the trees, it's in the grass, it's in the ground. *Shxwelí* is everywhere. . . . What ties us? What ties us to the sturgeon? It's the *shxwelí*. The sturgeon has a *shxwelí*, we have a *shxwelí*. So we're connected to that." (Carlson, 55)

Echoes of these ideas can also be heard in the Lakota notion of *mitakuye oyasin* or the Anishinaabe idea of *gakina indinawemaaganag*, both translated as "all my relations." These are terms used as prayerful affirmation and entreaty, continual reminders that we exist in a mutually dependent network of relationships and that forgetting that essential truth comes at great cost.

Indigenous Pedagogy: Learning in Place

As a textbook, this book is intentionally crafted around Indigenous theories and pedagogies. We draw here upon the work of Inés Talamantez, Vine Deloria, Lawrence Gross, Rodney Frey, Greg Cajete, Joann Archibald, and Linda Tuhiwai Smith, among others, in suggesting that Indigenous pedagogies are guided by several key themes: holistic, place-based learning, relational responsibility, beauty, respect, and a commitment to decolonization. We encourage educators to consult works by these authors, and consider ways that Indigenous pedagogies might be integrated into their own classrooms.

Indigenous pedagogies emphasize holistic learning, addressing the whole person: mind, body, spirit, and community. This sense of an interconnected whole is reflected in the understanding that "religion" is not an isolated aspect of life but can be found in natural-resource-management programs, health and wellness initiatives, poetry, artwork, and philosophy.

Indigenous pedagogies also emphasize *place-based* learning. What sets Indigenous cultures apart from settler cultures is their relationship with place. Nuu-chah-nulth scholar Charlotte Cote puts it this way: "Indigenous culture is a manifestation in human terms of the environment that has been its sustaining foundation" (Cote, 205). Indigenous cultures are those cultures birthed from a particular place. Their language, worldviews, and ethic emerge from that ecosystem. And Indigenous religions, in turn, are the expression of a people's millennia-old relationship with a living place. Because of this, the study of Indigenous religions and cultures means working to understand the relationship between people and place, why these places must be protected, and how we can all live in better relationship with a particular place.

At the same time, this book challenges stereotypes of Native people as intrinsically spiritual or "at one with the earth," stereotypes that burden Indigenous people with an expectation that they live in harmony with nature, and castigate them mercilessly should they appear to fail to do so. By contrast, Indigenous traditions again and again show how *challenging* it is to live in balance with the natural world. This is no biologically or ethnically inborn trait. Rather, *it's hard work*. Gross reflects on this in his work as a teacher of Anishinaabe traditions when he writes: "By the end of the semester, I have dissuaded most of the students from their romantic notions about Indians being close to nature and instead have instilled them with a sense of the hard work and satisfaction that can come from maintaining healthy spiritual relationships with the Creator, spirits, other-than-humans, and human beings" (Gross 2010, 21). Stereotyping Native people as magically in tune with nature is also deeply problematic because it lets everyone else off the hook. Instead, Indigenous traditions and spiritual leaders do just the opposite: they remind us of the ethical imperative we all share to do the hard work required in order to live in good relationship with the land.

Indigenous pedagogies also guide students toward *relational responsibility*. This means that all people exist within networks of relationships that give us obligations and responsibilities to others. Within this context, the ideal of pure objectivity is not possible, nor is it ultimately desirable. Instead, elders demand that we consider the web of relationships in which we exist. Who are your relatives, both human and otherwise? What obligations do you have to them? How do these relationships influence how you see the world?

Indigenous cultures and traditions also teach about the importance of a *beautifully lived* life, one that exists in harmony and balance with other living things. This idea is found in the Diné (Navajo) notion of *hózhó*: "to walk in beauty." Within this book, we work to point out those ways in which Native communities are seeking to achieve and maintain this balance of the beautiful, ethical, and practical, and the ways their non-Native allies can support those efforts.

These pedagogies also emphasize the core value of *respect* in teaching, learning, and research. Historically, settler colonialism has exploited Indigenous communities, removing information and artifacts rather than empowering those communities to survive. Elders and other leaders remind non-Native scholars that they should work in partnership with tribal communities, producing scholarship that benefits those communities. Likewise, it is our hope that this book will in some way be a giving-back—an affirmation of the good work being done by Native communities and scholars, and a call to stand alongside tribal communities in the hard work they are doing.

Finally, Indigenous pedagogies are united by a commitment to *decolonization*. This book calls attention to the historical realities and ongoing consequences of colonialism. The displacement of Native people did not end in the nineteenth century but is still ongoing. To that end, this book challenges political systems that suppress Native people and cultures, and affirms the restoration of Indigenous sovereignty and cultural vitality. We acknowledge that Native elders and cultural leaders are the true experts, and that scholarship is validated only to the extent it is affirmed by those authoritative voices.

As stated earlier in this chapter, learning how to listen to other-than-human people is a profound and world-changing lesson, and an entrance to other kinds of listening. At the same time, this emphasis on respectful listening takes on a particular salience within the colonial context of Native North America, where Indigenous communities have been systematically displaced, targets of genocide, or simply erased from much of the dominant culture's imagination. As this book works to affirm, settler-colonial society must also learn how to listen to Indigenous people. For most of U.S. and Canadian history, settler scholars have spoken for Native people, appropriating their voices—rather than stepping back so they can speak for themselves. The written record has largely been a monologue—rather than a dialogue. When Ilarion Merculieff and Libby Roderick titled their book *Stop Talking: Indigenous Ways of Teaching and Learning*, they were in part pointing to the pedagogical emphasis on observation and experience among Alaska Natives. But they hoped to convey something else as well. The title "was also a plea to the privileged people of the dominant Western culture to still their voices for a change, and to listen to other voices they may never have heard before" (Merculieff and Roderick, iv).

As Ridington argues, listening "is possible only when every person can realize a place in every other person's story. It is possible only when the circle of stories includes all the relations of a world that is alive with meaning" (Ridington, 469). Non-Native readers who would learn from Indigenous traditions and cultures, therefore, must challenge themselves to be *quiet*, and to *listen* to show respect for the moments of silence and to honor the boundaries of those places where they are not meant to go.[2]

An excellent example can be seen in the work of theologian Lily Oster. After supporting Native-led protests against a proposed oil pipeline at Standing Rock, Oster was prompted to consider what she would come to call "the revelation of *no*," the lessons learned by remaining *outside the circle*, respecting Native leadership and privacy. Oster cited Chief Arvol Looking Horse (Lakota), and his request that non-Native people refrain from entering the ceremonial Sun Dance circle. Looking Horse explained: "Our purpose for the Sundance is for the survival of the future generations to come, first and foremost. If non-Natives truly understand this purpose, they will also understand this decision and know that their departure from this Ho-c-o-ka (our sacred altar) is their sincere contribution to the survival of future generations."[3] Oster writes that such a request is a learning opportunity for members of settler society. By *departing from the center*, she suggests, one might find the transformative potential of stepping back and *listening*. Lest seeker spirituality becomes yet another extractive economy (one built upon the extraction of resources without concern for the long-term consequences of local cultures or ecologies), Oster challenges her fellow non-Native admirers of Native traditions to eschew a tendency toward appropriation, to instead attend to the complexities and diversity of Indigenous cultures, to join the struggle, and to consciously remain on the periphery. In other words, to listen.

About This Book

I approach this book as a scholar of Native American religious traditions, an advocate for Indigenous sovereignty, and an ally of Native communities. As I work, I often find myself meditating on my ancestors, stretching back like cedar roots to Scotland, England, Germany, eastern Europe, and Native North America. Such meditations continue to inspire my passion for social justice, ecological justice, and a profound curiosity about religious experience. These commitments prompted my leap into graduate studies in religion—a wildly impractical path for a blue-collar kid from Portland, Oregon. But it was there that I met and began working with my mentor Inés Talamantez.

Dr. Talamantez received her PhD from the University of California, San Diego, then taught at Dartmouth College and held post-doc positions at Harvard before joining the Religious Studies faculty at the University of California, Santa Barbara. There she founded their program in Native American Religious Studies, mentoring dozen of students through their PhD work. Her scholarship focuses on the ceremonial and ethnopoetic traditions of her own Mescalero Apache people, with particular emphasis on their girls' coming-of-age ceremony. As one of her graduate students, I was privileged to accompany her to Mescalero to observe, support, and participate in that weeklong ceremony. Over the years, we have continued to work together, collaborating on conferences and sharing in the trials of life. This book is the result of our two-decades-long friendship and collaboration.

Dr. Talamantez was involved throughout the writing of this book. Together, we talked about initial ideas and how we wanted to frame the work, devised an outline, and decided upon our sources. I wrote first drafts of chapters, and she reviewed them, challenging my ideas, offering clarifications, and continuing the conversation. In our initial discussions, we decided this book should reflect the concerns and commitments of contemporary tribal communities, not the normative categories dictated by academia. Hence, you won't find chapters on "mythology," "ceremony," and "rites of passage." Instead, you'll find examinations of climate change, water rights, diabetes prevention, and food sovereignty. We wanted, as much as possible, for this book to uplift the work being done by Native scholars and communities around these pressing issues.

In chapter 2, we explore the central importance of the earth as a source of power and life, introducing readers to sacred places at risk of destruction, and Native communities fighting to protect them. In chapter 3, we continue this discussion by focusing on the impacts of climate change and the possibilities of conservation. We consider: If the earth is so central to Indigenous spirituality, what happens when the earth begins to change? How does this affect Native American religious life? How are tribal communities combatting climate change and working to restore vital ecosystems? Chapter 4 explores water rights (the history of Native struggles for access to clean water) and water rites (the sacred nature of water within a variety of Native religious traditions). As Indigenous water protectors step up in the fight for clean water, they remind us that water is life, and water is alive. Chapter 5 shifts the focus toward traditional foods and Indigenous food sovereignty: the right of Native people to access and maintain their traditional foods. Indigenous food sovereignty includes efforts to preserve salmon, protect wild rice, restore bison, and maintain Indigenous farming practices. These efforts illuminate the sacred nature of food, how foods are seen as ancestors and teachers, and how they are honored in ancient first-foods ceremonies and agricultural traditions.

Chapter 6 builds on this work to consider the religious nature of health and healing. It explores different ritual, ceremonial, and medicinal healing practices, while looking at the ways in which tribal nations are adapting biomedicine to combat ailments such as diabetes, addiction, and cancer. Chapter 7 discusses gender and sexuality, reminding readers that in Indigenous cultures, women have had access to different forms of spiritual and political power, while sexual diversity has traditionally been respected and honored. The chapter considers the ways in which Indigenous people are decolonizing gender and sexuality, reclaiming a world where women and girls are safe and empowered, and where gender nonconformity is a sign of spiritual power, not shame. Finally, chapter 8 considers Christianity within Indigenous communities. It discusses the painful history of missionization, as well as the ways in which Native North Americans are indigenizing Christianity, challenging and transforming Eurocentric theologies and practices through the lessons of Indigenous values, worldviews, and sacred teachings.

We ask in closing that readers remember: this book is only a place to start. It is an introduction to the important work being done by Native communities, scholars, and their allies. At the end of each chapter, readers will find recommendations for further reading (books, articles, poems, and websites) and for viewing (films and videos). We hope this book will inspire further exploration and that it will help us all consider how we might better support contemporary Indigenous communities in their fight to protect their people, their lands, and their cultures. Just like the story that began this piece, we hope this book inspires readers to reconsider who we are, why we're here, and what our responsibilities are to the other-than-human persons with whom we share this earth.

Notes

1. A full version of this prayer can be found at https://www.narf.org/thanksgiving -address-greetings-to-the-natural-world/. A conversation about the Onandaga prayer between Whatweni-nah Frieda Jacques (Turtle Clan) and Kateri-Riley Thornton (Snipe Clan) can be found at "Haudenosaunee Thanksgiving Address," https://www.youtube.com/ watch?v=swJs2cGNwIU.

2. For an example of Ridington's collaborative scholarship, see Dane Wajich: Dane-zaa Stories and Songs: Dreamers of the Land digital resource. http://www.virtualmuseum.ca/ sgc-cms/expositions-exhibitions/danewajich/english/project/index.php.

3. https://www.manataka.org/page108.html.

References and Recommendations

Archibald, Jo-Ann. *Indigenous Storywork: Educating the Heart, Mind, Body and Spirit*. Victoria: University of British Columbia Press, 2008.

Cajete, Greg. *Look to the Mountain: An Ecology of Indigenous Education*. Durango: Kivaki Press, 1994.

Cajete, Greg. *Indigenous Community: Rekindling the Teachings of the Seventh Fire*. St. Paul: Living Justice Press, 2015.

Carlson, Keith. *You Are Asked to Witness: The Sto:lo in Canada's Pacific Coast History*. Chiliwack, BC: Sto:lo Heritage Trust, 1997.

Cote, Charlotte. *Spirit of Our Whaling Ancestors: Revitalizing Makah and Nuu-chah-nulth Traditions*. Seattle: University of Washington Press, 2015.

Deloria, Vine, Jr., and Daniel Wildcat. *Power and Place: Indian Education in America*. London: Fulcrum, 2001.

Frey, Rodney. *Landscape Traveled by Coyote and Crane: The World of the Schitsu'umsh*. Seattle: University of Washington Press, 2001.

Gross, Lawrence. "Silence as the Root of American Indian Humor: Further Meditations on the Comic Vision of Anishinaabe Culture and Religion." *American Indian Culture and Research Journal* Vol. 31 No. 2 (2007): 69–85.

Gross, Lawrence. "Some Elements of American Indian Pedagogy from an Anishinaabe Perspective," *American Indian Culture and Research Journal* Vol. 34 No. 2 (2010): 11–26.

Kimmerer, Robin Wall. *Braiding Sweetgrass: Indigenous Wisdom, Scientific Knowledge, and the Teachings of Plants*. Minneapolis: Milkweed, 2013.

Merculieff, Ilarion, and Libby Roderick. *Stop Talking: Indigenous Ways of Teaching and Learning and Difficult Dialogs in Higher Education*. Anchorage: University of Alaska Press, 2013.

Oster, Lily. "Notes from Standing Rock: Non-Extraction as Spiritual Practice," paper delivered to the American Academy of Religion. Boston, 2017.

Ridington, Robin. "Voice, Representation, and Dialogue: The Poetics of Native American Spiritual Traditions," *American Indian Quarterly* Vol. 20 No. 3/4 (1996): 467–88.

Ross, Julie Burns. "Indigenous Intergenerational Teachings: The Transfer of Culture, Language, and Knowledge in an Intergenerational Summer Camp," *American Indian Quarterly* Vol. 40 No. 3 (2016): 216–50.

Ryan, Esme, Willie Smyth, and Vi Hilbert. *Spirit of the First People: Native American Music Traditions of Washington State*. Seattle: University of Washington Press, 1999.

Smith, Linda Tuhiwai. *Decolonizing Methodologies: Research and Indigenous Peoples*. London: Zed Books, 2012.

Smith, Theresa. *The Island of Anishnaabeg: Thunderers and Water Monsters in the Traditional Ojibwe Life-World*. Caldwell: University of Idaho Press, 1995.

Talamantez, Inés, *Becoming: Introducing Apache Girls to the World of Spiritual and Cultural Values*. Albuquerque: University of New Mexico (forthcoming).

Zogry, Michael. "Lost in Conflation: Visual Culture and Constructions of the Category of Religion," *American Indian Quarterly* Vol. 35 No. 1 (2011): 1–55.

Websites and Films

"Dane Wajich: Dane-zaa Stories and Songs: Dreamers of the Land" digital resource. http://www.virtualmuseum.ca/sgc-cms/expositions-exhibitions/danewajich/english/project/index.php

"Haudenosaunee Thanksgiving Address," Whatweni-nah Frieda Jacques (Onondaga Turtle Clan) and Kateri-Riley Thornton (Onondaga Snipe Clan). https://www.youtube.com/watch?v=swJs2cGNwIU

Teachings of the Tree People: The Work of Bruce Miller (New Day Films, 2006).

"Thanksgiving Address: Greetings to the Natural World." https://www.narf.org/thanksgiving-address-greetings-to-the-natural-world/

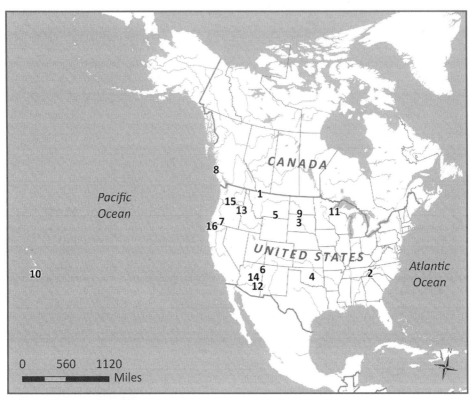

1 Blackfeet Indian Reservation
2 Eastern Band of Cherokee Indians
3 Cheyenne River Sioux Tribe
4 Choctaw Nation
5 Crow Tribe of Indians
6 Diné (Navajo) Nation
7 Klamath Tribe
8 Kwakiutl (Kwakwa̱ka̱'wakw)
   Territories
9 Lakota Territories
10 Mauna Kea
11 Ojibwe (Anishinaabe) Territory
12 San Carlos Apache Reservation
13 Wallowa Territories
14 White Mountain Apache Tribe
15 Confederated Tribes and Bands of
   the Yakama Nation
16 Yurok Tribe

Map 2.1. Map of North America locating the tribal communities, nations, and cultural groups mentioned in this chapter. Basemap data made with Natural Earth. (Liz O'Dea Springborn)

Earth

2

I̲N 1877, AFTER YEARS OF RESISTANCE, Hinmatóowyalaht'qit (Chief Joseph), finally agreed to negotiate terms of surrender with the United States Army. Chief Joseph tried his best to explain to General Oliver O. Howard the essential challenge he faced in being asked to surrender claims to his homeland. He explained:

> The Earth was created by the assistance of the sun, and it should be left as it was. . . . The country was made without lines of demarcation and it is no man's business to divide it. . . . The Earth and myself are of one mind. The measure of the land and the measure of our bodies are the same. Understand me fully with reference to my affection for the land. I never said the land was mine to do with as I choose. The one who has the right to dispose of it is the one who created it.

In response, General Howard replied: "We do not wish to interfere with your religion, but you must talk about practical things. Twenty times over you have repeated the Earth is your mother, and that chieftainship is from the earth. Let us hear it no more, but come to business at once" (LaDuke, 223).

The two were at an impasse. To General Howard, religious notions were all well and good, but they had little to do with "practical" matters—such as federal laws that sought to confine Native people to reservations. But for Chief Joseph, there were sacred laws that preexisted and overruled those of the United States. Encapsulated in this exchange are fundamentally different ways of understanding religion, the sacred, the supernatural, and one's relationship to the earth.

As was discussed in chapter 1, Indigenous cultures are *Indigenous* because they are *autochthonous*: they are cultures born from a particular place and exist in relationship with that place. It is the ground of their being. And as this story demonstrates, Indigenous perspectives of the earth differ markedly from those held by settler-colonial culture. According to traditional First Nations teachings, the earth is central to Indigenous religious traditions because it is the source of life and spiritual power, the home of powerful other-than-human people, and because it provides a palpable connection to their ancestors.

Photo 2.1.   Chief Joseph (Hinmatóowyalaht'qit). (Photoprint by Rudolph B. Scott, Spokane, Washington, October 17, 1899. Library of Congress Prints and Photographs Division, Washington, DC)

A Living Earth, Full of Many Nations

One of the primary differences between Native American and Euroamerican teachings about the earth is the understanding that the earth is spiritually endowed, and that it is inhabited by other-than-human people, all of whom are related, and all whom have equal value. Consider, by contrast, a worldview common throughout European history and exemplified in the 1579 drawing *The Great Chain of Being*.

Here we find a strict hierarchy of all matter and life, arranged in a clear progression from basic materiality to pure spirit. At the base level are earth and stone. As the image tells us, rock possesses only existence; it is devoid of life or spirit. The hierarchy ascends to plants, which we are told have life but lack motion or spirit. Animals are separated into wild and domesticated (wild having more force of will). These creatures are considered superior to plants because they have life, motion, and appetite, but no spirit. Human beings then enter in—carefully arranged on a hierarchy from peasant, to aristocrat, to king. Humans hold their exalted position over other created beings because they have existence, life, motion, appetite, and an immortal spirit. Above these are the angels (ranked) and God the Father overlooking all. This careful classification of existence privileges that which is pure

Photo 2.2. Great Chain of Being, from *Retorica Christiana*, written by Didacus Valdes in 1579. The image provides a powerful illustration of the hierarchical worldview expressed in classical Christian cosmology. (Wikimedia Commons, Public Domain, https://commons.wikimedia.org/wiki/File:Great_Chain_of_Being_2.png)

spirit, and therefore unchanging, over that which is perceived as lifeless matter—the earth.

The implications of this worldview can be seen in the rationale given for the Catholic Church's efforts to build a telescope and observatory on Mt. Graham. Traditional Apache people fought to prevent development of the site, claiming that it was a sacred mountain, a site of pilgrimage, and home of the *Gahe*, or mountain spirits. A representative from the Vatican dismissed their concerns. "No mountain is as sacred as a human being. . . . It is precisely the failure to make the distinction [between insignificant nature and immortal human souls] that has created a kind of environmentalism and a religiosity which must be suppressed with all the force that we can muster" (LaDuke, 28, 31). For such religious authorities, this distinction between human beings and the rest of creation is fundamental.

In contrast to this hierarchical classification, Indigenous traditions offer world-views more akin to a family tree: with interconnected branches, where no part is more important than another. The challenge issued here is not to transcend lesser beings but to realize one's *interdependency* with them. Indigenous and settler-colonial worldviews thus diverge in a remarkable way: Is humanity the apex of creation, the central concern of the universe? Or is it part of an interconnected web of obligations and responsibilities to other created persons? This perspective can be seen in Christi Belcourt's work *Wisdom of the Universe*. Belcourt, a Métis visual artist, said this about the piece:

> In Ontario, over 200 species of plants and animals are listed as threatened, en-dangered or extinct. Of those, included in this painting are the Dwarf Lake Iris, the Eastern Prairie Fringed Orchid, the Karner Blue butterfly, the West Virginia White butterfly, the Spring Blue-eyed Mary, the Cerulean Warbler and Acadian Flycatcher. Globally, we live in a time of great upheaval. The state of the world is in crisis. We are witness to the unbearable suffering of species, including humans. Much of this we do to ourselves. It is possible for the planet to return to a state of well-being, but it requires a radical change in our thinking. It requires a willingness to be open to the idea that perhaps human beings have got it all wrong. All species, the lands, the waters are one beating organism that pulses like a heart. We are all a part of a whole. The animals and plants, lands and waters, are our relatives each with as much right to exist as we have. When we see ourselves as separate from each other and think of other species, the waters and the planet itself as objects that can be owned, dominated or subjugated, we lose connection with our humanity and we create imbalance on the earth. This is what we are witnessing around us. The planet already contains all the wisdom of the universe, as do you and I. It has the ability to recover built into its DNA and we have the ability to change what we are doing so this can happen. (Belcourt)

This view of the world as alive and full of other people, both human and more-than-human, can be found throughout Native American teachings and origin stories. Diné (Navajo) ceremonialist Frank Mitchell put it this way: "When First Man and First Woman created the mountains, they said, 'I wonder by what means the mountains will be made alive? Let some beings take standing positions within them. In matter of fact, if there be none standing within them, they are but things that lie around without a purpose'" (Cousins, 500). Within Diné (Navajo) tradition, the earth is alive, and its inner form is Changing Woman, the *ye'ii* (holy person) who gave life to the first people. In the Diné language, the earth (along with plants, animals, and other aspects of the natural world) is referred to with kinship terms, suggesting respect, reverence, and affection. The earth is *shima*, mother. And young people are taught that "one should have compassion and respect for people and things in nature and think and behave toward these things in the context of kinship" (Lewton and Bydone, 480).

Photo 2.3. *Wisdom of the Universe* by Christi Belcourt (Metis). (Art Gallery of Ontario. http://artmatters.ca/wp/2014/08/artists-statement-christi-belcourt-on-the-wisdom-of-the-universe/)

When Alfred Hallowell studied with Great Lakes Ojibwe (Anishinaabe) elders in the early twentieth century, he was taught a similar lesson about the person-hood of the living world. The Ojibwe language codes the earth and features of the landscape such as mountains, rivers, lakes, and stones as animate. Hallowell recalls, "Since stones are grammatically animate, I once asked an old man: 'Are all stones we see about us alive?' He reflected a long while, and then replied, 'No! But some are'" (Smith, 50).

What does it mean to be alive? To be a person? Theresa Smith explains that in Anishinaabe cultures, "an animate being is a *person* by virtue of its membership and participation in an actual network of social and moral relationships and prac-tices with other persons. So moral agency is at the core of the Native conception of personhood. This means that one cannot be a person in isolation" (Smith, 90). Consider this: those who fail to live within this nexus of relationships give up their status as *true people*. In this sense, a field mouse fully living in proper relationship with its fellow creatures is acting like a *person,* while a human being who rejects his or her kinship with the world around them is not.

The earth is full of persons who exist, communicate, and uphold obligations to each other. A thunderstorm signals not only shifts in atmospheric pressure but also the arrival of powerful spiritual people (Smith, 66). As Smith found in her work with the Anishinaabe,

> Any object may hold within it a potential personhood. . . . But humans have no privileged or even unique status in this world, for *all* beings necessarily exist as will-ful personalities who are responsible for themselves. The Anishnaabeg do not look upon the world as instruments and they do not *project* themselves into the world but *find* themselves in and through a relational interaction with other persons, human and otherwise. The alternative which Anishnaabe life-world presents is, in short, not one in which we anthropomorphize nature, but one in which we open our category of personhood to include non-human beings." (Smith, 193)

Origin Stories

Origin stories help to make clear humanity's place within this inhabited earth. In many creation stories indigenous to North America, humans are latecomers, and their key to survival rests on their ability to enter into reciprocal relationships with the plant and animal people who preceded them. Because spiritual power and par-ticular gifts are distributed throughout the cosmos, each being is called to honor and uphold their particular gifts. Human beings soon find themselves in debt to these other species. In transformer, trickster, and culture hero stories, humans learn about the values and protocols necessary for taking part in the broader society of living things. Some stories describe how human tribes or clans are descended from inter-species marriages, their progeny embodying a kinship relationship between humanity and the star people, the salmon people, the bear people. And where kin-ship exists, so too should respect, cooperation, and reciprocity.

For the Yakama peoples of central Washington, understanding who they are meant to be has everything to do with their understanding of creation. Michelle Jacob and Wynona Peters explain:

> Yakama peoples believe that they have been placed on their homeland by the Creator and that they have lived on the land for hundreds of generations. According to tribal teachings, land is sacred and gendered. In the tribe's own written history of the Yakama people, the land is central to Yakama identity and spirituality: "My Mother is the Earth, my Father the Light . . . when I die, my body returns to my Mother and my spirit to my Father."

In contrast to a settler-colonial culture that takes a "dominant cultural view of land as solely an economic resource to be exploited for individual monetary profit, in the Yakama perspective, land is sacred and relational, as 'the people and the land are one entity married through constant companionship for thousands of years'" (Jacob and Peters, 42). This notion of being in a spousal relationship with a place demands that human beings care for, nurture, respect, and defend the land. Religious and ceremonial life provides a key place where this can happen. White Earth Anishinaabe activist and author Winona LaDuke explains:

> Native American rituals are frequently based on the reaffirmation of the relationship of humans to the Creation. Many of our oral traditions tell of the place of the "little brother" (the humans) in the larger Creation. Our gratitude for our part in Creation and for the gifts given to us by the Creator is continuously reinforced in Midewiwin lodges, Sundance ceremonies, world renewal ceremonies, and many others. (LaDuke, 12)

Daisy Sewid-Smith (Mamaliliqala Kwak'wa'wakw) clarifies the significance of ceremonial exchange even further. She notes that early Euroamerican observers had recoiled in horror at what they thought were examples of Native people worshipping elements of nature. To settlers, such interactions smacked of idolatry. But, Sewid-Smith explains, a great deal was lost in translation. There are three words for honoring sacred things in her Wakashan language, *hawax'ela* (to pray), *c'elwaqa* (to praise), and *7em'yaxa* (to worship). When Franz Boas described her people's traditions, he mistranslated *c'elwaqa* as *worship*.

> So the way it's written [in Boas's book] it looks like we're worshiping everything in nature, that we're nature-worshippers, but we're not. We are stewards of nature. Yes, we did acknowledge a plant, a tree, a salmon, an animal, for giving its life so that we may live. There's a big difference between *c'elwaqa* [and worship]. I could *c'elwaqa* a person; I can *c'elwaqa* you. . . . I'm not worshipping you. I am praising you for things you've done. (Sewid-Smith, Dick, and Turner, 203)

Because the world is spiritually alive, it is difficult—and perhaps unhelpful—to distinguish between the *natural* (which suggests an inanimate materiality governed by fixed laws) and the *supernatural* (which suggests a momentary suspension of those laws through the intrusion of some external spiritual force). Instead, Indigenous philosophies suggest a world imbued with spirit, animated by persons who have agency and who insist upon respectful, ethical behavior. That a spiritual being may make itself known during a ceremony is profound and meaningful, but it is not outside the *natural* order of things.

Thinking about the world as a network of relationships with fellow persons can have radical consequences, challenging the way we eat, the way we live, and the way we do business. When Sewid-Smith critiques the logging industry on Vancouver Island, for instance, she does so because it fails to consider the relationships that undergird the entire ecosystem. "We are thinking holistically of the whole environmental damage," she explains, and so are able to see that after clear-cutting, hills are "sliding down, damaging more plants. Some of them are sliding into the river, and blocking the rivers, so that salmon can't go up or destroying spawning grounds" (Sewid-Smith, Dick, and Turner, 205).

High Places, Sacred Places

In the 1990s, the United States Forest Service and its private-business partners proposed a new ski resort on Mt. Shasta in Northern California. Native communities and environmental groups protested, claiming that the mountain was sacred. In response, the Forest Service requested that the concerned parties draw a line on a map: Where did the mountain begin to be sacred? What line divided the sacred from the profane? To Native Northern Californians, the question was nonsensical.

What makes a place sacred?

This is a trick question. From Indigenous perspectives, all land is sacred because all land is alive. Devout Catholics would surely be scandalized if they were asked to distinguish between human lives that are sacred and those that are profane. Similarly, Indigenous philosophies do not draw a line between the sacred and the profane because all living persons who make Mt. Shasta their home have value and ought to have rights. At the same time, this doesn't mean that every place or every thing is the same. As Emily Cousins puts it: "While all land is sacred, certain places have qualitatively distinct sacred power" (Cousins, 505).

In other words, some places are more powerful or more important than others. Lakota scholar, philosopher, and activist Vine Deloria describes four kinds of sacred places: first, places sanctified by human action, where an important event in human history is commemorated; second, places where something holy has appeared or happened in an otherwise mundane or secular locale; third, sites of overwhelming holiness where a powerful spirit has made itself known; fourth, possible future sites of future revelations. To these, I would add a fifth: places that are homes for certain plant and animal people, creatures who are particularly powerful, endangered, or at risk of being lost.

There are countless sacred places in Native North America: a hollow in a stone on an ancient riverbed, a shrine built beside a cornfield, a Sun Dance circle. Some of the most powerful of these are on mountaintops: homes of important plant and animal people; dangerous spiritual beings; and sites of vision quest, pilgrimage, and prayer. Taking a closer look at several of these high places helps to convey a sense of what makes a place sacred, and what is at risk when they are lost.

Heart Mountain, Wyoming

Apsáalooke (Crow) elder Grant Bulltail tries hard to explain the importance of Heart Mountain. "I don't want to call it a sacred site because your idea of something sacred and my idea of something sacred are a little bit different," he told religious studies scholar Mary Keller (Keller, 83). His ancestors are buried there. For generations, his people have gone there for ceremony. It is the site of a great revelation given to one of his people. But the processes of colonialism have separated him and other Apsáalooke from the site. In 1851, the Apsáalooke signed a treaty with the United States government ceding territories in return for a thirty-three-million-acre reservation that included Heart Mountain and present-day Cody, Wyoming. But when gold was discovered in the western Plains, the federal government broke the treaty, reducing the promised reservation to a mere 2.2 million acres north of the Wyoming-Montana border, effectively stripping them of access to their sacred mountain.

At 8,123 feet, Heart Mountain is geologically remarkable: somehow, its summit is at least 300 million years older than its base—an oddity that scientists are still trying to understand. But for Bulltail and other Apsáalooke, the mountain matters for reasons that don't easily translate into Euroamerican parlance.

> I don't want to call it a sacred site because your idea of something sacred and my idea of something sacred are a little bit different. We feel that there are places that are located on the earth that have special power. When the Creator created the earth he went along and created things. And when you carry a cup of water, no matter how careful you are, you're going to spill some. We feel that power has spilled in some of them and Heart Mountain is one of those places. And if you have the right state of mind and you want powers, you'll get powers. But if you don't, you don't think in that manner, then nothing will happen. So that's why it's a sacred place to us. And a lot of people fasted there. One of them is a man called Foretop who had his vision that he was going to live as long as Heart Mountain was intact. And then when it collapsed [in a major landslide], he died. . . . And it's not sacred in the sense that if you go there there's going to be weird sounds and ghosts are going to come out and thunder is going to strike—it's not going to happen. But it's still, we believe, that there's something special there. . . . When I see Heart Mountain, I know that I am in the center of my homeland." (Keller, 88, 90)

There are, as Bulltail explains, places in the world with extra power, places where the Creator's great spirit extends and is maintained. In Apsáalooke, the term is *akbahii laashée*: a force that is overcoming, with limitless powers.

Heart Mountain's story is about the sacred. And it is also a story of colonialism and forced displacement. During World War II, Heart Mountain overlooked a Japanese internment camp. And until 1999, the north and east slopes of the mountain and the surrounding sagebrush flats were owned by a non–Native family. When a golf course and recreation community were proposed for the site, the Nature Conservancy stepped in. Citing the mountain's importance as a home to sage grouse, peregrine falcons, and golden eagles, as well as an incredible concentration of rare plants, they successfully preserved fifteen thousand acres for habitat, research, and educational programs. They pointed to the distinctly important nature of this place: it is a site sacred because of its ceremonial and visionary history and also because of its distinctive and powerful spirit. Geologists are drawn to its remarkable rock formations. Ecologists value its rare plants and bird habitat. For the Crow it is *akbahii laashée*.

Bulltail has worked with the Nature Conservancy to found the Restoring Sacred Land on Common Ground Alliance, a group supporting the Heart Mountain Reconnection Project. In collaboration with the Nature Conservancy and academics like Mary Keller and Laura Scheiber, Bulltail works to bring Apsáalooke people back into a relationship with Heart Mountain. For one weekend each July, Apsáalooke tribal members gather at the mountain, where they raise ceremonial tipis, conduct pipe ceremonies, consider traditional teachings, and participate in sacred drumming, song, and dance.

Sweet Grass Hills, Montana

The Sweet Grass Hills in Montana provide another example of sacred high country. According to Blackfeet history, a young man named Scarface conducted his fasts on the Sweet Grass Hills. Here he met the spirit of East Butte, who gifted him with spiritual power. Scarface spoke with the Creator, and from the Sun received instructions for the Sun Dance, one of the most important ceremonial traditions in North America today. For centuries, the Hills have hosted Sun Dances, reciprocating for the sacrifice and suffering of prayerful penitents with spiritual power, visionary guidance, and hundreds of medicinal and ceremonial plants (Cousins, 505). In 1992, several mining companies proposed a heap-leach gold mine in the Hills. The Blackfeet and the Chippewa-Cree fought back, insisting the Hills were sacred and central to their creation accounts. Partnering with ranchers and conservationists, the tribes petitioned Congress and the secretary of the interior. The Bureau of Land Management (BLM) suspended the mine's permit for two years, then approved it, arguing that it would not cause any harmful impacts. The Federal Advisory Council on Historic Preservation interceded, insisting that the tribes had not been adequately consulted.

During a second two-year study, tribes were asked to identify which parts of the Sweet Grass Hills were sacred, to, in effect, separate the sacred from the profane. Tribal leaders tried to explain that the entirety of the Hills were sacred, not just a single site. As a living ecosystem, its health required preserving it as a whole, not simply building fences and constructing signage around particular shrines or points of interest. Eventually the BLM withdrew its support for the mine, citing "high value potential habitat for the reintroduction of endangered peregrine falcons, areas

Photo 2.4.   Curly Bear Wagner stands at Writing-On-Stone Provincial Park in the Sweet Grass Hills on the Montana-Canada border, Thursday, September 17, 1998. Wagner leads a campaign to make the Sweet Grass Hills a United Nations World Heritage Site. (AP Photo/*Great Falls Tribune*, Stuart S. White)

of traditional religious importance to Native Americans, aquifers that currently provide the only potable water in the area, and seasonally important elk and deer habitat" (Department of the Interior). In 1998, Montana citizens voted to ban heap-leach mining for twenty years, and in 2017, the BLM voted to extend the moratorium for another twenty years.

The story of the Sweet Grass Hills helps us see Deloria's discussion of sacred and powerful places in practice. The Hills have historical significance as a site of vision questing and ceremony. They have mythological significance as the site of Scarface's visionary encounter with East Butte and Sun. They are the home of powerful spiritual beings: medicinal plants and animal people, including falcons, deer, and elk. And, in the late twentieth century, they gained another layer of sacrality when they became the sacred center of a powerful coalition of relationships built between groups of people who had previously been in conflict: Indian tribes, ranchers, hunters, and conservationists. If a sacred place can be understood as a place where spiritual relationships are experienced, symbolically articulated, and maintained, then that certainly happened in the Sweet Grass Hills: relationships were forged between animal people, plant people, and human communities.

Mauna Kea

On June 24, 2015, an *ahu* (shrine) was constructed on the broad shoulder of Mauna Kea, a mountain looming 13,803 feet above sea level on the island of Hawaii. The *ahu* was built by *Kia'i* (protectors), who opposed the construction of a thirty-meter telescope on a mountain sacred to Native Hawaiian people. One of the largest telescopes in the world, it was to be built near the summit of a revered *wahi pana* (sacred place) that figures prominently in Native Hawaiian oral traditions and ritual practices. The Kia'i came to block the road and prevent construction of the proposed telescope. Having occupied the mountain for ninety-one days, preventing construction crews from arriving on-site and enduring harsh conditions at high elevations amid the constant threat of arrest, the Kia'i built a shrine.

To Native and non-Native Hawaiians, the shrine held power, standing as a symbol of Indigenous resistance to settler colonialism, and of the powerful presence of Native Hawaiian ancestors. Hawaiian police officers reluctantly arrested protestors. But the protests proved at least temporarily successful, preventing construction vehicles from passing and halting construction. The *ahu* had symbolic and sacred power.

Hawaii's state Board of Land and Natural Resources continues to advocate for the construction of the telescope, arguing in a document filed on September 28, 2017, that the summit already hosts twelve other observatories nearly as large as the proposed new telescope and that it will not pollute groundwater, damage any historic sites, harm any rare plants or animals, or release toxic chemicals. It argues that the new observatory would be located in a place not currently used for ceremonies, out of view of most ceremonial locations, and would not impact ceremonies to any greater degree than current observatories already do. State representatives argue instead that the observatory is actually in line with Native Hawaiian traditions, which portray Mauna Kea as the child of Wakea (Sky Father) and Papa (Earth Mother), and see the summit of the island as the union of heaven and earth. Such a place, they argue, is surely the best place to study the heavens. The Kia'i disagree, and continue to fight the proposed project.

Dzil Nchaa Si An (Mt. Graham)

In 1997, Wendler Nosie (San Carlos Apache) traveled to Dzil Nchaa Si An (Mt. Graham) to pray for his daughter's coming-of-age ceremony. Preparations for this rite of passage include pilgrimages to the sacred mountain. Soon after his arrival, Nosie was arrested, and accused of trespassing on private property owned by the University of Arizona. After Nosie's arrest, the University of Arizona responded by creating a permit system for Apache people wishing to pray at this ancient site of pilgrimage.

At 10,720 feet, Dzil Nchaa Si An is a site of prayer and vision questing for Apache people, home of mountain spirits and other sacred beings. Despite continuous protests from the Apache and other Native American people in the surrounding region, the University of Arizona partnered with the Vatican and German-based Planck Institute to build enormous telescopes and microwave towers on Dzil Nchaa Si An. Apache traditionalist Brad Allison explains his opposition: "This is where we pray. This is where our ancestors are. [The telescopes are] like looking into the womb of a woman. We don't do that. Why don't you go somewhere else and do it? This is our home" (LaDuke, 28).

Dzil Nchaa Si An is ecologically unique, home to incredible biodiversity, with rare plant and animal species, and the largest property on the National Register of Historic Places. While sacred to all Indigenous tribes in the region, it holds particular importance for the White Mountain Apache because the mountain was included within the original boundaries of their reservation, as determined in an 1872 treaty. But when Euroamerican settlers laid claim to water and mineral resources, the reservation was summarily reduced, and Mt. Graham was lost. As early as 1890, private companies began harvesting timber on the sacred mountain.

Plans to build a twenty-telescope observatory were first introduced in the 1980s, prompting vocal opposition from Apache people. Despite protests from tribes, environmentalists, and their own faculty, University of Arizona regents approved construction. White Mountain Apache leaders continued to protest and petition for an end to construction, but the university had powerful allies, including Arizona senator John McCain, who waived environmental laws so that construction could continue. Conflicts over proposed microwave systems occurred between 2003 and their installation in 2008. Apache leaders insisted that artificial structures, radio waves, and microwaves "impinge and infringe upon, interfere with, distort, and detract from communications [with sacred power]," and demanded "no additional observatory-related impacts without commensurate restoration of our sacred Southern Mountain" (Welch, Riley, and Nixon, 42). Vernelda Grant, director of the San Carlos Apache tribe's Office of Historic Preservation and Archaeology, wrote in February 2005: "If you put up this microwave . . . it will hurt us by scrambling our prayers. . . . Apache resources can best be protected by managing our land to be as natural as it was in pre–white settlement times" (Welch, Riley, and Nixon, 43).

In 2005, the new president of the university issued a supportive statement declaring his intent to restore harmony among the university, Native people, and the mountain itself. He recognized the sacred nature of the mountain, supported full access to the mountain for Apache people, declared that there were no plans for expansion of existing observatories, and committed to instead devote the administration's energy to collaborative work. However, within eighteen months, the university changed administrations, and reversed its policy. By 2007, the microwave towers were in place.

There is much to be learned from the story of Dzil Nchaa Si An. Respectful and genuine consultation with Apache people from the beginning—including giving the Apache a real voice in co-managing the mountain—would have created a space for compromise rather than antagonism. Instead of using political power and material wealth to overrule their concerns, scientists might have considered how to partner with Apache wisdom keepers to learn more about the mountain and its complex biodiversity. In doing so, they might have learned a different way of engaging with this powerful place.

When White Mountain tribal council chairman Dallas Massey Sr. described the appropriate means of engagement with Dzil Nchaa Si An, he used the term "respectful avoidance" (Welch, Riley, and Nixon, 42). This, he said, is the best

English translation of an ancient Apache stewardship tenet. Sacred sites should not be interfered with, except by ceremonial practitioners who know how to minister to them. In this case, construction should be deferred or rejected until its impacts are completely understood, particularly within such a fragile and complex ecosystem. Massey and the San Carlos tribal council called for joint management of the site, with the goal of returning Dzil Nchaa Si An to pre-1870 conditions.

Sacred Places at Risk

One might wonder: How did we get to a situation where such sacred, powerful places are at risk? To understand this, we have to consider the history of colonial policies in North America and, in particular, the history of Indigenous land loss. Historically, the drive to acquire Native lands was at the heart of most federal Indian policies in the United States and Canada. Perhaps the best example of this can be seen in the removal policies of the 1830s, exemplified in what we now refer to as the Trail of Tears. In the American Southeast, the Cherokee, Choctaw, Chickasaw, Creek, and Seminole were historically known as the "Five Civilized Tribes." They had largely adopted settler culture and technology, converting to Christianity, printing the Bible in their own language, adopting plantation farming, and entering into Euroamerican systems of centralized governance and free market capitalism. Many had intermarried with Euroamericans. Many were wealthy and successful.

If, as settlers claimed, colonialism existed to "lift the savages out of barbarism," these communities should have been celebrated. But when their land proved valuable for farming and mineral extraction, the federal government passed the 1830 Indian Removal Act, forcibly removing and relocating them to Indian Country in present-day Oklahoma. Over a quarter of the population died along the way. Today, this forced march is commemorated as the Trail of Tears.

The Removal Act was an act of economic and political injustice, removing people from their lands and stripping them of their property. It was also a spiritual injustice, cutting people off from Indigenous homelands, sacred places, and the plants and animals they had been in relationship with for millennia.

The Reservation Era

Many treaties with Native American tribes were signed during the 1850s, requiring Native people to cede vast tracts of land in exchange for reservations and assurances of amenities like rations, farming supplies, schools, medical care, and protection from settler violence. However, while Native compliance to these treaties was enforced by the United States Army, many treaties were never ratified by Congress. Of those that were, the United States government broke provisions in all of them.

Implications of the reservation- and treaty-making processes can be seen in the case of the Lakota and the Black Hills. As early as 1804, Lewis and Clark had observed Lakota hunters in the Black Hills. Oral traditions, rawhide pictographs (winter counts), Lakota cosmology, and ancient Sun Dance sites all tie the Lakota to the Black Hills and identify the Hills as their place of emergence and the origin of many of their ceremonies. But by 1841, settlers had begun encroaching on Lakota territory, and conflicts arose. The 1851 Fort Laramie Treaty sought to curtail violence and provide safe passage for settlers moving through Lakota territory by guaranteeing to the Lakota a reservation of seventy million acres. With increasing pressure from white settlers, the U.S. government replaced the 1851 treaty with an 1868 treaty assuring the Lakota the undisturbed use of thirty-one million acres west of the Missouri River, including the Black Hills. It also ensured them hunting rights to an additional fifty million acres between the Platte River and the Yellowstone River. But this treaty would also be disregarded.

The Lakota were soon prevented from hunting in their reserved territories. Promised rations did not arrive, and farming on the Northern Plains proved nearly impossible. The Lakota were starving. When gold was discovered in the Black Hills, prospectors rushed to the territory, trespassing on Lakota land. The Lakota protested, but the military sided with prospectors, protecting squatters. In 1876, yet another new treaty was forced upon the Lakota demanding that they cede the Black Hills. Many leaders refused to sign the treaty, and open conflict erupted between the Lakota, Euroamerican settlers, and the army.

The Lakota never surrendered the Black Hills, and they continue to fight for their return. In 1979, after over a century of legal battles, the Lakota and some Dakota people were awarded $102 million in compensation for the Black Hills. But the tribes refused the money, which may now be worth over a billion dollars. Despite their economic struggles—Lakota reservations include some of the poorest counties in the United States—they continue to refuse the money. They want the Black Hills.

Allotment and Termination

As these stories attest, the establishment of reservations separated many Native people from their sacred places: original reservation boundaries left many sacred places out, or omitted important resource-gathering sites. More sites were lost when those original treaties were disregarded—as was the case for the Crow and Heart Mountain, the White Mountain Apache and Mount Graham, and the Lakota and the Black Hills. Unless places fell within revised reservation boundaries, tribes had no access to pilgrimage sites, nor could they protect them from development or exploitation. Those tribal communities that did not secure treaty rights and federal recognition lacked any ability to intervene on behalf of powerful living places.

Access and ability to protect lands and resources were further compromised through two federal policies: allotment and termination. The 1887 General Allotment Act, also known as the Dawes Severalty Act, imposed the concept of private property on tribal communities, breaking up reservation land and allotting each individual a parcel of their own. As Senator Henry L. Dawes himself argued, tribes could never advance into civilization because they lacked an essential quality of "selfishness, which is at the bottom of civilization." They must, he insisted, be introduced to the "mystique of private property" (Cousins, 499).

Most important, the Dawes Act removed reservation lands from collective tribal ownership, freeing up "surplus" land for Euroamerican settlement. Each Native family head received 160 acres; single people received 80, and persons under the age of 18 received 40. But under the concurrent Homestead Acts, Euroamerican settlers could claim up to 640 acres—far more than Native people could claim under the Allotment Act. "Surplus" reservation land was then opened up for settlement and sale to Euroamericans. Over the forty-seven years of the Dawes Act's life, Native American reservations were reduced by 90 million acres: *two-thirds* of the 1887 land base.

The Dawes Act was adopted with the assumption that Native people would assimilate into the dominant society, that tribes would eventually cease to exist, and that reservations would thus not be necessary forever. Hence, a child under eighteen could receive only forty acres—with no provision for increasing that allotment after they had come of age, nor were provisions made for future generations. The result was that families were forced to divide allotments into increasingly smaller parcels among their offspring until some became too small to be usable. Distributed in checkerboard fashion, allotments were not adjacent, and often on the least desirable land, all with the intention of preventing long-term investment or shared tribal property. The Dawes Act equated "selfishness and private property with civil life and social progress" (Jacob and Peters, 48). By imposing these values on Native people the United States government further devastated already struggling communities.

Termination dominated federal Indian policies during the mid-twentieth century. Like Allotment, Termination had as its main agenda the elimination of Native identities and tribal communities and assimilation into the dominant society. With or without their consent, Native people would be forced to enter into mainstream society. Termination policies disregarded treaties, denied the sovereignty of Native tribes, stripping them of reservation lands and the rights guaranteed them in treaties. Termination was an open invitation to private business, "freeing up" tribal land for resource extraction and development. More than one hundred bands and tribes were terminated during this era, impacting more than 1.5 million acres of land.

The Klamath Nation of southern Oregon provides a particularly compelling case study for the application of Allotment and Termination policies. Guaranteed a 1.1-million-acre reservation in their 1864 treaty, by 1957 that 1.1-million-acre reserve had been reduced to a mere 75,000 acres. The Allotment Act alone carved away two-thirds of their lands. Then, terminated under the Klamath Termination Act of 1954, their status as Indian people and their reservation were lost. After decades of sustainable forest management by the tribe, the largest stand of ponderosa pine in the United States was handed over to private timber companies, who were soon logging Klamath forests at five times the tribal rate.

Author and activist Winona LaDuke has argued: "The Klamath had managed their fisheries, livestock, and timber industries well enough to give a modest annual

stipend to each tribal member, along with maintaining a hospital and medical team.
. . . Termination cut to shreds the tribal safety net" (LaDuke, 55). The health of the
Klamath people declined dramatically in the years after Termination, and within a
decade, a Senate investigative committee found that the policy's implementation
had led to "extreme social disorganization," with many tribal members suffering
physical and mental illness as a result. The Klamath fought back, regaining federal
recognition in 1986, though much of their forests had already been lost.

Protecting and Reclaiming Sacred Places

As the above case studies make clear, protecting sacred places is fraught and complex. There are fundamental philosophical differences between Indigenous and
settler worldviews. Within Indigenous cultures, the earth is understood to be alive,
filled with persons with whom one ought to be in relationship. Settler-colonial culture tends to insist that human beings are the only sentient beings, the only beings
with souls, and the only beings who ultimately matter. In this worldview, the earth
is inert, existing only to provide resources for extraction and profit. While the latter
does not represent all of non-Native culture, it is unfortunately the perspective that
has dominated our legal and political system. A history of displacing Native people
from their lands, through legislation, reservations, and violation of laws, have left
places vulnerable to development and desecration, and Native communities continue to be in conflict with private interests and state and federal governments over
sacred sites and resources.

In the late nineteenth century, Indigenous religious traditions were effectively
outlawed, through acts such as the 1883 Indian Religious Crimes Code, which pro-
hibited the practice of Indigenous religious traditions and made it a crime to lead or
even attend a ceremony. Federal funds were allocated to support residential schools,
where Native children were (at times forcibly) removed far from their families, placed
in remote institutions, and forbidden from speaking their own languages, singing
their songs, or practicing their traditions. In these schools, Indigenous cultures were
actively denigrated as superstitious and backward, and children were trained to be
domestic servants and laborers. Conditions were harsh. Severe physical punishments
were the norm. Students reported being lashed or hung from their wrists if caught
speaking their Indigenous languages. Schools were unsanitary and lacked proper
nutrition or health care. Mortality rates were astronomically high. Sexual abuse ran
rampant. In some institutions, rates of abuse were nearly 100 percent.

In 1978, Congress passed the American Indian Religious Freedom Act
(AIRFA), intended to remedy this long history of federal policies explicitly targeting Indigenous religions, languages, and cultures. Affirming the importance of
Native American religious traditions and the government's history of suppressing
those traditions, AIRFA stated that whereas

> American Indians had been denied access to sacred sites required in their religions,
> including cemeteries; Whereas such laws at times prohibit the use and possession of

sacred objects necessary to the exercise of religious rites and ceremonies; Whereas traditional American Indian ceremonies have been intruded upon, interfered with, and in a few instances banned; Now, therefore, be it Resolved by the Senate and the House of Representatives of the United States of America in Congress Assembled, That henceforth it shall be the policy of the United States to protect and preserve for American Indians their inherent right of freedom to believe, express, and exercise the traditional religions of the American Indian, Eskimo, Aleut, and Native Hawaiians, including but not limited to access to sites, use and possession of sacred objects, and the freedom to worship through ceremonials and traditional rites. (95th Congress, Public Law 95-341)

Lyng v. Northwest Indian Cemetery Association

Many Indigenous people were initially hopeful that AIRFA would give them the legal means of protecting sacred places, but these initial hopes were soon disappointed. While AIRFA declared that Native people had the right to hold ceremonies and access sacred sites, it did not actually protect those resources or places. The bill could not enforce its own provisions. That this was true became painfully clear during the famous *Lyng v. Northwest Indian Cemetery Association* case. Brought by the Yurok and other Native Northern Californians, the suit sought to protect sacred high country in the Siskiyou Mountains from a proposed Forest Service logging access road. Such locations were powerful because of their purity, remoteness, isolation, and the powerful spiritual beings dwelling there. Spiritual doctors—*kegey*—underwent extensive training and purification before visiting these sacred high places to seek spiritual power.

Lyng went on to the Supreme Court, which found that AIRFA did not in fact protect sacred spaces from destruction. The majority opinion determined that the construction of a public road outweighed the religious rights of individuals, basing its decision on the notion that the road posed no threat to Native people's religious *beliefs*. Indigenous people could continue to believe whatever they liked. Logging "did not preclude beliefs even though it would inhibit the practice" (Welch, Riley, and Nixon, 34). The sacred high country was eventually protected, but not because of the AIRFA. The state of California declared the area a wilderness, preventing further development or construction. But, the damage of *Lyng* was still profound: the decision devastated future legal efforts to protect sacred places under AIRFA.

Indigenous sacred sites are also vulnerable to the changing policies of state and federal administrations. Consider, for example, the role of executive orders when it comes to protecting sacred places. Bill Clinton's Executive Order 13007 (1996) directed federal land managers to accommodate access to and ceremonial use of Indian sacred sites and to "protect the physical integrity of those sites" (Welch, Riley, and Nixon, 35). Clinton's Executive Order 13175 (2000) directed federal agencies to be guided by respect for American Indian self-government, sovereignty, and treaty rights and responsibilities and to create spaces for tribal elected officials to provide "meaningful and timely" input. But such executive orders only applied to federal agencies and lands, and they changed at the whim of shifting administrations. The George W. Bush administration ignored these executive orders. The Obama administration sought to revive them. The Trump administration actively opposed them, undermining tribal efforts to protect public lands and promoting the interests of private companies seeking to extract resources and profit from those public lands.

Given the weaknesses within AIRFA and executive orders, some tribal communities have turned to the National Historic Preservation Act (NHPA) as a possible way of protecting sacred sites. Listing on the National Registry of Historic Places means that any proposed development on a site must be reviewed for negative impacts, but it does not actually prevent the development from taking place. For instance, listing Mt. Graham with the National Register of Historical Places acknowledged "the legitimacy of Western Apache oral and religious traditions" and recognized "the significance of the mountain as home and source for *gaan* (mountain spirits), sacred power, prayer places, and plants and other materials used in Apache religion" (Welch, Riley, and Nixon, 39). But its new status did not mean that existing development had to be removed, nor did it prohibit future construction. NHPA is also problematic because the very nature of a historic registry suggests that these places are relics of the past, that they are monuments to a previous moment in time, rather than a living manifestation of an active religious tradition. The act also assumes that a discrete boundary can be drawn around a site, demarcating the sacred from the profane. The nature of NHPA suggests that a particular shrine or rocky outcropping is sacred. The rest of the hillside is not.

In part, we can better understand why AIRFA and NHPA fail to protect sacred sites when we consider that U.S. laws are largely informed by Protestant notions of sacred places. Thus, the laws memorialize *events* that took place in history, prioritizing those that either celebrate the political history of the United States or that commemorate historical examples of Christian faith. These laws and policies are built on an understanding of religion as being fundamentally about individual *belief*, not about communal practice in a *place*. They are built on a notion of protecting *rights* (particularly to private property), not on an understanding of ongoing *responsibility* to live in relationship with a living earth.

Legal battles suggest that treaty rights provide the most promising path toward protecting sacred spaces. Because they guarantee access to particular resources, such as salmon or suckerfish, bison, elk, or huckleberries, treaties ensure legal rights to the healthy ecosystem needed to sustain these resources. The courts have repeatedly upheld these rights, suggesting treaties may provide a means of protecting Native American religious freedom and sacred lands.

Tribes have also found success in protecting sacred spaces through the strategic negotiation of alliances. Recall the story of the Sweet Grass Hills. Dangerous heap mining was prevented because of a coalition of ranchers, environmental groups, and local communities. Another example is found with the Cheyenne River Sioux, who experienced a degree of success through their alliance with the National Park Service when they sought to protect the sacred nature of Mato Tipila, the Lodge of the Bear, also known as Devil's Tower. A popular climbing destination, the National Park Service responded to Native concerns by instituting a voluntary no-climb policy during the month of June to accommodate the ceremonies that take place near and around the lodge. Climbing decreased by 79 percent after the voluntary ban was put into place, suggesting that many non-Native people are willing to make compromises to protect Native American rights and cultures (Freedman, 4, 13). The chapters that follow discuss other alliances and partnerships that may prove successful in protecting these important places.

Conclusion

While Indigenous religious traditions vary widely, they share in common the importance of place. These are, by very definition, sacred beliefs and practices that have emerged out of a people's relationship with a particular ecosystem, built upon their relationships with the plant and animal people that live there, and drawing upon inherent sacred power. The earth is a place of sacred power—and particular places are particularly powerful. Some of these places are elevated locations—mountaintops that were locations of sacred encounters and are ongoing manifestations of the numinous and powerful. But fundamentally different understandings of the natural world, alongside colonial agendas of conquest, have placed such places at risk. Chief Joseph (Hinmatóowyalaht'qit) did his best to explain that he and his people shared their very being with the earth, and that she ultimately could only be the property of her Creator. But such notions flatly contradicted assumptions upon which much of settler-colonial culture was based: private property and the extraction of resources for personal gain. In spite of these philosophical differences, Native people have continued to seek a variety of legal avenues and strategic alliances to protect these places, with varying degrees of success.

All of this raises an important question: If the sacred earth is the heart of Native American religious and cultural life, then what happens if that relationship is fundamentally challenged? Not just by legal frameworks or international borders, but by the earth itself? In the next chapter, we'll discuss the impacts of climate change on Native American cultures and traditions and how tribal communities are fighting back by opposing the use of fossil fuels, preserving forests, and protecting endangered species.

References and Recommendations

Cousins, Emily. "Mountains Made Alive: Native American Relationships with Sacred Land," *Cross Currents* Vol. 46 No. 4 (1996): 497–509.
Deloria, Vine. "Sacred Places and Moral Responsibility," in *God Is Red: A Native View of Religion*. London: Fulcrum, 2003.
Department of the Interior, Public Land Order 7254, "Withdrawal of Public Mineral Estate Within the Sweet Grass Hills Area of Critical Environmental Concern and Surrounding Areas; Montana," (April, 1997). https://www.gpo.gov/fdsys/pkg/FR-1997-04-10/pdf/97-9222.pdf

Freedman, Eric. "Protecting Sacred Sites on Public Land: Religion and Alliances in the Mato-Tipila-Devils Tower Litigation," *American Indian Quarterly* Vol. 31 No. 3 (2007): 1–22.

Jacob, Michelle, and Wynona Peters. "The Proper Way to Advance the Indian: Race and Gender Hierarchies in Early Yakima Newspapers," *Wicazo Sa Review* Vol. 26 No. 2 (2011): 39–55.

Johnson, Greg. "Materializing and Performing Hawaiian Religion(s) on Mauna Kea," in *Handbook of Indigenous Religions*, edited by Greg Johnson and Siv Ellen Kraft. Leiden: Brill, 2017.

Keller, Mary. "Indigenous Studies and 'the Sacred,'" *American Indian Quarterly* Vol. 38 No. 1 (2014): 82–110.

Kelley, Dennis. "Political Activism as Ceremony: Experiencing the Sacred through Protest," in *Tradition, Performance, and Religion in Native America: Ancestral Ways, Modern Selves*. Abingdon, UK: Routledge, 2014.

LaDuke, Winona. *Recovering the Sacred: The Power of Naming and Claiming*. Boston: South End Press: 2005.

Lewton, Elizabeth, and Victoria Bydone. "Identity and Healing in Three Navajo Religious Traditions: Sa'ah Naagháí Bik'eh Hózho," *Medical Anthropology Quarterly* Vol. 14 No. 4 (2000): 476–97.

95th Congress, Public Law 95–341. "Joint Resolution: American Indian Religious Freedom." https://www.gpo.gov/fdsys/pkg/STATUTE-92/pdf/STATUTE-92-Pg469.pdf

Ostler, Jeffrey. *The Lakotas and the Black Hills: The Struggle for Sacred Ground*. New York: Penguin, 2010.

Perdue, Theda, and Michael Green. *The Cherokee Nation and the Trail of Tears*. New York: Penguin, 2007.

Schremp, Gregory. "Distributed Power: An Overview. A Theme in American Indian Origin Stories," in *Stars Above Earth Below: American Indians and Nature*, edited by Marsha Bol. Lanham, MD: Robert Rinehart Publishers, 1998.

Sewid-Smith, Daisy, Chief Adam Dick, and Nancy Turner. "Sacred Cedar Tree of the Kwakwaka'wakw People," in *Stars Above Earth Below: American Indians and Nature*, edited by Marsha Bol. Lanham, MD: Robert Rinehart Publishers, 1998.

Smith, Theresa. *Island of Anishnaabeg: Thunderers and Water Monsters in the Traditional Ojibwe Life-World*. Lincoln: University of Nebraska, 2012.

Welch, John, Ramon Riley, and Michael Nixon. "Discretionary Desecration: Dzil Nchaa Si An (Mt. Graham) and Federal Agency Decisions Affecting American Indian Sacred Sites," *American Indian Culture and Research Journal* Vol. 33 No. 4 (2009): 29–68.

Websites and Videos

AGO People's Choice. http://christibelcourt.com/ago-peoples-choice/

Apache Stronghold. http://www.apache-stronghold.com/assets/us_congress_letter_3-8-16.pdf

Belcourt, Christi. http://artmatters.ca/wp/2014/08/artists-statement-christi-belcourt-on-the-wisdom-of-the-universe/

"The Energy of Heart Mountain." https://vimeo.com/83604524

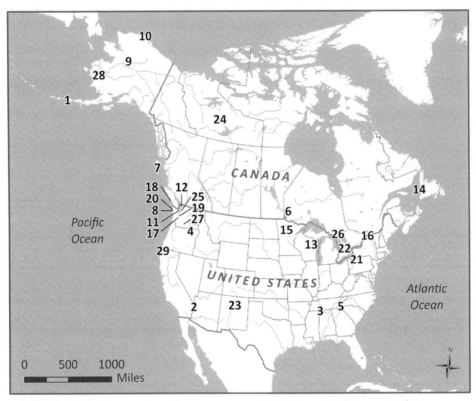

1 Aleut Territories
2 Chemehuevi Indian Tribe
3 Chicasaw Territories
4 Confederated Tribes of the Umatilla Nation
5 Cowee Mound
6 Grassy Narrows First Nation
7 Haida Nation
8 Hoh Indian Tribe
9 Huslia Koyukon
10 Iñupiat
11 Jamestown S'Klallam Tribe
12 Lummi Nation
13 Menominee Indian Tribe
14 Mi'Kmaq Territories

15 Minnesota Chippewa Tribe
16 Mohawk Nation
17 Nisqually Indian Tribe
18 Nuu-Chah-Nulth
19 Puyallup Indian Nation
20 Quileute Tribe
21 Seneca Nation of Indians
22 Six Nations of the Grand River
23 Tewa Speaking Communities
24 Tlicho Dene Territories
25 Tulalip Tribes
26 Whitefish River First Nation
27 Yakama Indian Tribes
28 Yupiaq Territories
29 Yurok Tribe

Map 3.1. Map of North America locating the tribal communities, nations, and cultural groups mentioned in this chapter. Basemap data made with Natural Earth. (Liz O'Dea Springborn)

Climate and Conservation

3

Climate change is a potential culture killer.

—ZOLTÁN GROSSMAN

A s EARLY AS 2003, INUPIAT HUNTERS AND FISHERS on the North Slope of Alaska reported seeing evidence of climate change with dire implications for subsistence fishing and hunting: "The sea ice is gone; there's no main pack ice anymore. All of it is just floating ice. . . . In the 1970s and 1980s, the ice was close. You didn't have to go far to see it. . . . [Now] the ice is thinner. It is more dangerous with more open water; there are more waves. Now the ice is three hundred miles out. It is dangerous" (McBeath and Shepro, 46–47). More rain and unpredictable weather have meant increased erosion along riverbanks and shores, more sediment, and warmer rivers and lakes. Melting permafrost has caused slumping land and increased mud. Willows, land otters, rabbits, and porcupines have moved north; fish have declined in number; flocks of migrating birds and caribou herds are smaller and sicker. Oil production facilities have polluted air, land, and water. By 2013, western James Bay First Nations were reporting changes in weather patterns: extreme weather events were increasing, and animal behavior had altered (Tam et al., 2013).

Nearly 3,000 kilometers away on Vancouver Island, Nuu-chah-nulth elder and educator Charles Atleo describes the situation this way:

> While climate change remains a question among the scientific and scholarly community, it is not a question for those with direct (and threatening) experience of it. For the latter, the evidence for climate change is clear in its destruction of homelands, in its degradation of rivers that formerly spawned millions of salmon, and in its destruction of habitat with the consequent disappearance of many species. (Atleo 2011, 18–20)

If, as the previous chapter discussed, the spiritually endowed earth lies at the heart of Indigenous religious life, what happens when that very earth is at risk? How

Photo 3.1.   Ice Watch, Utqiagvik, Alaska. A man looks out at the Chukchi Sea. August 2013. (https://www.flickr.com/photos/air_traveller/15392797787, Christopher Griner)

might a sickening planet impact Native religious and cultural life? And in turn, how might Indigenous religious and cultural traditions provide tools for responding to this growing crisis? Restoring a harmonious and balanced relationship with the natural world is not easy. But ancestors' stories, rituals, and ceremonies provide much-needed guidance to undertake that hard work. This chapter considers tribal responses to environmental crises such as climate change, deforestation, and habitat loss showing how Indigenous knowledge can be employed to mitigate climate change and protect threatened ecosystems. While the climate crisis poses a dire threat, solutions lie within the traditional ecological knowledge of Indigenous cultures, and collaborative partnerships with First Nations communities.

Climate Change

Climate change disproportionately impacts Indigenous people. As Terry Williams and Preston Hardison of the Tulalip Tribes Fisheries and Natural Resources Department put it: "Climate change is pulling the living carpet out from under tribal nations" (Williams and Hardison, 61). Indigenous people are rooted in their ancestral lands, the places "from which they emerged, where their ancestors dwell, about which their stories and language refer, and to which they have continuing spiritual and collective obligations." Because of this, "large scale environmental decline would cut them off from their origins, from the places of their collective memory, and the rights to self-determination the Tribes possess as peoples" (Grossman 2008, 15–16). Indigenous people pay a steep price for the global consumption of fossil fuels: their lands are developed without their consent, their health damaged by impacts to air, water, and food chains. In North America, tribal communities battle growing heat waves, wildfires, and invasive species. Imported diseases and parasites threaten forests and sea life. Ocean acidification weakens shellfish and other marine species, while their ranges are shifting as plants and animals migrate north, away from tribal territories.

Williams and Hardison make clear that these changes have profound impacts for Indigenous cultures and communities:

> The living world is a core part of tribal identity, as animals, plants, fungi, and even microbes are often embedded in tribal stories, are a co-equal part of their kinship relations with their human kin, and are used for subsistence, economy, medicines, architecture, clothing, artistic expression. Climate change threatens to move culturally important species away from both the legal territories and lands to which they have usufruct rights to use resources. (Williams and Hardison, 58)

Consider, for instance, the Quileute and Hoh Nations of the Washington coast. Prior to colonialism, they traveled seasonally, harvesting resources from across a traditional territory that spanned nine hundred square miles. Today, while their reservation is one square mile, they still maintain their ancient fishing traditions, having protected their rights to the sea. In coastal origin stories, it was Transformer (K'wati) who discovered the coastal people. When K'wati first saw them, they were walking on their hands. "Walk on your feet!" he commanded them. And then, he taught them to fish. "Go and fish smelt. You shall catch much fish when you fish smelt. Ever since then there has been smelt at Hoh" (Papiez, 75). But climate change has meant low oxygen levels in ocean waters, resulting in dead zones and leading to massive kill-offs. It has meant decreasing winter snow pack, warmer rivers, faster floods, and more sediment. Smelt, a species at the heart of their creation story and a gift from Transformer that shapes who they are as a people, are growing scarce. A millennia-old subsistence culture is at risk of being lost, unless something is done.

Ceremonies of Protest

Acknowledging the role of fossil fuels in climate change, Native nations have joined in opposition to these industries. In 2014, a huge coal terminal was proposed for the banks of the Columbia River. The Yakama Tribes fiercely protested, determined to protect their river. Not long afterward, another coal terminal was proposed on the site of an ancient Lummi village in western Washington. If built,

Photo 3.2.   Amanda Polchies of the Elsipogtog First Nation, at an anti-fracking demonstration on October 17, 2013. (Ossie Michelin and APTN National News)

this second terminal would be the largest such facility in North America. The massive $665 million terminal would host 487 massive coal barges every year, each of them traversing the treacherous waters of the Strait of Juan de Fuca and the Salish Sea. Ignoring tribal protests and in violation of the law, the company conducted site surveys, bulldozing an archaeological site and damaging an ancient burial ground.

But the Lummi, Yakama, and their tribal allies responded with powerful weapons: the sacred and the ceremonial. The Yakama took to the waters of the Columbia, holding fish-ins at the proposed terminal site, declaring their treaty rights to fish, and demanding the rejection of coal. Master carver Jewell James carved a cedar totem pole, and Lummi tribal members took the pole on a tour around the country. At each stop, they sang traditional songs, led prayers, and told stories, raising awareness and securing allies. Within two years, both projects were dead: their permits denied by the Army Corps of Engineers.

Puyallup tribal members continue to fight a proposed liquid natural gas plant on the tidal flats of Commencement Bay in Tacoma, Washington. In 2018 they employed a powerful symbolic arsenal: Puget Sound Energy employees arrived at

Photo 3.3.   Nancy Shippentower (right), an elder with the Puyallup tribe, holds tree branches as she stands in in front of a sign marking an area at the Port of Tacoma as traditional Puyallup territory during a protest in front of Puget Sound Energy's liquefied natural gas facility being built at the port, Friday, May 24, 2019, in Tacoma, Washington. Tribal members and other supporters are hoping to halt the construction of the project, and earlier in the month, Washington governor Jay Inslee, who was seeking the Democratic nomination for president on a platform focused on climate change issues, withdrew his earlier support of the project. (AP Photo/Ted S. Warren)

work one Monday morning to discover a miniature version of a longhouse built outside the entrance to their headquarters—replete with solar panels on the roof. "This is how it feels when your consent is taken from you," Puyallup tribal member Dakota Case told the local news. "We're building without permission on PSE property, just as PSE is doing on our land" (Ruud, 2018).

Throughout North America, Indigenous people are fighting back against climate change, working to mitigate its effects, building partnerships to preserve lands and resources, and protesting fossil fuels and deforestation. Such battles accomplish more than raising awareness or transforming political discourse. As religious studies scholar Dennis Kelley (Chumash) helps to make clear, for those who participate, political action on behalf of the earth provides space for sacred work. As he puts it, "Indian political activism is the valorization of traditional American Indian worldviews, providing community support and opportunities for regular ritual participation" (Kelley, 46). Resistance lights the fire of cultural and linguistic revitalization. Ceremonies of protest heal the bonds among human communities, individuals, and the earth. A march, a blockade, a prayer circle, a potluck, a pole raising, a drum circle: these all become ceremonies when they do the sacred work of renewing the earth and restoring Indigenous peoples' relationships with it. Two examples help illustrate the ways in which a protest can become a ceremony, restoring bonds between people and place as they seek to protect their homelands.

"Nothing Gets the Attention of Canada Quicker Than a Good Ol' Mohawk Barricade": Drawing a Line at Six Nations

On March 17, 2006, Haudenosaunee women linked arms across a road, intent on blocking the progress of logging and construction equipment. Women with infants, small children, and elders were facing hundreds of angry Eurocanadian residents and armed riot police. At issue was a new housing development, one that would mean logging their forest and the construction of hundreds of new homes, every year, for twenty years. The Six Nations of the Grand River Reserve in southeastern Ontario bordered the proposed development within unceded Haudenosaunee territory, lands guaranteed to the people in the Haldimand Treaty of 1784. Tribal members were outraged. Their protest began with potlucks, but culminated in a months-long occupation that changed the Canadian political landscape.

As organizer Janie Jamieson (Dodayotahahkwane) recalled, the protest wasn't just political, it was spiritual, inspiring pride and a renewed commitment to culture and language.

> This unity created in the people a pride that renewed an interest to learn and participate in our original teachings. . . . Our people have felt helpless not just for years but for generations. Our grandparents dealt with this helplessness in different ways, some became band council members, and some entrenched themselves into Christianity or both. While others drank and did nothing. . . . But the gathering of the people sparked a fire. . . . Right now, like I firmly believe with the psychological war that is going on, the best way to equip our kids is self-identity. They can't take that away. You can't make my son unlearn Mohawk anymore. You can't take away these ceremonies. He's still going to practice them. . . . Now my son is immersed in who he is, and there's nothing that they can do to take that away from him. (McCarthy, 252)

Awaiagon Agadaeoga, a young Seneca activist participating in a blockade at Tyendinaga put it this way: "It showed me who I really am, put meaning to my life. It started my walk on ceremony road. Without it I'd still be like a zombie wandering the world, trying to find where I belong" (McCarthy, 107).

Lighting the Sacred Fire at Grassy Narrows

It was December, which is a really cold time of year to set up camp in western Ontario. But three young members of the Anishinaabe Grassy Narrows First Nation were doing just that. Near the shores of Slant Lake, they positioned fallen trees across a snow-covered logging road, lit a fire, and built a tipi. Then they settled in for a long wait, determined to stop logging trucks and equipment from moving into their traditional lands. Escalating concerns over large-scale industrial logging had grown throughout the 1990s. By 2002, the people had had enough. The Grassy Narrows blockade became a site of cultural revitalization, finding its center in a sacred fire kept continually burning. One of the original three activists recalled: "I remember an elder once told me on my healing journey I should start with myself, my family, my community, and then our nation. I never understood that, until the day my sister, another man and I went to lay logs over the road. We did it because we were sick and tired of watching our lives slowly disappear" (Willow 2012, 103).

In her book about the Grassy Narrows blockade, Anne Willow explains that for the Anishinaabe activists, preserving the land and preserving the people were inseparable concerns: their land-based culture required healthy ecosystems to survive. Their burial grounds had been flooded, native rice crops threatened by pollution, forests clear-cut. A pulp mill had polluted their rivers with mercury, poisoning children, raising infant mortality rates, and destroying the local fishing economy by putting nearly 90 percent of their men out of work. In response, many turned to drugs, alcohol, and suicide. Their history, Willow writes, is "heartrending . . . a source of rage" (Willow 2012, 69).

But things were changing. Willow explains: "While activists at Grassy Narrows today continue to conceive of the environment as 'powerful' and to position themselves humbly within it, they are simultaneously—and without any apparent incongruity—able to envision themselves in the role of environmental defenders" (Willow 2012, 79). Their protest, centered on a sacred fire and ceremonial tipi, did just that.

The blockade was a success. After five hard-fought years the logging company withdrew. By 2012, the Grassy Narrows First Nation was co-managing the forest with the provincial government, and the blockade site along Slant Lake had become a community gathering place. At this former site of conflict, families camp, tend the sacred fire, offer tobacco, share meals, build canoes, and work with elders, reclaiming traditional ways of life. The blockade inspired a cultural renewal. It was a sacred fire, inspiring them to fight back, to protect Anishinaabe ways of life (Willow 2012, 140). Such case studies are important to note because they show the connection between Indigenous people and place, between protest and sacred tradition. Doing the work of protecting intact ecosystems—by protesting fossil fuel extraction or protecting carbon-sequestering forests—is not separate from, but vitally interrelated with, the health of Indigenous people and the survival of Indigenous cultures.

Traditional Ecological Knowledge

Mike Williams (Yupiaq), vice chairman of the Alaska Inter-Tribal Council, is well aware of the challenges posed by climate change and environmental degradation. But he is also aware of the potential solutions held by Indigenous communities:

> Throughout the nation in Indian Country, traditional foods are declining, local landscapes are changing, rural infrastructure is being challenged, soils are drying, and

lake and river levels are declining. Tribes are experiencing droughts, loss of forests, fishery problems, and increased health risks from heat strokes and from diseases that thrive in warmer temperatures. [But] tribes offer some of the greatest resources for helping the nation with renewable energy development, particularly wind, solar power, biomass, and geothermal power. . . . It is important that our traditional knowledge be incorporated and respected, that we be consulted, and that our values and needs be honored. (Williams, 37)

"Traditional knowledge" here refers to the vast wealth of scientific knowledge and philosophical wisdom maintained by Indigenous cultures, often referred to as Traditional Ecological Knowledge (TEK) or Indigenous Knowledge (IK).

Deborah McGregor (Whitefish River Anishinaabe) defines IK as a system of careful observation of and attending to the natural world, in order to articulate responsibilities that "ensure the continuation of Creation (or what academics or scientists might call 'sustainability')" (McGregor 2004, 389). Martha Johnson, executive director of the Dene Cultural Institute in the Northwest Territories describes TEK as:

A body of knowledge built up by a group of people through generations of living in close contact with nature. It includes a system of classification, a set of empirical observations about the local environment, and a system of self-management that governs resource use. The quantity and quality of traditional environmental knowledge varies among community members, depending upon gender, age, social status, intellectual capability, and profession (hunter, spiritual leader, healer, etc.). With its roots firmly in the past, traditional environmental knowledge is both cumulative and dynamic, building upon the experience of earlier generations and adapting to the new technological and socioeconomic changes of the present. (Johnson, 393)

While sharing much in common with Western science, TEK differs in that it includes spirituality. Knowledge comes as "a gift from the Creator, the ancestors, acquired through dreams, or in direct conversations with the spirit world, the plant people, the animal people, or other spiritual origins. Indigenous peoples regard their traditional knowledge as both practical and spiritual" (Williams and Hardison, 62). Here deep spiritual insights intertwine with and undergird pragmatic management techniques, such as how to protect biodiversity, restore habitat, or provide critical analysis of mitigation techniques and potential adverse impacts.

Marie Battiste (Mi'kmaq) and James Youngblood Henderson (Chickasaw) explain that TEK, or IK, rests upon a *relationship* between a people and their place.

[IK] is the expression of the vibrant relationships between people, their ecosystems, and other living beings and spirits that share their lands. . . . All aspects of knowledge are interrelated and cannot be separated from the traditional territories of the people concerned. . . . Developing these ways of knowing leads to freedom of consciousness and to solidarity with the natural world. (McGregor 2004, 390)

In a similar vein, Gregory Cajete (Tewa) argues that TEK isn't just knowledge about relationships with the natural world, but "the relationship itself" (McGregor 2004, 391). For Cajete, TEK is something one *does* rather than something one *knows*. It is the act of relating ethically with the world around you. As Cajete explains,

> Native people traditionally lived a kind of communal environmental ethics that stemmed from the broadest sense of kinship with all life. The underlying aim of the science of ecology, therefore, the understanding of the web of relationships with the "household" of Nature, is not modern science's sole property. Understanding the relationship scientifically is not enough—living and nurturing these relationships is the key. This is the ecology of the Native community. (McGregor 2004, 394)

This is important: while scientists may be tempted to extract answers and solutions from Indigenous communities, the very definition of TEK means that taking such knowledge out of context won't work—without a lived relationship with a place, it is no longer Indigenous Knowledge.

Executive director of Sustainable Nations PennElys Droz (Anishinaabe) and Leann Simpson (Anishinaabe) caution against the temptation to see TEK as another resource to be extracted. As Simpson says: "My land is seen as a resource. My relatives in the plant and animal worlds are seen as resources. My culture and knowledge is a resource. My body is a resource, and my children are a resource. . . . The act of extraction removes all of the relationships that give whatever is being extracted meaning. . . . That's always been part of colonialism and conquest" (Droz, 106). Rather than a body of information to be exploited, TEK is a guide for healthy relationships in "a world made up of interconnected other-than-human persons," who have "intelligence, knowledge wisdom, and ability to discern right from wrong." TEK provides guidelines for living in the world—which necessitates taking life and altering the landscape—but doing so in a way that "respects the rights of other families to exist" (Droz, 110).

TEK is passed on through storytelling, ritual, and ceremony. In her book *Walking the Land, Feeding the Fire: Knowledge and Stewardship among the Tłicho Dene*, Alice Legat explores the way in which stories are imprinted on the landscape among this Athabaskan First Nations people of Canada's Northwest Territories. Tłicho Dene territory is a storied landscape, and in walking its trails, one passes through stories, each teaching a vital lesson about how to live.

Koyukon Luck and TEK

In a similar fashion, Orville Huntington and Annette Watson show how TEK is passed on through oral traditions in their Koyukon village of Huslia, another Northern Athabaskan–speaking community across the border in Alaska. Huntington and Watson emphasize that they "are particularly concerned with climate change because it is so rapid. In the lands around our village of Huslia, we must live with these changes daily. The permafrost that kept stable the riverbanks and lake systems has melted, so the banks more rapidly erode, destabilizing our homes and subsistence resources ever faster" (Huntington and Watson, 52). Loss of permafrost, drying lakes, and warmer temperatures have all meant changes in plant life—fewer berry bushes, fewer hardwoods, fewer salmon—and changes in animal migrations. Flowers are blooming at the wrong time; sleepless bears are wandering into winter villages; new invasive pests are causing trouble.

But these authors argue that solutions to these new challenges can be found in ancient oral traditions, such as the Koyukon notion of "luck."

> These old ways of knowing, the ways to show respect, are our very belief and spiritual grounding in our natural world. There is no difference in the sacred stories of the distant time we Koyukon Athabaskans call *Kk'adonts'idnee* and our current lives, what we see with our own eyes, and what we feel in our hearts to be true. . . . Riddles tell us the way to have luck. Luck is very important to the survival of our people; it indicates that we have been respectful to the animals and lands where we live. (Huntington and Watson, 54)

Rather than suggesting random chance or good fortune, the Koyukon notion of "luck" is instead akin to social capital: it suggests good favor accrued over a lifetime of following protocols that include proper speech, thought, and action. Failing to show respect or gratitude ruins one's luck. Considering these core ethical principles, and the way they help guide relationships with the natural world, offers a new path forward.

Huntington and Watson also emphasize that Koyukon ecological knowledge is not simply factual information that can be extracted from stories and integrated into Western scientific systems. "The problem with 'integration,'" they explain, "is that it erases Indigenous ethics and Indigenous solutions to contemporary challenges" (Huntington and Watson, 59). Removing knowledge from context omits the "kincentric ecology," of the Koyukon worldview, where human beings exist in reciprocal kinship relations with the natural world. When caribou populations are threatened by fossil fuel extraction, for example, Koyukon riddles provide more than a means of tracking caribou migration patterns. They provide a different way of seeing who caribou are. Koyukon riddles teach an ethical and spiritual worldview. They teach how to live in a place, and in relationship with that place, and they ought to be taken seriously. For example, rather than regulations that separate people from animals, Koyukon natural-resource managers recommend policies that "encourage our ethical kinship with fellow beings" (Huntington and Watson, 66).

Nuu-chah-nulth Principles and TEK

E. Richard Atleo (Umeek) is a hereditary chief of the Ahousaht First Nation, the first aboriginal person in British Columbia to earn a doctorate degree, and cochair of a scientific panel for sustainable forest practices in Clayoquot Sound on Vancouver

Island. His book *Principles of Tsawalk: An Indigenous Approach to Global Crisis* provides an example of the ethical philosophies underlying TEK. In his work, Atleo argues that Nuu-chah-nulth origin stories "serve the same purpose as does scientific theory, since they provide insight into the nature of existence" (Atleo 2012, 53). Like science, knowledge is accrued through observation and trial and error. Unlike science, it is also accrued through prayer, fasting, ritual restrictions, and ceremonial bathing (in Nuu-chah-nulth, this is called *ʔuusumč*). Cultivating humility through ritual purification helps individuals encounter spiritual powers, gifts, songs, and direction. Like science, such knowledge is to be shared with the community. But traditional knowledge is reported back to the community not with "papers or PowerPoint slides, but rather, with rattles, chants, songs, dances, regalia, and demonstrations of spiritual powers and medicinal gifts" (Atleo 2012, 53).

Atleo identifies three key values within the Nuu-chah-nulth ethical system that help to regulate harmonious relationships between human beings and the natural world: recognition, consent, and continuity. To *recognize* someone is not just to greet them, but to acknowledge their personhood and the relationship that binds you together. True recognition, Atleo says, requires humility because it implies acknowledging the others' right to exist, on their own terms and in their own way. *Consent* is also vital if we want to address the crises of climate change and vanishing species. A vital principle for sustainable relationships, consent requires the recognition of another being's personhood. "For example, consider what occurs when Nuu-chah-nulth take down a great cedar tree to transform it into a canoe or into parts of a house and household items and utensils. The tree is acknowledged as a personage and paid much respect and honor. It is recognized as an organic and living part of a larger entity that scientists today refer to as *nature*" (Atleo 2012, 102).

Recognition and consent should not just govern interactions with nature, but with other human beings as well. Atleo explains:

> Most of the previous five hundred years of colonization can be characterized as a period of continuous violation of consent towards women in general and Aboriginals and other dispossessed groups in particular. . . . When a people are not recognized, it is difficult, if not impossible, to allow them the privilege of consent. (Atleo 2012, 102–3)

All life forms have a "sacred right to continue to live in their own integrity of being," to be what the Creator intended them to be. This, he suggests, should be considered a "co-management principle," a path toward honoring not just the necessity but the sacrality of biodiversity (Atleo 2012, 121–22).

Continuity concerns the notion that all of life is interconnected and comes from the same source. With this perspective, individualism and isolation are deeply problematic. "In the Nuu-chah-nulth worldview, it is unnatural, and equivalent to death and destruction, for any person to be isolated from family or community" (Atleo 2004, 27). Consider the Nuu-chah-nulth word *aphey*, which Atleo translates as *kind*. To be kind, he tells his readers, is to show generosity and hospitality, and to ask for help when you need it. Rather than a one-way gesture of compassion, here kindness is contingent on recognizing and honoring the interconnected nature of our existence. To be kind, one must both give help and ask for it.

Or, consider the Nuu-chah-nulth word *isaak*, which Atleo translates as *respect*. *Isaak* "necessitates a consciousness that all creation has a common origin" with a common Creator (Atleo 2004, 15). In Nuu-chah-nulth, the term for Creator is *Qua-ootz*, translated as owner-of-reality. (Interestingly, Atleo notes that this same word is used to refer to grandchildren—because both they and the Creator create the future that is becoming a reality.) Because all of creation has the same origin, all things share in the same spirit, and all things are ultimately one. This notion of respect is thus not an expression of fear but rather "a pragmatic stance in keeping with creation's original design of wholeness" (Atleo 2004, 16).

While the truth of Creation is ultimately a story of interconnection, settler colonialism challenges this fundamental truth. Atleo argues: "The state of affairs in postmodernity might justifiably be described as a tyranny of individual rights to the exclusion of, or to the detriment of, group rights. There appears to be an imbalance of the two" (Atleo, 2004, 55). Whereas in traditional Nuu-chah-nulth culture, individual self-interest and self-expression "are intended to serve the interests of family and community" (2004, 57), a focus on individualism obscures the fundamental unity of reality, leading to imbalance and disharmony.

Attempting to explain this central idea, Atleo and his peers coined a Nuu-chah-nulth phrase: *heshook ish tsawalk* (everything is one). The phrase draws from the notion that "biological differentiation is understood as the result of transformations from a common source of being" and an "essential unity between spiritual and physical beings" (Atleo 2012, 86–88). "Since reality is a unity, what befalls one part of this unity must befall the whole. The Nuu-chah-nulth worldview . . . sees the global crisis in relational terms, in terms of a creation filled with mutually interdependent life forms that require mutually acceptable protocols in order to maintain balance and harmony. From this point of view, the global crisis is one of relational disharmony" (Atleo 2012, 37).

Traditional Ecological Knowledge at Work

Having considered different principles of Traditional Ecological Knowledge, this section pivots to consider what these ideas and values look like when put into practice. Kat Anderson's book *Tending the Wild: Native American Knowledge and the Management of California's Natural Resources* explores Indigenous Knowledge at work. In this historical and archaeological analysis, Anderson makes the case that pre-colonial California was not a wilderness, but a carefully tended garden. For millennia, Indigenous Californians had been weeding, pruning, transplanting, and employing controlled burns and pest management techniques as they cared for the bioregion. Over twelve thousand years, plants and animals evolved alongside Native Californians, shaped by these interventions. Considering this wealth of knowledge, Anderson argues that Native people should co-manage public lands with a real voice in decision making within their traditional territories. Integrating Native communities into research and co-management of their lands, she suggests, could provide a wealth of benefits for settler scientists and Native communities alike.

This kind of integrative work can be seen throughout Native North America, where, collectively, Indigenous communities manage approximately 95 million acres of land. In many instances, this management is informed by TEK. For instance, in British Columbia, strategic watershed analysis teams are collaborating to interview elders and harvesters, gather field data, and use GPS to produce digital sharable maps that identify hazards and changing conditions, and are sharing information around how to manage, care for, and harvest migrating resources. Other tribal communities are working together to promote renewable energy. In Washington State, the Makah Nation has invested in the Makah Bay Offshore Wave Energy Project; the Tulalip Nation is investing in biomass energy; and the Skokomish recently installed one of the largest tribally owned solar-power systems on the West Coast. The Gitga'at in British Columbia are designing small-scale hydroelectric dams designed to aid salmon passage rather than impede it. Lakota Solar Enterprises is an entirely Native-owned and -operated renewable energy company, serving the Pine Ridge tribal community, and providing green job training to Native American communities throughout the United States. As founder Henry Red Cloud explains: "My biggest dream is for First Nation communities to become energy independent before mainstream America."

Perhaps the most important concern guiding this work is Native people's relationships with place. As Alan Parker (Chippewa Cree) argues, Indigenous peoples' survival depends on their ties to their land:

> These connections have served as a wellspring of spiritual energy and have linked them to their ancestors. These links provide a body of knowledge that defines who they are in the cosmos and how they must structure their lives in order to survive. If future generations of Indigenous people are to continue the traditional practices that make culture a source of spiritual nourishment, these vital connections must be maintained. (Grossman 2008, 22)

Taking a closer look at several case studies will help illustrate this practice.

St. Paul Island Aleut

The Aleut people of St. Paul Island in northwest Alaska provide a compelling example of what this might look like. Known as the People of the Sea Lion, their very identity has been challenged as sea lion populations have declined by 80 percent over three decades. The impact has been devastating, severing the ties between young men and older hunters who maintain the ancestral practices and ceremonial traditions. Without this connection to their heritage and to a meaningful vocation, many young people floundered. Larry Merculieff observes:

> In one generation of that happening—in the mid-eighties to mid-nineties—we lost 70 percent of our young men, due to accidental death due to alcohol, suicide,

murder, and incarceration for felony crimes. That never happened to our young men before, but nobody from the outside would study what occurred, so there's no documentation. This is some indication again of what science priorities are; they're collecting data to see what the climate is doing, rather than also assessing the human impacts on St. Paul Island. (Merculieff, 46)

The Aleut drew on their traditional knowledge as they responded to the crisis, founding a stewardship camp to teach young people about their land. "With the guidance of stories and storytelling, with the elders present, [the camp is] bringing songs back to restore the intimate and profound connection that people had with the environment" (Merculieff, 47).

Bridging the link between Western science and traditional Aleut knowledge, local high school students studied the changes on the island and their impact on bird populations. They employed Western scientific research methods, combining them with Aleut methods of interpretation and presentation. Instead of using PowerPoint, students performed their research through storytelling, dancing, or other culturally relevant forms. A community member recalled: "The students made up a song in Aleut, and they did sign dancing along with it. It was fantastic. The whole community got together and these students performed it to a standing ovation" (Merculieff, 49).

Menominee Forest

Another example of TEK at work can be seen in the Menominee Nation of northeastern Wisconsin, which utilizes traditional values and teachings to ensure productive and sustainable forest management. Comprising 235,000 acres, 220,000 of which are forested, Menominee land contains 330 miles of trout streams and 44 lakes. Thousands of tribal residents depend on these forests for their livelihood. Considered a model of sustainable forestry, Menominee forests are famous for their health and biodiversity. Rich in large, older trees, they produce more timber per acre than adjacent National Forest lands that are managed using typical forestry techniques.

In his book *Sustaining the Forest, the People, and the Spirit*, Thomas Davis emphasizes that this success is due to the traditional values and knowledge that inform Menominee practices, affirming their responsibility to the land and its ecosystems, and teaching that the health of the people is inseparable from that of the forest. Traditional songs, dances, and ceremonial celebrations keep these values alive. The Menominee are religiously diverse: Indigenous religions coexist with the Catholic Church, the Church of Jesus Christ of Latter-day Saints, and the Native American Church, but all Menominee share an ethos when it comes to the land. Management decisions follow a consensus model that values the community over individual gain and affirms the equity of generations (those present, those before, and those yet to come). This demand for consensus means that change must come slowly and never at the cost of a healthy forest. Here, cutting-edge science and the free market are balanced by traditional values, which ensure a commitment to future generations, the human community, and the other-than-human community.

Swinomish Climate Change Assessment

The Swinomish Nation in Washington State provides another example of a tribal community integrating TEK and Western science to combat climate change. In their 2009 Executive Summary of the Swinomish Climate Change Initiative Impact Assessment Technical Report, the Swinomish argued that "human health, ecological health, and cultural health" are all "woven together, all equally important." The tribe has developed ways of integrating these concerns, including "participation in spiritual ceremonies, intergenerational education opportunities, and traditional harvesting practices" (Swinomish Nation, 139). While settler-colonial society might draw lines between science and religion, the Swinomish case illustrates how TEK requires the integration of spirituality, sacred philosophy, and critical participant observation. Traditional teachings make clear how human health is tied to ecological health. "Ceremonial use is more than the ceremonies and gatherings themselves. It also means the importance of giving thanks to the spirits of the natural resources when harvesting and preparing them, and the necessity to feed the spirit of oneself by consuming natural resource foods or feeding the spirit of a relative who has passed by offering natural resources." Ceremonies cultivate resilience, and "resilience is important because certain impacts of climate change may lead to grief and despair" (Swinomish Nation, 141–42).

For the Swinomish, climate change and environmental devastation are expressions of colonialism, seen within "externally imposed habitat destruction, economic dislocation, food security interruption, social order disruption, physical relocation, and natural resource piracy" (Swinomish Nation, 142). Healing the people and healing the land requires decolonizing. It requires tribal self-determination, regaining access to traditional foods and medicine, reclaiming Native languages, and restoration of habitats.

Umatilla Natural and Cultural Resources

Confederated Tribes of the Umatilla, located in northeastern Oregon, are also putting TEK into practice to address climate change and find a path toward conservation of valued species. Natural Resources Director Eric Quaempts explains how TEK informed a reorganization of their department. In a remarkable move, the tribe decided to merge the Department of Cultural Resources with the Department of Natural Resources. This decision led them to structure their scientific studies and resource management around traditional teachings of the "first foods." As Quaempts explains, the first foods (roots, salmon, berries, venison) are honored in seasonal ceremonies that form the foundation of Umatilla spiritual life.

> The first foods comes from a tribal creation belief, that when the world was created, the Creator asked the different animals, who was going to take care of the Indian

people. This was the order that they promised themselves. And that promise is remembered in the way the foods are served in the community longhouse. They're
served in that same order. And water is first, because all life depends on water.
(Drummond and Steele)

Throughout the year, the first foods ceremonies honor each food in turn, moving from the lowest elevation to the highest, from river basins to mountains. The
Umatilla Natural and Cultural Resources Department integrated this elevation and
seasonal organization into their systems, drawing on oral traditions and ceremonial
practices as they track changes in the landscape, to see how species are changing:
coming earlier or later, or moving farther upland. As he explains, this focus on first
foods directly shapes their work.

> It takes us from in-stream in the flood plain, to the mountains, where the huckle-
> berry grow. This is why we can't separate natural resources from cultural resources.
> They're the same thing. The biggest concern to me, is that if climate change pre-
> dictions are accurate, and if you see shifts in the suitability of habitat and range for
> entire species like salmon or maybe even other foods like roots or berries, if those
> foods shift in their distribution significantly, then it's kind of like they're leaving the
> community behind. (Drummond)

Collaborative Conservation

In addition to integrating TEK with their own tribal land management, tribal communities are responding to climate change, protecting ecosystems, and caring for
endangered species by leading strategic partnerships with nontribal groups. Such
collaborative conservation partnerships preserve lands, reclaim Indigenous access to
those lands, and honor their obligation to care for them.

An early example of successful co-management of Indigenous territories is
the Gwaii Haanas National Park Reserve. In the 1970s and 1980s, clear-cutting
was transforming the Haida landscape on the coast of British Columbia, changing
forests to tree farms, destabilizing hillsides, and warming rivers choked with silt
(and, as we now know, contributing to climate change). Moved to protest, the
Haida responded by blockading a new logging road. Elders were first at the site,
and news coverage showed powerful images of Haida elders in traditional regalia
aligned against big business and a police state. The issue was complex. Many Haida
people were loggers, and some were among the police called upon to break up the
blockade. An observer recalled, "One of the RCMP officers was a Haida. That
was a really, really hard day for him. He had tears in his eyes as he led one of the
female Haida elders to the helicopter. It was a really emotional day for everyone.
There was so much at stake" (Von der Porten, 91).

In a powerfully symbolic move, the Haida hosted a feast for both sides of the
blockade. First Nations leaders traveled to Japan to meet with the head of the logging company and plead with them to cease operations on Haida lands. Later court

Photo 3.4.   Diane Brown uses hemlock branches and water to bless the Gwaii Haanas legacy totem pole before its raising in Windy Bay, British Columbia, on Lyell Island in Haida Gwaii on Thursday, August 15, 2013. The 13-meter totem was the first monumental pole to be raised in the area in 130 years. It was carved to celebrate the 20th anniversary of the Gwaii Haanas Agreement, a document that allows the government of Canada and the Haida Nation to co-manage and protect the region. Haida Gwaii is made up of more than 150 islands about 90 kilometers west of British Columbia's north coast. (AP Photo/The Canadian Press, Darryl Dyck)

hearings included traditional songs, family stories, and the testimonies of elders. In the end, the protests succeeded in sparking a move toward more sustainable logging practices and in calling new attention to Indigenous rights. In 1986, Lyell Island became the Gwaii Haanas National Park Reserve. Today, the park is co-managed by the Haida Nation and the Canadian National Park Service. Guujaaw (Haida) explained: "[At Lyell Island] we wanted to make it real clear that our culture is our relationship to the land, that's where our songs come from, where our language comes from, and the dances are all about the creatures that we share this land with. And so we brought the song back to the land to express exactly who we are in relationship to the land" (Von der Porten, 96). Gwaii Haanas National Park has become a model for what it means to do collaborative conservation.

Anthropologist Anna Willow contrasts collaborative conservation with "fortress conservation." In a fortress-conservation model, nature is seen as pristine and healthy only when it is removed from human contact. While done with good intentions, the establishment of wilderness areas and national parks often enforced a fortress-conservation model, removing Native people from traditional territories that they had cared for and been in relationship with for millennia. In contrast to this exclusionary model, collaborative conservation is an "organized attempt to unite diverse individuals and interests for the common purpose of environmental protection" (Willow 2015, 32). In her book *Trust in the Land: New Directions in Tribal Conservation*, Beth Rose Middleton likewise calls for a shift toward environmental justice and away from historical conservation methods that restrict Native people from accessing their territories. "Lands that had been stewarded for centuries were declared forest reserves, then national forests and national parks. They were off-limits, except for certain permitted uses, and Native land management practices were criminalized. . . . Often, Indian people were not even allowed to engage in permitted use of these lands" (Middleton, 37). Such policies had severe consequences for Indigenous communities, cultures, and identities.

Middleton and Willow both call for conservation practices that partner with Indigenous communities and are informed by the needs and rights of all people, particularly people of color and those from lower-income communities. Middleton argues, "Non-Native land trusts, agencies, and private conservationists will be working toward environmental justice and undoing historical wrongs if they give priority to establishing relationships with local tribal governments, Native organizations, and Native families, and to accompanying them in this work, rather than opposing it by further enclosing Native homelands" (Middleton, 5). This movement toward environmental justice was supported by the creation of the Tribal and Native Lands program by the U.S. Federal Trust for Public Lands in 1999. The program "focuses on collaborating with tribes and tribal governments to protect and return Native homelands to Native people" by ensuring tribal access to public lands, and supporting tribal conservation goals (Middleton, 28). Elders teach that some places do indeed need to have restricted access, such as burial sites, places of prayer, or key habitats for endangered species, provided such restrictions are undertaken in consultation with Native communities. The key issue is that tribes be recognized as real partners in decision making and co-management, and that such co-management be guided by Indigenous Knowledge.

Intertribal Sinkyone Wilderness Council

The Intertribal Sinkyone Wilderness Council (ISWC) is another example of such collaborative partnerships. A nonprofit land conservancy governed by representatives of ten Northern California tribes, ISWC collectively manages the 3,845-acre Sinkyone Wilderness. Created to avert plans by Georgia-Pacific to log the forests, the alliance oversaw the transfer of half its lands to the Sinkyone State Park, while the other half went to the ISWC. Executive director Hawk Rosales explained that the people's relationship with the land was key to their efforts. "We were able to show important connections between the Sinkyone land, the Sinkyone ancestors, and the Sinkyone descendants of today. That struck a chord in everyone's heart" (Middleton, 48). Supported by the Bay Area Friends of Sinkyone, the ISWC works to preserve and restore important resources, providing access for Native basket weavers, salmon habitat restoration, seasonal culture camps, and workshops where tribal youth learn about harvesting, using, and caring for native plants.

The Salt Song Project

A nonprofit land trust, the Native American Land Conservancy (NALC) has both Native and non-Native board members working together to buy back and preserve lands. Based in California, NALC focuses on the "introduction to Native steward-ship and land ethics, including learning to recognize the visible and invisible (story, song, energetic) elements of a landscape" (Middleton, 68). Its mission is to "steward healing landscapes, perpetuate ancestral knowledge, and provide educational and cultural experiences" (Middleton, 69). The Salt Song Project protects sacred sites and the songs associated with them along a pilgrimage route that stretches one thousand miles from southern California to Arizona, southern Utah, and western Colorado. Each stop along the route is rich with stories and songs that tell the story of the Chemehuevi people and their relationships with the land. NALC Executive Director Kurt Russo explains: "We do ethnohistory learning during the day, [and] at night [we are] by the fireside, and the singers are singing songs from that rock, for three hours, incredible songs, and every one of those youth were singing those songs. . . . They are not just good for the youth and the elders, but [they are] good for the rock too" (Middleton, 78).

The Dungeness River Management Team

The Jamestown S'Klallam Tribe of Washington State co-leads the Dungeness River Management Team (DRMT). In partnership with the North Olympic Land Trust, Clallam County, and the Washington Department of Fish and Wildlife, the DRMT preserves riparian lands on the Dungeness River and its floodplain by purchasing properties and securing easements to protect the watershed and restore salmon habitat. No fewer than twenty-seven partners joined together in collaboration in a $7 million project to restore Jimmycomelately Creek and Estuary.

The Cowee Mound

For 175 years, one non-Native family owned the most intact Mississippian archae-ological site in western North Carolina. Then, descendants of the original owners decided to return the Cowee Mound to the Eastern Band of Cherokee Indians. Working in collaboration with the Land Trust of the Little Tennessee, they did just that. The site includes 0.6 miles of riverfront property, valuable habitat for threat-ened fish and endangered mussels, and is a key migration stopover for waterfowl.

Billy Frank Jr. Nisqually Wildlife Refuge

In 1856, the Nisqually tribe signed a treaty that guaranteed them a 4,717-acre reservation. But in 1884, much of this land was lost to the allotment process, and in 1917, 3,300 acres of the reservation were seized for the construction of the Fort Lewis-McChord Joint Army–Air Force Base. Then, in 1974, after decades of protest, the Nisqually reclaimed their treaty rights to fish and co-manage their waterways. As part of this work, they partnered with the army to build their Clear Creek Hatchery on the base, reintroducing salmon fry to the river. Then they partnered with farmers and ranchers along the watershed, working to restore salmon habitat. Since then, the tribe has conserved more than 2,800 acres of the Nisqually watershed, and salmon are showing signs of recovery.

Nisqually Tribe Natural Resources Program Manager Georgiana Kautz explains:

> We're telling people to take a look at watersheds that have tribes on them; there is a lot of collaboration . . . because in order for us to get to salmon recovery, it's not

Photo 3.5.   Billy Frank Jr. (Nisqually) points out a spot where he used to fish along the Nisqually River near Olympia, Washington, Thursday, April 14, 2005, where he was born and lived as a child. The Nisqually Indian elder and activist contributed leadership and multiple arrests to the battle fought by Northwest Indian tribes for their treaty-negotiated salmon-fishing rights. (AP Photo/Ted S. Warren)

going to be just us alone, it's going to take everybody within the watershed: the agencies, the farmers, the tribes, and Fort Lewis! Sometimes I do get angry at what happens, but I also know that I want to be positive, I want to move forward, and I want my children to have these same type of beliefs that you can do whatever you want, accomplish whatever you want, and that we'll be able to exist as Nisqually tribal members, today, tomorrow, and forever. (Interview with Emily Gwinn, Jennifer Johnson, and Joe Nance on April 18, 2009, cited in Middleton, 190)

Perhaps most well-known is the Nisqually partnership with U.S. Fish and Wildlife Service and Ducks Unlimited to restore the wildlife refuge and estuary at the mouth of the Nisqually River. Removing dikes and restoring tidal flows to hundreds of acres of saltmarsh transformed the river's mouth and began a process of recovery. In 2015, President Obama renamed the refuge in honor of Billy Frank Jr., famed Nisqually fishing rights activist and cultural leader.

Yurok Condor Restoration

In northern California, the Yurok Tribe has taken the lead in the reintroduction and recovery of the critically endangered California condor (*Gymnogyps californianus*). Tribal biologists spent years conducting scientific assessments to determine

Photo 3.6.   Yurok Wildlife Program biologist Tiana Williams releases a turkey vulture, which was used in a long-term contaminant study. The Yurok Tribe used the carrion eater as a surrogate for condors to determine if the far northern part of California and southern Oregon are still suitable for condors. Based on the tribe's research, it was determined that the region has ample, clean habitat for condors. (Yurok Condor Program)

if the region remained a suitable habitat for the birds, concluding that tribal lands provided an ideal environment with plenty of food, particularly that emerging from the marine environment, and low levels of environmental contaminants. The tribe engaged in extensive outreach efforts to hunters in southern Oregon and northern California, raising awareness of the impacts of lead bullets. One of the greatest threats to condor health is elevated lead levels, largely due to their eating carcasses or offal remains that contain lead ammunition fragments. In 2014, after years of hard work, the Yurok were able to formally bring federal agencies (the National Park Service and the U.S. Fish and Wildlife Service) as well as nongovernmental organizations (NGOs) and private industry on board within a memorandum of understanding. By 2018, this agreement had been expanded to include sixteen partners, including the aforementioned groups and two state agencies. Currently, the tribe is co-leading the National Environmental Policy Act (NEPA) procedure for condor reintroduction and if, as expected, the initial efforts are successful, the tribe will act as co-managers of the condor release site, overseeing all direct hands-on management of the reintroduced flock for the foreseeable future.

With only 488 condors alive as of December 2018—and only 312 in the wild—this is important work. It matters to the Yurok in particular: the condor is sacred to them, holding a revered place in Yurok oral traditions, cosmology, and ceremony. But this initiative is not just about condors. It is part of a broader tribal commitment to restoring the ecosystem within their territories, returning them

Photo 3.7.   Yurok Condor Reintroduction Initiative: To prepare for the future release of condors in Yurok Country, Yurok Wildlife Program biologist Tiana Williams releases a bird (condor) at a training put on by Pinnacles National Park. (Yurok Condor Program)

to the greatest extent possible to their pre-colonial condition. Accomplishing that requires tribal leadership guided by traditional ecological knowledge and collaboration with other regional partners.

The Cowboy and Indian Alliance (CIA)

A coalition of ranchers, fishers, farmers, environmentalists, public health workers, and Native communities, the CIA successfully fought off a proposed bombing range in the Black Hills in the 1980s and 1990s. In the 2000s, they again joined forces to stop a proposed coal train. Despite the cliché of cowboys versus Indians, these communities find common ground in their love of the land. "Many white ranchers and farmers see their lifestyle as endangered by modern economic trends, much as tribal members have seen their land-based cultures under siege" (Grossman 2005, 24). In more recent years, the organization has brought together Indigenous communities and individuals, ranchers, and farmers living along the Keystone XL Pipeline route in northern Nebraska and southern South Dakota. With shared concerns about the safety of their lands and waters, members work together in their opposition to fossil fuel pipelines. In 2014, the CIA organized Reject and Protect, a four-day demonstration in Washington, DC, in opposition to the Keystone pipeline. That same year, they began Seeds of Resistance: in acts of ceremonial (and agricultural) protest, the group planted Ponca sacred corn on a Nebraska farm that lay in the path of the proposed Keystone XL pipeline.

Walla Walla Basin Watershed Council

A final example of collaborative conservation can be seen in the Walla Walla Basin Watershed Council. In their 1855 treaty, the Confederated Tribes of the Umatilla (the Umatilla, Walla Walla, and Cayuse) agreed to reduce their 6.4-million-acre territory to 500,000 acres. But in the decades that followed, their reservation would be reduced to a mere 172,000 acres. Despite this loss of land, the Umatilla have retained their rights to fish and hunt in usual and accustomed places. As they work to protect these rights, they have partnered with the Walla Walla Basin Watershed Council. The Council brings together farmers, ranchers, and city, state, county, and industry representatives to protect and enhance biological and cultural resources in the basin. Their work includes removing barriers to fish passage, diversion improvements, constructing fish ladders, and extensive monitoring of the health of fish populations.

More and more non-Native advocates are seeing the benefits of partnering with tribes when it comes to protecting resources. As Liz Hamilton of the Northwest Sportfishing Industry Association insists, "If the federal government fails us, the tribes will use treaty rights to breach the dams. It could be treaty rights that save the salmon." In a similar fashion, third-generation wheat farmer Richard Thieltges praised successful collaborative efforts to protect the Sweet Grass Hills: "Farmers-ranchers, Native Americans and environmentalists are three sides of a natural alliance.

We are the only people who truly have to bear the burden of what's happened to the land. So the mining industry tries to drive wedges between us" (Grossman 2005, 31). Puget Sound commercial fisherman Larry Carpenter likewise sees tribal rights as key to continuing his work. "If there hadn't been treaty rights, there wouldn't be a resource. . . . Thanks to that, there are fish" (Grossman 2005, 54).

Negotiating these relationships is not always easy. Contested sacred sites and resources are often more of a cause for conflict than collaboration. And yet, a common cause and a willingness to engage with different notions of the sacred can make the difference. Cultural geographer Zoltán Grossman explains,

> Differing views of sacredness can enable an alliance to go beyond an environmental issue to build greater cultural understanding. But this happens only if both communities view the sacredness in a nonexclusive way. . . . Whether or not they view the land as sacred, many local white residents value the land more than corporate or governmental "outsiders" and can therefore make some common links with Native values. Two neighboring communities fight over a place because they value it highly, but that same value can be used to defend the same place against a threat from outsiders who do not share their values. (Grossman 2005, 33)

With such collaborations, Indigenous communities can bring TEK and Indigenous values and ethics to bear upon complicated problems such as climate change and endangered ecosystems. As Dennis Martinez of the National Park Service has said, such collaborations are utterly vital because they come "at a time when the earth and its inhabitants are most in need of healing. Native cultures, although badly fragmented by the impacts of industrial societies, still hold onto significant ecological wisdom based on long ecological experiences in particular places. To ignore that millennia-long experience and knowledge is to risk doing poor science" (Cronin and Ostegren, 89).

Conclusion

Native cultures are at risk from the impacts of climate change and related environmental destruction. At the same time, Indigenous people have resources upon which they can draw: strong community ties, tribal sovereignty, and TEK. As Grossman and Parker have explained, "Indigenous self-determination is not a matter of going backwards to reclaim museum-preserved Native cultures, but a matter of applying traditional knowledge to solve twenty-first century problems" (Grossman and Parker, 160).

Climate change violates treaty rights: when greenhouse gases alter the climate, pushing key species to extinction or forcing them to move, tribes are denied rights guaranteed them in treaties and protected under federal law. When deforestation or resource extraction contributes to climate change and threatens the viability of ecosystems, it threatens the survival of Native cultures, communities, and spiritual traditions. Tribes are challenging these threats through protest, court action, and collaborative partnerships. Their strongest assets, however, are the teachings of their elders. As this chapter shows, environmental destruction and climate change are religious and cultural issues for Indigenous people. Indigenous science—TEK—bridges the gap between religion and science: sacred worldviews, stories, and enduring values inform and are informed by empirical observation. In many ways, the religious traditions of Native North America are the science of sacred relationships, and restoring these relationships lies at the heart of Indigenous environmental activism.

Indigenous Scholars and Allies Statement in Support of the March for Science

April 22, 2017

As original peoples, we have long memories, centuries old wisdom and deep knowledge of this land and the importance of empirical, scientific inquiry as fundamental to the well-being of people and planet.

Let us remember that long before Western science came to these shores, there were Indigenous scientists here. Native astronomers, agronomists, geneticists, ecologists, engineers, botanists, zoologists, watershed hydrologists, pharmacologists, physicians and more—all engaged in the creation and application of knowledge which promoted the flourishing of both human societies and the beings with whom we share the planet. We give gratitude for all their contributions to knowledge. Native science supported indigenous culture, governance and decision making for a sustainable future—the same needs which bring us together today.

As we endorse and support the March for Science, let us acknowledge that there are multiple ways of knowing that play an essential role in advancing knowledge for the health of all life. Science, as concept and process, is translatable into over 500 different Indigenous languages in the U.S. and thousands world-wide.

Western science is a powerful approach, but it is not the only one.

Indigenous science provides a wealth of knowledge and a powerful alternative paradigm by which we understand the natural world and our relation to it. Embedded in cultural frameworks of respect, reciprocity, responsibility and reverence for the earth, Indigenous science lies within a worldview where knowledge is coupled to responsibility and human activity is aligned with ecological principles and natural law, rather than against them. We need both ways of knowing if we are to advance knowledge and sustainability.

We acknowledge and honor our ancestors and draw attention to the ways in which Indigenous communities have been negatively impacted by the misguided use of Western scientific research and institutional power. Our communities have been used as research subjects, experienced environmental racism, extractive industries that harm our homelands and have witnessed Indigenous science and the rights of Indigenous peoples dismissed by institutions of Western science.

While Indigenous science is an ancient and dynamic body of knowledge, embedded in sophisticated cultural epistemologies, it has long been marginalized by the institutions of contemporary Western science. However, traditional knowledge is increasingly recognized as a source of concepts, models, philosophies and practices which can inform the design of new sustainability solutions. It is both ancient and urgent.

Indigenous science offers both key insights and philosophical frameworks for problem solving that includes human values, which are much needed as we face challenges such as climate change, sustainable resource management, health disparities and the need for healing the ecological damage we have done.

Indigenous science informs place-specific resource management and land-care practices important for environmental health of tribal and federal lands. We require greater recognition and support for tribal consultation and participation in the co-management, protection, and restoration of our ancestral lands.

Indigenous communities have partnered with Western science to address environmental justice, health disparities, and intergenerational trauma in our communities. We have championed innovation and technology in science from agriculture to medicine. New ecological insights have been generated through sharing of Indigenous science. Indigenous communities and Western science continue to promote diversity within STEM fields. Each year Indigenous people graduate with Ph.D.'s, M.D.'s, M.S.'s and related degrees that benefit our collective societies. We also recognize and promote the advancement of culture-bearers, Elders, hunters and gatherers who strengthen our communities through traditional practices.

Our tribal communities need more culturally embedded scientists and at the same time, institutions of Western science need more Indigenous perspectives. The next generation of scientists needs to be well-positioned for growing collaboration with Indigenous science. Thus we call for enhanced support for inclusion of Indigenous science in mainstream education, for the benefit of all. We envision a productive symbiosis between Indigenous and Western knowledges that serve our shared goals of sustainability for land and culture. This symbiosis requires mutual respect for the intellectual sovereignty of both Indigenous and Western sciences.

As members of the Indigenous science community, we endorse and support the March for Science—and we encourage Indigenous people and allies to participate in the national march in DC or a satellite march. Let us engage the power of both Indigenous and Western science on behalf of the living Earth. Let our Indigenous voices be heard.

Source: https://www.esf.edu/indigenous-science-letter/

References and Recommendations

Anderson, Kat. *Tending the Wild: Native American Knowledge and the Management of California's Natural Resources.* Berkeley: University of California Press, 2005.

Atleo, Richard E. *Tsawalk: A Nuu-chah-nulth Worldview.* Vancouver: University of British Columbia Press, 2004.

Atleo, Richard E. *Principles of Tsawalk: An Indigenous Approach to Global Crisis.* Vancouver: University of British Columbia Press, 2012.

Cajete, Gregory. "Western Science and the Loss of Natural Creativity," in *Unlearning the Language of Conquest,* edited by Wahinkpe Topa. Austin: University of Texas Press, 2006.

Cronin, Amanda, and David Ostergren, "Tribal Watershed Management: Culture, Science, Capacity and Collaboration," *American Indian Quarterly* Vol. 31 No. 1 (2007): 87–109.

Davis, Thomas. *Sustaining the Forest, the People, and the Spirit.* Albany: SUNY Press, 2000.

Droz, PennElys. "Biocultural Engineering Design: An Anishnaabe Analysis for Building Sustainable Nations," *American Indian Culture and Research Journal* Vol. 38 No. 4 (2014): 105–26.

Grossman, Zoltán. "Unlikely Alliances: Treaty Conflicts and Environmental Cooperation between Native American and Rural White Communities," *American Indian Culture and Research Journal* Vol. 29 No. 4 (2005): 21–43.

Grossman, Zoltán. "Indigenous Nations' Responses to Climate Change," *American Indian Culture and Research Journal* Vol. 32 No. 3 (2008): 5–27.

Grossman, Zoltán. "Indigenous Responses to the International Climate Change Framework," in *Asserting Native Resilience: Pacific Rim Indigenous Nations Face the Climate Crisis,* edited by Z. Grossman and A. Parker. Corvallis: Oregon State University Press, 2012.

Grossman, Zoltán, and A. Parker. *Asserting Native Resilience: Pacific Rim Indigenous Nations Face the Climate Crisis.* Corvallis: Oregon State University Press, 2012.

Haudenosaunee Clan Mothers Statement on Land and Environmental Issues, Haudenosaunee Environmental Forum, Six Nations of the Grand River Territory. *Tekawennake* (July 2007).

Huntington, Orville, and Annette Watson. "Interdisciplinarity, Native Resilience, and How Riddles Can Teach Wildlife Law in an Era of Rapid Climate Change," *Wicazo Sa Review* Vol. 27 No. 2 (2012): 49–73.

Johnson, Martha. *Lore: Capturing Traditional Environmental Knowledge.* Hay River, Northwest Territories: Dene Cultural Institute, 1992. http://lib.icimod.org/record/9841/files/1418.pdf

Kelley, Dennis. *Tradition, Performance, and Religion in Native North America*. Abingdon, UK: Routledge, 2014.

Legat, Alice. *Walking the Land, Feeding the Fire: Knowledge and Stewardship among the Tlicho Dene*. Tucson: University of Arizona Press, 2012.

McBeath, Jerry, and Carl Edward Shepro. "The Effects of Environmental Change on an Arctic Native Community: Evaluation Using Local Cultural Perceptions," *American Indian Quarterly* Vol. 31 No. 1 (2007): 44–65.

McCarthy, Theresa. *In Divided Unity: Haudenosaunee Reclamation at Grand River*. Tucson: University of Arizona Press, 2016.

McGregor, Deborah. "Coming Full Circle: Indigenous Knowledge, Environment, and Our Future," *American Indian Quarterly* Vol. 28 No. 3, 4 (2004): 385–410.

McGregor, Deborah. "Traditional Ecological Knowledge: An Anishinaabe Woman's Perspective," *Atlantis* Vol 29 No 2 (2005): 103–9.

Merculieff, Larry. "Different Ways of Looking at Things," in *Asserting Native Resilience: Pacific Rim Indigenous Nations Face the Climate Crisis*, edited by Z. Grossman and A. Parker. Corvallis: Oregon State University Press, 2012.

Middleton, Beth Rose. *Trust in the Land: New Directions in Tribal Conservation*. Tucson: University of Arizona Press, 2011.

Papiez, Chelsie. "Climate Change in the Quileute and Hoh Nations of Coastal Washington," in *Asserting Native Resilience: Pacific Rim Indigenous Nations Face the Climate Crisis* edited by Z. Grossman and A. Parker. Corvallis: Oregon State University Press, 2012.

Ruud, Candice. "Protestors Build a Longhouse at PSE, Ask What It and LNG Have in Common," *Tacoma News Tribune* (April 2, 2018). https://www.thenewstribune.com/news/local/article207740454.html

Tam, Benita, et al. "The Impact of Climate Change on the Well-Being and Lifestyle of a First Nation Community on the Western James Bay Region," *Canadian Geographer* Vol. 57 No. 4 (2013): 441–56.

Tatum, Melissa, and Jill Shaw. *Law, Culture, and Environment*. Durham, NC: Carolina Academic Press, 2014.

Swinomish Nation. "Swinomish Climate Change Initiative, Executive Summary of the Swinomish Climate Change Initiative Impact Assessment Technical Report, October 2009," in *Asserting Native Resilience: Pacific Rim Indigenous Nations Face the Climate Crisis*, edited by Z. Grossman and A. Parker. Corvallis: Oregon State University Press, 2012.

United States Fish and Wildlife Service, National Parks Service, Bureau of Land Management, U.S. Forest Service, Yurok Tribe, et al. "Memorandum of Understanding on California Condor Conservation," June 14, 2016.

Von der Porten, Suzanne. "Lyell Island (Athlii Gwaii) Case Study: Social Innovation by the Haida Nation," *American Indian Culture and Research Journal* Vol. 38 No. 3 (2014): 85–106.

Williams, Mike. "Alaska: Testimony from the Front Lines," in *Asserting Native Resilience: Pacific Rim Indigenous Nations Face the Climate Crisis*, edited by Z. Grossman and A. Parker. Corvallis: Oregon State University Press, 2012.

Williams, Terry, and Preston Hardison. "Climate Threats to Pacific Northwest Tribes and the Great Ecological Removal: Keeping Traditions Alive," in *Asserting Native Resilience: Pacific Rim Indigenous Nations Face the Climate Crisis*, edited by Z. Grossman and A. Parker. Corvallis: Oregon State University Press, 2012.

Willow, Anna. *Strong Hearts, Native Lands: The Cultural and Political Landscape of Anishinaabe Anti-Clearcutting Activism*. Albany: SUNY Press, 2012.

Willow, Anna. "Collaborative Conservation and Contexts of Resistance: New and Enduring Strategies for Survival," *American Indian Culture and Research Journal* Vol. 39 No. 2 (2015): 29–52.

Films and Websites

Drummond, Benjamin, and Sara Steele. "Facing Climate Change: Plateau Tribes." https://vimeo.com/36951241

"Indigenous Scholars and Allies Statement in Support of the March for Science," April 22, 2017. https://www.esf.edu/indigenous-science-letter/

Jamestown S'Klallam Tribe. "Protecting and Restoring the Waters of the Dungeness: Watershed Based Plan," 2007. https://jamestowntribe.org/wp-content/uploads/2018/08/1-Protecting-and-Restoring-Dungeness.pdf

Latota Solar Enterprises. http://www.lakotasolarenterprises.com/

Looking Horse, Arvol. "Chief Arvol Looking Horse Seeks Face-to-Face Meeting with President Obama." http://nativenewsonline.net/currents/chief-arvol-looking-horse-seeks-face-face-meeting-president-obama/

"sčədadxʷ (salmon), in Memory of Billy Frank Jr." https://youtu.be/D15itTjuY-g

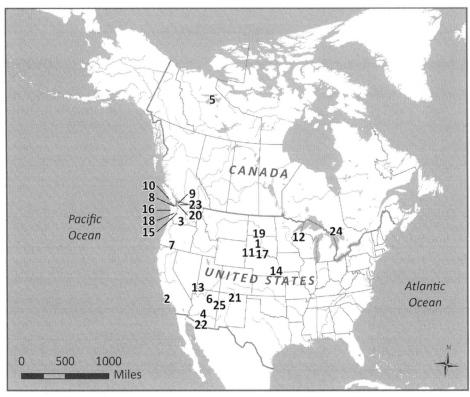

1 Cheyenne River Sioux Tribe
2 Chumash Territories
3 Confederated Tribes of the Yakama
4 Gila River Indian Reservation
5 Great Bear Lake, Sahtu Territories
6 Hopi Tribe
7 Klamath Tribes
8 Lower Elwha Klallam Tribe
9 Lummi Nation
10 Nuu-Chah-Nulth Territories
11 Oglala Lakota Territories
12 Ojibwe (Anishinaabe) Territorries
13 Paiute Territories

14 Ponca Tribe
15 Puyallup Indian Tribe
16 Quinault Indian Nation
17 Sicangu Lakota Territories
18 Squaxin Island Tribe
19 Standing Rock Indian Tribe
20 Swinomish and Samish Indian
   Nations
21 Taos Pueblo
22 Tohono O'odham Nation
23 Upper Skagit Indian Tribe
24 Whitefish River First Nation
25 Pueblo of Zuñi

Map 4.1.   Map of North America locating the tribal communities, nations, and cultural groups mentioned in this chapter. Basemap data made with Natural Earth. (Liz O'Dea Springborn)

Water

4

We don't want this black snake within our treaty boundaries.

—STANDING ROCK SIOUX TRIBAL CHAIRMAN DAVE ARCHAMBAULT II

IT WAS THE MIDDLE OF THE DAY on October 27, 2016, when elder and sacred pipe carrier Casey Camp-Horinek (Ponca) positioned herself in the middle of Highway 1806. Alongside her stood Russell Eagle Bear and Ben Rhodd, cultural preservationists with the Rosebud Sioux Tribe of South Dakota. Nearby, men were participating in an *inipi* (sweat lodge), steam rising into the air. Holding her pipe aloft, Camp-Horinek began to pray. Eagle Bear, Rhodd, and other water protectors gathered around her in a tight circle, bowing their heads in prayer and doing their best to ignore hundreds of nearby police officers and National Guardsmen in full riot gear. Within minutes, the scene would change: police and guardsmen advanced, forcibly pulling men from the *inipi*, while Camp-Horinek, Eagle Bear, and Rhodd faced pepper spray and arrest.

The encampment near Standing Rock had been in place since April 1, established by a Lakota youth group committed to fighting the proposed Dakota Access Pipeline. Tribal leaders on the Standing Rock Sioux and Cheyenne River reservations had been stunned to learn that the U.S. Army Corps of Engineers had approved the construction of a crude-oil pipeline within less than a mile of their reservation. The decision was made without the tribal consultation dictated by law. Indeed, the initial environmental assessment for the project had actually omitted any mention of the tribe on its maps or in its analysis, obscuring any potential impacts on the tribe's only source of potable water.

Outrage increased as tribal people learned that the pipeline had already been rerouted once before: its original route had taken it too close to Bismarck, North Dakota, provoking the ire of its predominantly white communities that feared it might impact their drinking water. Its new trajectory would take the pipeline under the Missouri River and Lake Oahe, through burial grounds, sacred memorials,

Photo 4.1.   Defend the Sacred. A water protector faces militarized police at Standing Rock, North Dakota. (Ryan Vizzions)

and prayer sites. Moving 570,000 barrels of crude oil across four states, the pipeline would eventually cross 209 rivers, creeks, and tributaries along the way.

Standing Rock and Cheyenne River tribes immediately filed a lawsuit, protesting the decision. But on August 8, 2016, the tribe learned that construction would begin in a mere forty-eight hours. News spread quickly. By the end of the day, hundreds of activists had gathered at Sacred Stone Camp. By the end of the week, a dozen people had been arrested, including Standing Rock Sioux tribal chairman Dave Archambault. The tribe's historic-preservation officer Jon Eagle Sr. explained what drove the community to protest. "The land between the Cannonball River and the Heart River is sacred. In the area are sacred stones where our ancestors went to pray for good direction, strength and protection for the coming year. Those stones are still there, and our people still go there today" (Taliman).

On September 2, 2016, concerned tribes filed documentation in federal court demonstrating that the pipeline would pass through multiple ancient burial and prayer sites, including the site of the 1863 massacre at Whitestone Hill, where on September 3, 1863, the U.S. Army killed 150 men, women, and children. The 156 survivors (124 of whom were women and children) were taken into custody. Today, Lakota and Dakota people consider the site to be a sacred place and do not venture there without prayer, even removing their shoes when visiting the site. But on September 3, 2016—the anniversary of the massacre—Dakota Access construction crews unnecessarily bulldozed the site (active construction work was still a long way off). As far as the tribes were concerned, the action and its timing was a clear assertion of colonial coercion and an insult to the memory of those who died in the massacre.

In November, the North Dakota governor issued a mandatory evacuation order: protestors must leave or face the consequences. Water protectors refused to go, braving frigid temperatures and dangerous conditions. Police turned water cannons on the water protectors, a potentially lethal tactic in the bitter cold, and there were serious injuries: one woman lost her arm, another lost her sight. The conflict came to a head on December 4, 2016, when two thousand veterans of U.S. armed forces arrived at Standing Rock to support the protest, determined to act as human shields between the water protectors and police. But as the veteran-allies arrived, the Army Corps of Engineers issued a statement: construction would be halted.

Jubilation was short-lived, however. Within two short months, the project was revived under the incoming Trump administration, which cut short environmental and cultural impact assessments, expediting construction. The pipeline was completed in April 2017. Within days, it had leaked 400 barrels (16,800 gallons) of crude oil. Within six months, it suffered a larger leak, spilling 210,000 gallons of oil near Amherst, South Dakota.

The protests at Standing Rock drew national media attention, highlighting Indigenous concerns about climate change, clean water, and tribal sovereignty, and illuminating deeply held religious convictions. It brought to national and international attention a teaching that is central to many Native American traditions: the sacredness of water. This chapter explores this importance of water within Indigenous traditions and considers the historical origins of contemporary water rights controversies.

Within Indigenous teachings, water is the living source of life, a home to powerful sacred beings, and ought to have rights of its own. Autumn Peltier, water protector and activist from Wiikwemkoong Unceded Territory, a First Nation reserve on Manitoulin Island in Ontario, Canada, first spoke before the United Nations when she was thirteen years old. In 2019, Peltier spoke before the United Nations for the second time. As she then explained: "When you ask the question about 'why is the water so sacred?' It's not just because we need it and nothing can survive without water. It's because for years and years our ancestors have passed on traditional oral knowledge that our water is alive and our water has a spirit" (Peltier).

Water Is Alive. Water Is Sacred

Understanding the passion behind the demonstrations at Standing Rock requires an understanding of Indigenous worldviews and values. One of these shared values is the notion that water is a sacred source of power, that water is *alive*. As a sacred living being, water plays a sacramental role in many ceremonies.

Photo 4.2.   Autumn Peltier is Anishinaabe-kwe, a member of the Wiikwemikong First Nation, and internationally recognized as a water protector and advocate for clean water. Peltier has twice addressed world leaders at the UN General Assembly and has met with Prime Minister Justin Trudeau on the issue of water protection and Indigenous water rights. (Linda Roy/ Irevaphotography)

Vi Waln (Sicangu Lakota) explains:

Water is essential in Lakota ceremony. The Lakota people who sun dance or *hanblecya* (vision quest) will tell you how painful life is without Water. Humanity should never be so arrogant as to take the Water we've been given for granted. . . . Here on the Rosebud Reservation, a majority of our Water is piped in from the Missouri River. Some of us get our Water from an underground aquifer. In either case, we must pray for our Water every time we use or drink it. Prayer transforms Water in Lakota ceremony. Water buckets and Water drums used in our Native American Church prayer services definitely transform the Water in those containers. Give your Water love and gratitude. There can be no life without Water. *Mni Wiconi*. Water is Life.

Many Indigenous traditions describe water as the lifeblood of the earth. For instance, in her seminal work *Navajo Religion* (1950), Gladys Reichard quoted an elder, who explained: "Each mountain is a person. The watercourses are their veins and arteries. The water in them is their life as our blood is to our bodies" (Reichard, 20). Several case studies from across the continent help to illustrate similar ideas of the powerful, vital nature of water.

Paiute Waterways and Sacred Power

Paiute traditions in the Great Basin associate spiritual power with water. As Jay Miller (Lenape) explains, *puha* (spiritual power) flows over the landscape, and while it is not the same thing as water, it can be found within it. A map of spiritual places overlaid on the landscape reveals a pattern that follows the flow and meandering of waterways. Spiritual power permeates the landscape, paralleling those web-like currents. Miller points out that in southern Paiute oral traditions, the world is created from Ocean Old Woman. Ocean Woman works together with the Animal People to shape the world, creating a network of kinship and reciprocal relations. It is water that binds this network together. Water is the keystone of southern Paiute religion "because power (*puha*) as the life force-and-energy has a very great affinity for all living things, all of which depend on water" (Miller, 344). In the dry region of the Great Basin, water determines the movement and existence of life. The sacred site of Paiute creation narratives is Snow-Having (Mount Charleston), so called because it holds snow for the spring melt, providing a vital source of water. Within Paiute traditions "all water sources are sacred because they are reservoirs of power, whether as clouds, rain, snow, springs, seeps, lakes, streams or rivers" (Miller, 345).

Zuñi River and Salt Lake, New Mexico

Among the Zuñi of western New Mexico, nearly every aspect of religious life is tied in some way to the Zuñi River. "Along its banks and in the stream, food offerings are made to the gods and the ancestral spirits for continued protection, spiritual guidance, and long life" (Ladd, 120). Ancestors return to Zuñi territory when masked dances are performed, traveling up the river in the guise of ducks. Ancestors return as rain during the summer and snow in the winter, replenishing the river and ensuring a good harvest. Here, water is the manifestation of one's ancestors, a river the visible link between this world and the next.

A sacred figure in Zuñi oral tradition is the Great Salt Mother, Ma'l Oyattsik'i. In the mythic past she traveled in search of a place to rest. When she came to what is now Zuñi Salt Lake, Ma'l Oyattsik'i finally lay down. The lake is a sacred site and a pilgrimage location for Apache, Diné, and Pueblo communities. At the center of the lake is a great salt cone. Known as the flesh of Salt Mother, pilgrims gather the sacred mineral, using it to bless new infants. When an energy utility proposed to develop a coal mine near the Zuñi Salt Lake, the Zuñi Salt Lake Coalition—made up of tribes and environmental groups that opposed the mine—fought back. After two decades of legal battles and twenty-four-hour prayer vigils, the utility relinquished its mining permits and coal leases. The Zuñi Salt Lake and six hundred acres of surrounding land were transferred back to the Zuñi, who now manage the site.

Bear Lake, Northwest Territories

Located in the Northwest Territories of Canada, Great Bear Lake has been declared a UNESCO Biosphere Reserve, the largest in North America, and the first led by an Indigenous community. For the Sahtuto'ine (or Bear Lake People) the lake is seen as the final refuge, a last resort for humanity. Sahtuto'ine oral traditions affirm that their lake is a living being. As one story explains, long ago a fisherman lived on the lake. One day, the man set out his hooks.

> When the fisherman returned to check on them, a lake trout had broken one of the lines and taken the hook. This bothered the fisherman, because in those days, hooks were extremely valuable. So that night, he transformed himself into a losch, also known as burbot, a freshwater version of cod. The fisherman swam down to the middle of the lake to look for the hook and heard a booming sound. There, at the bottom, he saw a gigantic beating heart. All the species of fish—trout, whitefish, pickerel, herring, suckers—faced the heart, surrounding and protecting it. He swam back to shore after seeing this, and the following morning when he went to check on his three hooks, he found three trout. One of them had the hook he had lost the day before dangling from its mouth. When the fisherman saw the water-heart, he realized Great Bear Lake was alive. . . . Some in Deline believe that the water-heart at the bottom of the lake gives life to all of the lakes, oceans and rivers in the world. (Kujawinski)

The Maiden of Deception Pass

Deception Pass is a narrow and dangerous strait separating Whidbey Island from Fidalgo Island, and connecting Skagit Bay with the Strait of Juan de Fuca in Washington State. Tidal flows reach eight knots here, reversing directions in a treacherous current. According to the Samish and Swinomish people, it is in this place that human beings and the spirit of the ocean came to an agreement.

In the mythic past, when the first people were living near Deception Pass, a young woman named Ko'kwal'alwoot was out clamming. But when she waded into deeper water, someone took hold of her hand. She heard a voice from the sea, wooing her. The next day, she returned. Again and again she came back to the water, where someone took her hand, and an unseen voice talked to her. Eventually, she agreed to marry this spirit of the sea if her father would give his permission. A young man rose from the water, went with her, and asked her father for his daughter's hand. The father refused. He would not let his daughter go down to the sea. The man told him how beautiful it was beneath the waves, but he refused to let his daughter go.

The young man went away. And so did the fish. And the shellfish. The salmon grew scarce, and the freshwater streams dried up. Finally, the young woman went back to the sea, pleading with the young man of the ocean to give her father another chance. This time, her father agreed, with the condition that the young woman would return every year so they could be sure she was happy and well. Each year, she came back. And each year, she was more and more like a creature of the sea: her hair was turning green; barnacles grew on her face. Soon it was clear that she was unhappy out of the water. The sea was now her home. Seeing that she longed for the ocean, her father released her from her promise. The young woman returned to the sea, but she kept watch over her people, making sure they had food and fresh water, protecting them when they traveled through Deception Pass, where they sometimes saw her long green hair floating on the water. The people knew they had a relative in the sea (Clark, 199). The story about people's kinship relationship with the sea is memorialized by Swinomish carver Tracy Powell in his work *Ko'kwal'alwoot: The Maiden of Deception Pass*.

Mishebeshu, Whitefish River First Nation, Ontario

Oceans, seas, rivers, and lakes are alive in and of themselves. They are also alive because they are home to powerful living things: plant people, animal people, fish people, and other spiritual beings such as Ko'kwal'alwoot and her young man of the sea. In her work, Theresa Smith describes traditions among the Anishinaabe of the Whitefish River First Nation that honor (and sometimes avoid) powerful spiritual beings who live under water. Such spiritual beings (*manitouk*) can take many forms: healing or dangerous, helpful or threatening, but are always treated with respect. Mishebeshu refers to certain underwater monsters that might take the form of serpents or lynxes. Such creatures wreak havoc, cracking ice, pulling boaters and swimmers to their deaths, or making the soft ground treacherous underfoot. In stories, Mishebeshu exists as a foil to Thunderbird. While Thunderbird is an ally of human beings, Mishebeshu is usually dangerous. But even this dangerous creature has benign possibilities. In some stories, it is Mishebeshu who gives the gift of the *midewiwin*, or medicine societies, to the people.

As these examples show, there are a variety of ways that water is understood to be a source of spiritual power in Native North America. Water is associated with the spirit of life and creation. Water is itself alive. And water is also the home to powerful spiritual beings.

Water as Source of Healing and Renewal

Healing Activism

Another key theme in understanding the importance of water in Native North America is that water is a source of healing and renewal. In some instances, healing comes as part of the struggle to protect water. In the case of the Standing Rock and Cheyenne River tribes for instance, the desire to protect sacred waters from pollution has quite literally saved lives. In 2016, youth suicide in these communities had reached epidemic levels. During a single summer, thirty Cheyenne River youth attempted and eight succeeded in committing suicide, this within a community of just over eight thousand people. But for those struggling with the structural violence wrought by colonialism, traditional culture and spirituality can be a path toward resilience. For Jasilyn Charger, it was her cousin who pointed her toward their culture. He advised her: "'Don't get high, let's go to a sweat.' He got me off drugs and into our culture" (Elbein). With her cousin and fellow tribal member Trenton Casillas-Bakeberg, Charger would go on to begin the One Mind Youth Movement (OMYM), a place where young people could connect with traditional culture and spirituality. In April 2016, OMYM founded the Sacred Stone Prayer Camp at the Dakota Access site; over the months that followed, the encampment would grow to become an international movement.

For OMYM, the pipelines were foretold in a dire prophecy about a devouring serpent. The black snake, an image from Lakota mythology and prophecy, "symbolizes a darkness, a sickness, whose only intention is to sow dysfunction and loss of life in our communities," explained Dallas Goldtooth, an organizer who worked with Charger (Elbein). The prophecy helped make the connection clear; the battle against the pipeline was also a battle against other colonial ills: addiction, abuse, and suicide. And the path toward healing was also here: in fighting to save sacred water.

OMYM organized a 500-mile run protesting the pipeline, with runners meeting with other Native communities along the way. Then they did it again, this time executing a 2,000-mile relay all the way to Washington, DC. Arvol Looking Horse, hereditary chief and spiritual leader of the Lakota, blessed the young people and their efforts, giving them a ceremonial pipe, and dubbing them *akicita*: warriors for the people. For OMYM members, learning about their traditional ways and fighting for their lands and waters was the path to healing future generations. Saving water saved their lives, inspiring purpose and forging a living link between the ancestors and the generations to come.

Ritual Bathing and Purification

Water heals through activism and is a call to return to traditional culture and spirituality. It also heals through ceremony, where it functions as a symbol and means of purification. Consider, for example, ritual bathing traditions on the Northwest coast. Among the Nuu-chah-nulth of Vancouver Island, this tradition is known as *ʔuusumč*. A complex ritual process of fasting, prayer, and meditation, the heart of *ʔuusumč* includes bathing in icy waters and scrubbing one's body with cedar boughs. *ʔuusumč* purifies the heart and mind, strengthens the body, and prepares one for important tasks. It is through *ʔuusumč* that one's spiritual eye is able to see clearly, interpret life, and receive guidance. Richard Atleo explains:

The experiences of the *?uusumč* were individual and personal, but the practice was universal. Every household necessarily had practitioners of the *?uusumč* because it was firmly believed that it was not possible to succeed in life without it. Not only did *?uusumč* reveal spiritual powers, spiritual gifts, songs, directions, and information, but its application culminated in successful hunts for food. (Atleo 2012, 53)

Ritual bathing in icy waters cleansed the mind, spirit, and body, and promoted humility. Atleo writes: "We know that one necessary condition for a successful *uusumč* is to maintain a deliberate state of inner smallness" (Atleo 2012, 64).

In a similar vein, Vi Hilbert, a Coast Salish cultural expert and educator, wrote about the importance of the Skagit River as a source of healing, spiritual renewal, and reflection for her and her family.

Everything about the river was spirit help: the ripples in the water, the whirlpools and the eddies. These things were recognized by the people as their help. People would bathe in the river when they were looking for their spirit help. It had to be unpolluted, clear, cold water. My son had to do that even just a few years ago. He'd come up out of that water and his hair would freeze with icicles. So it's a discipline and you have to have a mindset that says, "my body is going to endure this. I'm doing this for a special purpose." (Yoder, 65)

Water renews and transforms both body and spirit.

Throughout Native North America, water also holds a central place in the purification rites of the sweat lodge. While sweats vary by region, the most common contemporary practice follows Northern and western Plains styles, inspired in part by the writings of the Lakota spiritual leader Black Elk, who described the *inipi* ceremony in the book *The Sacred Pipe: The Seven Rites of the Oglala Sioux*. A domed structure made from willow boughs, and covered by blankets, hides, or sleeping bags, creates an enclosed space of complete darkness. A pit is dug at the center, and special heated rocks are ceremonially brought in. Water is poured over the rocks, and each person is given the opportunity to sing or pray and speak from the heart. After each round, the door is briefly opened to let in cool air and to bring in more stones. At the end of the sweat, participants might plunge into a nearby body of cold, pure water. The power of the sweat lodge comes from the renewing and cleansing steam. It also comes from the vulnerability and openness found within, where family members and friends can speak openly, from the heart, about concerns, fears, or anxieties, and can pray for each other. The *inipi* reminds participants of the sacred cleansing nature of water, and of our reliance on it for life. It purifies, strengthens, and prepares individuals for difficult tasks ahead. With that in mind, the presence of an *inipi* at Standing Rock (as mentioned in the opening paragraph of this chapter), and its use within a protest against a pipeline, is all the more striking, as are the implications of armed riot police pulling participants out of the lodge and away from their prayers.

The Native American Church

The ceremonial power of water can also be seen in the Native American Church, where water is acknowledged as the source of life and is a central symbol within their ceremonies. With an estimated quarter of a million members, the Native American Church has active chapters in reservation communities all over the nation. Incorporated in 1918, the church is based on ancient beliefs and practices rooted in the Huichol of northwestern and western Mexico, brought to the United States in the late nineteenth century and adapted for this context.

Members of the church regard partaking of peyote (*Lophodora williamsii*) as a holy sacrament, and do so during all-night prayer ceremonies. These ceremonies take place in a specially constructed tipi with a sacred fire and earth altar at its center. Ceremonial leaders (Roadmen) lead the services, directing those gathered in prayer and song. Native American Church ceremonies are places of vulnerability, for speaking from the heart, affirming core values, and supporting those hurting or at risk. Such ceremonies promote sobriety and renewal, supporting those in recovery or healing from abuse. As a symbol of life and purification, water is central to these services.

Many symbols in the Native American Church center on water and help to uphold these themes. Consider, for example, the Waterbird, the water drum, and the young woman who brings water at dawn after a long night of prayer and reflection. Played throughout the night, the water drum accompanies the songs, lending a tonal pitch that is distinct to peyote music. Such powerful symbols represent renewal and rebirth.

Holy Water, Holy Wine

Water's role in ceremony provides a means for bridging Indigenous lifeways and Christian traditions as well. John Hascall, Ojibwe member of the *midewiwin* (medicine society) and a Capuchin priest, describes a water rite within his congregation.

> All the symbols of our worship are natural gifts—like the gift of water. We begin many of our Eucharistic celebrations with a water rite to remind us of our baptism and our life within the community. We seek to restore harmony in our relationships with God, with each other, and the world. Coming to the water for healing, we restore our relationships and renew the harmonious community into which we were baptized. For native people, water is the basis of life. We learn the value of water when we fast three or four days on the mountain, in the forest or in some other sacred place. For many tribes this means we refrain from all water and food for four days. Our purpose in fasting is to create harmony in the world and within ourselves. As we pray in the fast, we pray that all people of the earth, all nations and cultures, may be strengthened. (Treat, 181)

In Hascall's liturgy, the water rite *precedes* the Eucharist: water is blessed and placed in the four directions. In his ritual adaptation, *east* represents the sunrise, newness of life, resurrection, baptism, and offerings of water to the earth, reminding congregants of the sweat lodge, where water is poured on hot stones. *South* is associated with women, the giving of life, and cedar, and includes a prayer for healing of women and of the world. *West* is associated with sage, thunderbirds that bring water and new life to earth as rain and storms, and is accompanied by prayers for remembrance of human suffering and intercession. *North* is associated with tobacco, prayer for elders and ancestors, and expressions of thanks for mother earth, creation, God as father, and spirit. Only after these sacred waters and directions are recognized, does the Eucharist begin (Treat, 182–83).

Taking to the Waters: Reviving Canoe Culture
It has been an honor to travel in your sacred waters.

—PHIL CHARLES, LOWER ELWHA KLALLAM "LIGHTNING" SKIPPER,
AT MAKAH, 2010

Throughout the Pacific Coast region, tribal communities are revitalizing canoe cultures and finding healing and restoration on the water. In the 1990s, Santa Barbara's Chumash community formed the Chumash Maritime Society and worked to build a traditional *tomol* (canoe). On September 8, 2001, the *'Elye'wun* (swordfish) entered the harbor of Santa Cruz Island, met by a cheering crowd. It was the first time the Chumash people had crossed the Santa Barbara Channel in a traditional hand-built canoe for 142 years. In 2011, the *'Elye'wun* would make an even further journey to the Swinomish reservation in Washington State. Dennis Kelley, one of those to make the crossing in 2001, was there to witness her arrival. "My nerves at watching the young paddlers come ashore at Swinomish were not concerns about their skill; they have clearly surpassed the abilities of us oldsters. I was more concerned about *'Elye'wun*, as the old girl has logged a lot of miles. My concerns were unfounded, however, because, like the people she has dutifully conducted, she is resilient and uniquely suited to her task" (Kelley, 40).

Throughout the West Coast, the revitalization of canoe culture is restoring people's relationship to water. Canoes serve as powerful symbols of survival and continuity: in British Columbia, coastal people tell stories of ancestors surviving floods by tying off to the tops of trees or even mountains. Canoes are described as tools of survival, carriers of the people, and containers of the culture. Prior to colonialism, canoes were also the best way to get around, as tribal people visited relatives, raided, and traded. Contemporary canoe culture likewise celebrates the canoe's ability to carry people great distances, build relationships, engage in competition with other tribal groups, and carry the culture forward into the future.

In 1989, Emmett Oliver (Quinault) led the Paddle to Seattle, an intertribal canoe journey commemorating the state centennial. Since then, the movement has grown. Today, Tribal Journeys is an annual event drawing together thousands of participants and over a hundred canoes and canoe families from Alaska to California. Throughout this multiweek event, canoes traverse hundreds of miles, stopping

Photo 4.3.   Canoes come ashore during Tribal Journeys, an intertribal canoe journey held annually in the Pacific Northwest. (Scott D. Hall)

at tribal communities along the way, until they arrive at their final destination—such as the 2011 landing at Swinomish described above. Hosted by a different tribe each year, the final stop culminates in a weeklong gathering, marked by "protocols," the public performance of songs, dances, oratory, and gift giving. Guided by elders, young people are taught traditional arts like carving (canoes and paddles), weaving (cedar hats, and other regalia), painting and design, dance, and song. They learn their language, as they are taught to request permission to land, to express thanks or welcome, and to sing their traditional songs. For two weeks a year, those participating in Tribal Journeys submerge themselves in Indigenous culture.

As Bruce Johansen says, canoes have become "a cultural and spiritual metaphor for emerging from the oppression that followed the immigration of EuroAmericans" (Johansen, 132). Canoes are not just symbols of *transportation*; they are symbols of *transformation*. In Coast Salish and Chinook territories, canoes served as coffins, carrying the soul to the spirit world. Perhaps in part because of this, the canoe was a central symbol within a Coast Salish healing ceremony known as the "soul retrieval" or "spirit canoe" ceremony, wherein healers and their helpers traveled to the land of the dead to retrieve a patient's lost soul. The spirit journey took multiple nights, and was a huge undertaking. Tribal council member and executive director of the Squaxin Island tribal museum Charlene Krise has argued that Tribal Journeys is a modern-day soul retrieval ceremony. As pullers undertake this great journey on the sea, they are retrieving their own souls, the souls of their people, and the spirits of their ancestors.

Participation in Tribal Journeys requires a commitment to abide by the Rules of the Canoe. These include a promise to abstain from drugs, alcohol, and violence; to respect yourself and those around you; to honor elders and the earth; and to treat canoes with respect. Joe Washington, a Lummi elder, commented on the healing potential of Tribal Journeys. "Drinking means nothing to my son now. All he wants is to get in that canoe. He's out on the water, paddling. He wants to carve. He wants to know the cedar" (Johansen, 134).

Water is alive. And so are the hand-carved cedar canoes moving over those waters. Carving a canoe is considered a spiritual undertaking, requiring prayer and spiritual help. Before entering the canoe, pullers say a prayer of blessing and thanksgiving, greeting the canoe by name. In 2004, when intoxicated non-Native tourists desecrated several canoes, the entire event was put on hold until a healing ceremony was held "to restore the spirit of the canoes their canoe families regard as sacred, living beings" (Johansen, 137). Canoes are seen as vital entities, embodying the spirit of the people, the water, the cedar, the ancestors, and the future.

Puyallup artist Shawn Qwalsius Peterson likewise describes canoes as a metaphor for cultural recovery. As he puts it, the culture capsized during the storm of colonialism and imported disease. But canoes illustrate the "means of up-righting culture after capsizing." The people have been culturally adrift, but the stories told at Tribal Journeys, carved on paddles and regalia, serve as anchors. Settler colonialism presents a host of negative and destructive behaviors: consumerism, isolation, drug and alcohol addiction, violence, and disregard for the natural world. But the canoe teaches that you must find a counterbalance, a way to restore equilibrium against these forces that would set you off course. Sometimes, he argues, you have to do a "Hard Fifty," a term for when pullers must work together extra hard to make it through a rough spot. As Peterson writes, the canoe teaches the importance of catching the tide. Settler culture isn't going away, but Native people can work with it, incorporating new technologies, and finding new means of staying afloat.

Water's Rights

In March of 2016, the New Zealand government granted the Whanganui River the same legal rights as a person. After 140 years of fighting for its recognition, the Whanganui tribes of the North Island had succeeded. "The reason we have taken this approach is because we consider the river an ancestor and always have." Gerrard Albert, the lead negotiator for the Whanganui *iwi* explained: "We have fought to find an approximation in law so that all others can understand that from our perspective treating the river as a living entity is the correct way to approach it, as an indivisible whole, instead of the traditional model for the last 100 years of treating it from a perspective of ownership and management." Under its new status, New Zealand law now sees no differentiation between harming the tribe and harming the river. They are legally one and the same. Albert explains: "Rather than us being masters of the natural world, we are part of it. We want to live like that as our starting point. And that is not an anti-development, or anti-economic use of the river, but to begin with the view that it is a living being, and then consider its future from that central belief" (Roy).

This example from New Zealand raises a question: If water is alive, if water is a source of life, healing, and spiritual power, does that have implications for how we treat water? Many Native cultures, traditions, and activists argue that this is indeed the case. As the water protectors at Standing Rock declared, water, as a gift from the Creator, as a sacred source of life, should have rights of its own.

Given this, it is all the more striking that Indigenous communities are more likely than any other North American group to lack access to safe drinking water. All of the wells on the Pine Ridge reservation in Nebraska have been tainted by uranium from the Crow Butte uranium mine. In Canada alone, there are ninety-one long-term drinking water advisories affecting First Nations people. In a 2011 piece for the *Lakota Country Times*, Candace Ducheneaux (Cheyenne River Lakota) put it this way:

> I come to you today in a most sincere and humble manner to speak to you about water. *Mni wakan.* Water is sacred. *Mni Wiconi*, water is life. As Lakota, this is something we have known since we first uttered words and it is evident in our language. *Mni.* Mi, I. Ni, live. *Mni*, I live or we live. We all need water to live. . . . Drinking water quality has been destroyed by oil spills, gold and uranium mine tailings, sewage and industrial waste, chemicals from household products, fertilizers and pesticides, and other contaminants that have been dumped and washed into our rivers, streams and ground waters. And, it is poisoning us. Here on Cheyenne River and amongst other Lakota tribes, there are elevated cases of normally rare diseases, such as cancer, lupus, heart anomalies, rheumatoid arthritis, etc. which have been linked to the deadly toxins in our waters. The incidents of these rare diseases among Lakota people are off the charts when compared to national averages. . . . Currently, the nation's longest river, the Missouri, is number four on America's Most Endangered Rivers list. (Ducheneaux)

Indigenous activism on behalf of water is informed and inspired by spiritual teachings such as those discussed in this chapter. Moccasins on the Ground, a nonviolent direct-action training camp led by Owe Aku International, emphasizes filmmaking, social media, and public education to encourage opposition to projects like tar sands oil extraction and the Keystone XL and Dakota Access pipelines. Debra White Plume, a Lakota grandmother explains:

> We must protect our Sacred Water. For us, this is spiritual work. . . . South Dakota's always been pro-mining, since back in the day when the gold miners came here and discovered gold in our sacred Black Hills, and they took it. . . . At that time our people were very oppressed, suppressed, repressed, and sick from the genocide

of small pox, tuberculosis, and even the common cold. They were weak physically. They were sick, and they couldn't fight them, but we can fight now. There are other ways to fight now. Back then it was only militarily, and now there are other methods of fighting. . . . We're talking about non-violent direct action, but it's still action. It's still being in the face of the enemy, being in the face of the police, being in the face of the corporation, being in the face of the corrupt tribal government, being in the face of whoever is threatening you and your right to sacred water and to a good life. Without sacred water, there is no life. . . . None of us will live without Mother Earth. That's what that means: *Mni Wicozani*. With water there is life, and that goes across all boundaries. (Last Real Indians)

Anishinaabe scholar Renée Bédard points to women's particular roles in praying and caring for water. Bédard explains that Anishinaabe women act as water carriers during ceremonies because they have an "intimate connection with water, and because of their ability to bring forth life" (Simpson, 99). Formed in 2002, Mother Earth Water Walkers is an Anishinaabe voice for water. Mothers and grandmothers have carried water from each of the Great Lakes to the Missouri River, walking hundreds of miles on pilgrimages of song and prayer. Josephine, one of the organizers, describes Water Walkers "as a calling, not just for herself, but for all women" (Simpson, 105).

Fighting for Water Rights

Why are teenagers from Standing Rock and Cheyenne River running a two thousand-mile relay to Washington, DC? Why are Native grandmothers carrying water from each of the Great Lakes and walking the length of the Missouri River? How did we arrive at a place where Indigenous communities do not have access to safe drinking water and struggle for the political means to protect it?

The history of tribal water rights can help provide some context. One can begin with the Winters Doctrine, which set standards for interpreting treaties and tribal water rights. The doctrine was affirmed in the Supreme Court case *Winters v. United States* (1908), which established several legal precedents. First, tribes hold title to all lands and rights to use those lands, unless rights are surrendered in treaties. Second, treaties should be interpreted as Indigenous signatories would have understood them at the time. Since treaties were written in English, a second language for many signatories, any uncertainties or ambiguities are to be read "from the standpoint of the Indians" (McCool). Finally, the Winters Doctrine also affirmed that reservations were intended to be self-reliant and self-sufficient, with water rights implicitly reserved within treaty rights to engage in agriculture and subsistence activities. The central principle is that tribes have rights to water needed to make reservations viable.

For many years, however, the Winters Doctrine was rarely enforced. State governments frequently overruled tribal rights, while the federal government failed to protect those rights. Tribal water claims were further complicated by doctrines of prior appropriation (the notion that whoever first started using a water resource had first rights), which often conflicted with the federal reserved water rights found in the treaties. Such competing claims arose in the 1862 Homestead Act and the 1877 Desert Land Act, which required homesteaders to irrigate and cultivate land in order to claim title. Tribal water rights were further complicated by the Dawes General Allotment Act of 1883 (also known as the Dawes Act). By breaking up reservation lands and opening "surplus" land to non-Native residents, allotment created a new problem: Did non-Native people on reservations share in Native water rights? For a long time, such complications and deliberations made it nearly impossible for Native people to advocate for their water. After all, litigation was expensive and complex and could go on for decades.

But in 1963, *Arizona v. California* provided a partial solution. Here, the courts ruled that tribes had substantial water rights to the Colorado River, including the right to agricultural irrigation. It further affirmed that these rights predated the signing of treaties and did not go away for lack of use. The case laid the foundation upon which other tribes could seek to reclaim sacred waters.

Blue Lake

In the 1970s, another landmark case affirmed the Taos Pueblo people's guardianship of Blue Lake. Located in the Sangre de Cristo mountains of New Mexico, Blue Lake is a shrine for Taos people, regarded as a source of life and site of creation. Traditionally, access to the site was restricted, permitted only at certain times and under certain conditions. When New Mexico became part of the United States in the Treaty of Guadalupe-Hidalgo, the Taos were guaranteed rights to their traditional territories, including Blue Lake. But in 1906, the United States disregarded the treaty, appropriating Blue Lake and making it part of U.S. Forest Service land. A camping and recreation site was built on its shores, and it was opened to the public. The Taos vigorously protested, insisting that the move violated Taos treaty rights and religious and privacy principles. The 1924 Pueblo Lands Act offered monetary compensation for Blue Lake, but the Taos refused it. Continued protests gained national attention, and in the 1960s, the National Council of Churches helped give voice to Taos demands. Finally, in 1970, President Nixon returned Blue Lake to the Taos Pueblo people, signing over 1,640 acres surrounding the lake.

Gila River

The Gila River Indian Community of Arizona comprises Akimel O'otham (Pima) and Pee-Posh (Maricopa) people, and provides a compelling case study of the federal government's historical failure to protect tribal water rights. As historian David DeJong explains, these cultures were built on agriculture, a practice they maintained and expanded upon during Spanish colonial rule. But by the early twentieth century, they had been reduced to poverty and were near starvation. By the late twentieth century, most Pima had been forced to find work off reservation and relied on highly processed and fast food for much of their diet.

The saga of their river began under the aforementioned 1862 Homestead Act and the 1877 Desert Land Act, both of which required irrigation and cultivation for farmers to gain title to land. In 1871, Euroamerican farmers upstream on the Gila River began to divert water from the reservation. In 1888, the Florence Canal Company began diverting more water from the river to irrigate wheat fields and fruit orchards. The impact on the Gila River Indian Community was dire: between 1887 and 1904, tribal grain production went from 105,000 bushels to 12,000. Tribal leaders appealed to Washington, DC, first in 1895 and again in 1903, but by 1904, the Gila River community faced starvation. The Bureau of Indian Affairs attempted litigation on their behalf, but the case proved too expensive and was soon dropped. In 1923, the Pima lost their entire wheat crop.

But the 1963 *Arizona v. California* case affirmed the tribe's rights to water, and the Gila River community gained new legal ground. It was another forty years before the Gila River Indian Community Water Settlement Act of 2004 was actually signed into law, guaranteeing the tribe's rights to agricultural irrigation and drinking water. By then, their agricultural system had collapsed, much traditional knowledge had been lost, diet and lifestyles had changed, and the people faced an uphill battle to regain their health and their relationship with the land. Nonetheless, the tribe has put enormous effort into reclaiming these traditions.

Black Mesa

Another example from the arid Southwest that helps to illustrate the fraught experience of Native communities and water rights is found on Diné (Navajo) and Hopi land at Black Mesa. Peabody Coal's Black Mesa Mine and adjacent Kayenta Mine are the largest coal strip mines in North America, scarring over seventeen thousand acres of Hopi and Diné land. The mines began during the 1960s, when a flurry of mining contracts was quickly pushed through tribal approval processes. The leases offered very low returns and no end date. It is perplexing why tribes would agree to such terms until one learns that John Boydon, the attorney representing the tribes, was covertly employed by the mining companies. Failing to disclose this conflict of interest, Boyden appears to have intentionally misled the tribes, advising them to accept the deal and assuring them the mine would not impact the underground aquifer. Though the tribes had insisted that the coal be transported by train, Boyden instead agreed on their behalf to slurrying the coal, a process that required the construction of a 273-mile pipeline from Black Mesa to Laughlin, Nevada, and would draw water from the Navajo Aquifer. (Boyden was also responsible for drafting the Hopi-Navajo Relocation Act, a document that led to the relocation of 10,000 Navajo and 1,000 Hopi citizens from the Black Mesa area.) For thirty-five years, Peabody drained 1.3 billion gallons—*annually*—of pristine water from the Navajo Aquifer: over 45.5 billion gallons of water to transport coal. The result has been devastating. In some places, water levels have dropped more than 100 feet, springs have run dry, and changes in water pressure have allowed contaminated water to leak into the pristine aquifer. Black Mesa's last day of operation was December 31, 2005. As of 2019, the Kayenta Mine continues to operate.

Former Hopi tribal chairman Vernon Masayesva explains that for Hopi people water is more than a resource; it is an expression of their spiritual link to their ancestors.

> Only water existed at the dawn of time. From water came land; from land and water all forms of life were created, including mankind. Because all life comes from the same source, we are all interconnected and I am as much a part of the clouds as they are of me. . . . Hopi see the water underneath us as a living, breathing world we call *Patuwaqatsi* or "water life." Plants breathe moisture from the sky, and cloud people reciprocate by pulling the moisture to the plants' roots. Hopi believe that when we die, we join the cloud people and join in their journey home to *Patuwaqatsi*, and so all Hopi ceremonies are tied to the water world, and all the springs along the southern cliffs of Black Mesa serve as religious shrines or passageways to water-life. The water model developed by western scientists does not include any of these values because they cannot be measured or quantified. (LaDuke, 35)

In traditions belonging to Pueblo cultures throughout the Southwest, springs are sacred places of prayer and veneration; they are sites of pilgrimage where individuals make offerings and seek guidance. Places of life and growth within an otherwise arid landscape, springs are richly symbolic of water's ability to bring life. Some are associated with powerful figures within Pueblo mythology, like Spider Woman and snake, figures of creation and renewal. Perhaps it is not surprising that tribal communities in the arid Southwest revere water. Water transforms the landscape in ways that are nothing short of miraculous, and a good rainy season can be the difference between starvation and survival. But tribal communities in the water-rich Northwest also revere water, and fight for their rights to water.

Klamath River

The Klamath tribe is one such community. Having struggled mightily under allotment and termination policies; their original 2.2-million–acre reservation was radically diminished before being lost altogether. While the Klamath regained federal recognition in 1986, they did not regain their land base or their river. The Klamath River is 263 miles long and includes 12,000 square miles of watershed. The river used to support between 600,000 and 1.1 million spawning salmon each year. Once the third-largest salmon-producing river in the country, the Klamath is now blocked by dams, pumping stations, canals, and irrigation ditches, and runs are less than 1 percent of what they once were. In some streams and tributaries, salmon and steelhead haven't been seen for nearly a century. Between 1905 and 1960, large-scale irrigation projects invited non-Native farmers into the region.

As more farmers were given yet more promises, the river was soon overcommitted. Today, the Klamath River faces competing demands: agriculture, endangered species, waterfowl, commercial fishing, sportfishing, subsistence fishing, electric power, recreation, and the cultural traditions of tribal people. Salmon and other fish runs have declined to near extinction: the shortnose sucker was listed as endangered in 1988, the coho salmon in 1997.

By the 1990s, the media described the region as being in the midst of "water wars," with farmers, fishermen, and conservationists battling over this limited resource. In 2001, courts issued an order that water be set aside to support threatened and endangered species. In retaliation, fourteen hundred farmers illegally pried open irrigation gates. The Bush administration (with the particular encouragement of Vice President Dick Cheney) defended the farmers. The irrigation spill triggered a massive fish kill: thirty-three thousand spawning salmon died in shallow, warm waters in a die-off that would have impacts for years to come.

For the Klamath, the river is not simply an economic concern. It has religious, spiritual, and cultural implications as well. Elwood Miller, former director of natural resources for the Klamath tribes explains:

> When we go out into the land, we can literally feel the permanent presence of our people throughout history, a sense of belonging that cannot really be described to others; in our neck of the woods, that's where the waters begin; it jumps out of the ground right there in Klamath country and begins its trek toward the ocean and ends up down in Yurok territory on the coast. (LaDuke, 29)

Dam construction and irrigation compromised water quality and caused fish populations to decline, impacting the ability of Klamath people to support themselves as fishers, but it also impacted ancient rituals, ceremonies, and rites of purification. The impact is not just economic, but spiritual as well. Rituals that relied on the river have been compromised and may no longer be practiced due to pollution, while some sacred sites are no longer accessible because of damming. Tribes argue that dams are to blame for high levels of heart disease, diabetes, and other ailments, as members no longer have access to traditional vocations, spiritual practices, or foods. As Jeanerette Jacobs-Johnny (Karuk) explains, the ceremonial work conducted along the river is part of a broader commitment to ecological sustainability and spiritual renewal. "We do prayers at the center of the world here, but they are not just for us. It is for the whole world. We are trying to save the world" (LaDuke, 47). Karuk vice-chairman Leaf Hillman explains: "Our dependence is reciprocal. The fish and the river have provided for us for all those years. Now it is our turn to pay them back" (LaDuke, 63).

An 1864 treaty had guaranteed the Klamath people the right to fish in the Klamath River, but that right was not secured until 1984, when it was upheld by the Ninth Circuit Court of Appeals, which agreed that the treaty guaranteed sufficient water in the river to support fish life. When the Klamath Tribe regained federal recognition in 1992, one of their first acts was to reinstate their First Sucker

Ceremony, honoring the once abundant suckerfish, *c'waam*. Erika Zavaleta recalls that the fish had once "choked the river on the day of the ceremony so that people could pick them up from the surface of the water." The people used to harvest tens of thousands of pounds of these fish. But declining runs closed their fishery in 1986, and today they are restricted to catching two suckerfish each year, and only for ceremonial purposes. In its revitalization of the first suckerfish ceremony, ceremonial leaders catch two precious fish, honor them, pray for their restoration, and then carefully release them back into the river. For the Klamath, the life of the fish closely parallels their own. The restoration of *c'waam* has become emblematic of the Klamath people's fight to reclaim their sovereignty, their lands, and their identity.

After years of conflict, Klamath tribes have joined the U.S. secretary of the interior, farmers, fishermen, and other federal, state, and local representatives to form the Klamath Basin Task Force. In 2010, they signed the Upper Klamath Basin Agreement, which called for the removal of four dams, wetland restoration, and provided funds for tribal economic investment. Tribes were hopeful that dam removal would help them reclaim currently submerged sacred sites as well as cultural and spiritual practices that centered on the river. Unfortunately, Congress failed to vote to enact the legislation necessary to adopt the agreement, and it was terminated in January 2018. A new agreement is currently in place, the Klamath Hydroelectric Settlement Agreement, which aims to remove four hydroelectric dams on the river by 2020.

Water Rights in Washington State

A discussion of tribal water rights ought to include a particular focus on Washington State, where the history of treaty making has resulted in a unique take on the issue. In the 1850s, territorial governor Isaac Stevens negotiated ten treaties. These treaties assured tribes: "The exclusive right of taking fish in all the streams, where running through or bordering said reservation, is further secured to said confederated tribes and bands of Indians, as also the right of taking fish at all usual and accustomed places, in common with citizens of the Territory" (*U.S. v. Winans*).

For years, these rights were virtually ignored and in many instances actively suppressed. Tribes fought back but did not receive legal assurance of their treaty rights until the Boldt Decision of 1974. Judge George Boldt's ruling affirmed the legal right of tribes to half of the annual salmon harvest, the right to fish at all "usual and accustomed places," without unnecessary regulation, and the right to co-manage the resource. Boldt also set legal groundwork for future efforts to preserve tribal rights to water.

In 1993, the Yakama Nation of central Washington sued the state, arguing that the right to fish required healthy habitat for fish. The courts found in their favor. Tribes (and thereby rivers) had the rights to "the absolute minimum amount of water necessary to maintain anadromous fish life in the Yakima River" (Osborn, 99). Courts determined that treaty rights guaranteed that salmon should have access to cool, unimpeded waters, both on and off reservation.

Photo 4.4.   Elwha Dam Removal. Aiyana Jackson, 9 (left), and Leo Lucas, 15 (right), members of the Lower Elwha Klallam tribe, watch as water flows over the Elwha Dam prior to a ceremony to mark the beginning of the removal of the Elwha Dam and the restoration of the Elwha River, Saturday, September 17, 2011, near Port Angeles, Washington. (AP Photo/Ted. S. Warren)

As climate change exacerbates water scarcity, particularly in the dryer central and eastern parts of Washington State, the Yakama Nation "has parlayed its treaty right into formal and informal co-management partnerships with Washington and the United States Bureau of Reclamation. Through these processes, the Tribe has successfully asserted its Stevens Treaty water rights to protect fish and habitat, and institutionalized processes to perpetuate protections" (Osborn, 100). Tribes in Washington State, Oregon, and Idaho have all successfully demonstrated that, as Nez Perce Tribal Executive Committee chairman Anthony D. Johnson asserted before the U.S. Congress, "fish and water are materially and symbolically essential to Nez Perce people both in the present and the past; and declines in fish and water availability, primarily due to human environmental alteration and restrictions on access, have had devastating effects on our people and their culture" (Osborn, 101).

In a similar manner, the Lower Elwha Klallam tribe on the Olympic Peninsula of northwestern Washington was able to parlay the Boldt decision into the removal of the Elwha River dams. When the Elwha Dam (1913) and the Glines Canyon Dam (1927) were built, they were already in violation of the law for their failure to provide for salmon passage. After 1938 and the establishment of Olympic National Park, the Glines Canyon Dam was in further violation of the law: dams are not allowed in national parks.

In 1992, the Elwha River Ecosystem and Fisheries Restoration Act was signed into law. Built on a partnership of the tribe, the National Oceanic and Atmospheric Administration (NOAA), the Washington Department of Fish and Wildlife, and the U.S. Geological Survey, the act provided for the removal of the dams. In August of 2014, the biggest dam-removal project in U.S. history was finally complete. As the dam waters receded, tribal members were once again able to visit sacred sites that had been inundated for nearly a century. Each year since the dam's removal, biologists have seen increasing numbers of returning Chinook, coho, chum salmon, bull trout, steelhead, and eulachon. New habitat has been created for Dungeness crabs, clams, other shellfish, and seabirds. S'Klallam tribal hatcheries are returning fish to the river, while first-salmon ceremonies honor the return of fish each year.

Conclusion

As this book goes to press, the Tohono O'odham Nation in Arizona, in cooperation with nine other regional tribal communities, is fighting the proposed construction of the Rosemont Mine. The open-pit copper mine would bury ancient Hohokan villages, burial sites, and the remains of an ancient ball court. The mine threatens the habitat of two endangered wildcats: the ocelot and the only known jaguar living wild in the United States. The mine area also includes over six thousand acres of tribal resource-gathering areas, where community members gather plants for medicines and basketry. But the impacts of the mine on local water are a particular concern. The mine will draw enormous amounts of water from underground aquifers, lowering the water table by approximately ten feet, while exposing existing waterways to toxic pollutants. Ned Norris Jr., former Tohono O'odham Nation chairman (2007–2015), explains: "There are springs there that are sacred to us. We go there for offerings, to get blessed, to offer prayers and ask the Creator to help us and give us strength. . . . That would be a desecration of holy water, as far as we're concerned, and the potential contamination of all water. You look at the sacredness, the need for water in southern Arizona, this has the potential for polluting the water for current generations, and for future generations ahead of us" (Tohono O'odham Nation).

Water is considered sacred and alive. It is a source of spiritual power and the home to powerful spiritual things. Water provides spiritual renewal, a means of purification and transformation through ritual, ceremony, and prayer. It is something to be honored, experienced with gratitude, and has rights of its own. Tribal communities have had to fight for their water rights, for their rights to irrigate crops, to have safe drinking water, and to protect the rivers and waterways that define them as a people. For Indigenous communities who have lived alongside particular rivers, lakes, and springs, their waters are ancestors and relatives. When those waterways are compromised by pollution, dams, or diversion, the people themselves are compromised. Dammed rivers can lead to suicide or drug and alcohol epidemics. Drained aquifers and depleted springs mean spiritual damage to ancestors, or to one's own participation in the cycle of life and death.

For water protectors, preserving and protecting waters thus becomes not simply a matter of activism, but a kind of sacred work. As Autumn Peltier has explained, advocating for the rights of First Nations people to access safe drinking water is a sacred calling. "I've said it before. We can't eat money, or drink oil. . . . I hope one day I will be an ancestor, and I want my descendants to know, I used my voice, so they can have a future" (Peltier).

References and Recommendations

Atleo, Richard E. (Umeek). *Principles of Tsawalk: An Indigenous Approach to Global Crisis.* Vancouver: University of British Columbia Press, 2012.

Brown, Joseph Eppes. *The Sacred Pipe: Black Elk's Account of the Seven Rites of the Oglala Sioux.* Norman: University of Oklahoma Press, 1989.

Clark, Ella E. *Indian Legends of the Pacific Northwest.* Berkeley: University of California Press, 1953.

DeJong, David. "The Sword of Damocles? The Gila River Indian Community Water Settlement Act of 2004 in Historical Perspective," *Wicazo Sa Review* Vol. 22 No. 2 (2007): 57–92.

Ducheneaux, Candace. "Water Is Life," *Lakota Country Times* (July 11, 2012). https://www.lakotacountrytimes.com/articles/water-is-life/

Elbein, Saul. "The Youth Group That Launched a Movement at Standing Rock," *New York Times* (January 31, 2017). https://www.nytimes.com/2017/01/31/magazine/the-youth-group-that-launched-a-movement-at-standing-rock.html

Jaffe, Sarah. "Standing Firm at Standing Rock: Why the Struggle Is Bigger Than One Pipeline." (September 28, 2016). https://www.commondreams.org/views/2016/09/28/standing-firm-standing-rock-why-struggle-bigger-one-pipeline

Johansen, Bruce. "Canoe Journeys and Cultural Revival," *American Indian Culture and Research Journal* Vol. 36 No. 2 (2012): 131–42.

Kujawinski, Peter. "Guardians of a Vast Lake, and a Refuge for Humanity," *New York Times* (February 7, 2017). https://www.nytimes.com/2017/02/07/travel/great-bear-lake-arctic-unesco-biosphere-canada.html

Ladd, Edmund James. "Ethno-ornithology of the Zuni," in *Stars Above Earth Below: American Indians and Nature,* edited by Marsha Bol. Lanham, MD: Robert Rinehart Publishers, 1998.

LaDuke, Winona. *Recovering the Sacred: The Power of Naming and Claiming.* Boston: South End Press: 2005.

McCool, Daniel. *Native Waters: Contemporary Indian Water Settlements and the Second Treaty Era.* Tucson: University of Arizona Press, 2006.

Miller, Jay. "Numic Religion: An Overview of Power in the Great Basin of Native North America," *Anthropos* (1983): 337–54.

Monet, Jenni. "For Native 'Water Protectors,' Standing Rock Protest Has Become Fight for Religious Freedom, Human Rights" (November 3, 2016). https://www.pbs.org/newshour/nation/military-force-criticized-dakota-access-pipeline-protests

Osborn, Rachel Paschal. "Native American Winters Doctrine and Stevens Treaty Water Rights: Recognition, Quantification, Management," *American Indian Law Journal* Vol. 2 No. 1 (2013): 76–113.

Peterson, Shawn Qwalsius. "The Journey Has Just Begun," in *S'abadeb—The Gifts: Pacific Coast Salish Art and Artists*, edited by Barbara Brotherton. Seattle: University of Washington Press, 2008.

Reichard, Gladys. *Navajo Religion: A Study in Symbolism.* Tucson: University of Arizona Press, 1950/1983.

Roy, Eleanor Ainge. "New Zealand River Granted Same Legal Rights as Human Being," *The Guardian* (March 16, 2017). https://www.theguardian.com/world/2017/mar/16/new-zealand-river-granted-same-legal-rights-as-human-being

Sarvis, Will. "Deeply Embedded: Canoes as an Enduring Manifestation of Spiritualism and Communalism among the Coast Salish," *Journal of the West* Vol. 42 No. 4 (2003): 74–80.

Saulters, Oral. "Undam It? Klamath Tribes, Social Ecological Systems, and Economic Impacts of River Restoration," *American Indian Culture and Research Journal* Vol. 38 No. 3 (2014): 25–54.

Simpson, Leanne. *Lighting the Eighth Fire: The Liberation, Resurgence, and Protection of Indigenous Nations.* St. Paul: University of Minnesota Press, 2009.

Smith, Theresa. *Island of Anishnaabeg: Thunderers and Water Monsters in the Traditional Ojibwe Life-World.* Lincoln: University of Nebraska Press, 2012.

Taliman, Valerie. "Dakota Access Pipeline Standoff: *Mni Wiconi*, Water Is Life," *Indian Country Today* (August 16, 2016). https://newsmaven.io/indiancountrytoday/archive/dakota-access-pipeline-standoff-mni-wiconi-water-is-life-FuSZ5CeNIUi-bq1oDyXs1w/

Treat, James. *Native and Christian: Indigenous Voices on Religious Identity in the United States and Canada.* Abingdon, UK: Routledge, 1996.

United States v. Washington. 384 F.Supp. 312 (1974).

United States v. Winans. 198 U.S. 371 (1905).

Waln, Vi. "Mni Wiconi. Water Is Life. There Is No Life without Water," *Lakota Country Times* (February 9, 2017). https://www.lakotacountrytimes.com/articles/water-is-sacred/

Wilkinson, Charles. *Fire on the Plateau: Conflict and Endurance in the American Southwest.* Washington, DC: Island Press, 2004.

Wilkinson, Charles. *Blood Struggle: The Rise of Modern Indian Nations.* New York: W.W. Norton and Co., 2006.

Yoder, Janet. *Writings about Vi Hilbert by Her Friends.* Seattle: Lushootseed Press, 1992.

Websites and Videos

ABC News, "Meeting the Youths at the Heart of Standing Rock Protests." https://abcnews.go.com/US/video/revealing-documentary-youth-heart-standing-rock-protests-dakota-45674446

Celletti, Mark, and Robert Satiacum. *Canoe Way: The Sacred Journey.* Cedar Media. 2009.

Last Real Indians, "Sacred Water Protection: Moccasins on the Ground Unified Messaging." http://lastrealindians.com/sacred-water-protection-moccasins-on-the-ground-unified-messaging/

Lundahl, Robert. *Song on the Water: The Return of the Great Canoes.* Freshwater Bay Pictures. 2004.

Peltier, Autumn. "Water Protector Autumn Peltier Speaks at UN," CBC News. https://www.youtube.com/watch?v=OusN4mWmDKQ

Reel Northwest, KCTS 9, "Maiden of Deception Pass." (July 15, 2016). https://www.youtube.com/watch?v=A0-JpuOkfRU

Tohono O'odham Nation, "Ours Is the Land." https://vimeo.com/223976575

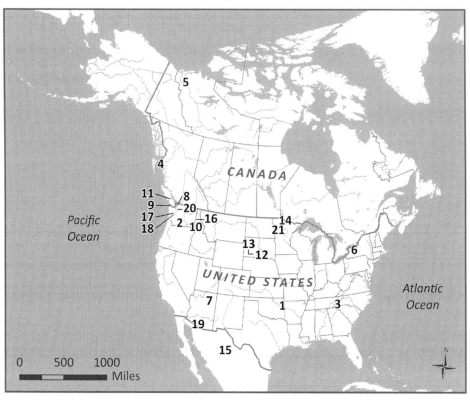

1 Cherokee Nation
2 Confederated Tribes of the Yakama Nation
3 Eastern Band of Cherokee
4 Gitxaala Nation
5 Gwich'in Lands
6 Haudenosaunee (Iroquois) Territory
7 Hopi Tribe
8 Lummi Nation
9 Makah Tribal Nation
10 Nimiipuu (Nez Perce) Tribe

11 Nuu-Chah-Nulth Territories
12 Oglala Lakota Territory
13 Oglala Sioux Tribe (Pine Ridge)
14 Rainy River First Nation
15 Rarámuri Territory
16 Schitsu'umsh (Coeur D'Alene) Tribe
17 Skokomish Indian Tribe
18 Squaxin Island Tribe
19 Tohono O'odham Nation
20 Tulalip Indian Tribes
21 White Earth Nation

Map 5.1. Map of North America locating the tribal communities, nations, and cultural groups mentioned in this chapter. Basemap data made with Natural Earth. (Liz O'Dea Springborn)

Food

5

WHEN THE TATANKA FOOD TRUCK PULLS UP, you know you are in for something good, and something different. Specializing in pre-contact foods of the Dakota and Minnesota territories, chef Sean Sherman (Oglala Lakota) introduces his diners to the foods of his ancestors. Sherman is the owner of Sioux Chef, a catering business with a food-education mission, committed to revitalizing Indigenous foods and training Native people to prepare and explore their cuisine. For Sherman and those working with him, this effort isn't just about what happens in the kitchen: it includes a commitment to revitalizing Indigenous modes of agriculture, harvesting, preparation, and land stewardship. Food, it turns out, is about a lot more than just a full belly.

Basic nutrition is required for our survival, and sheer necessity drives us to revere the things that give us sustenance. Food is part of a life well lived: it gives us joy, comfort, inspiration. Sharing food is also an expression of relationship. The things we eat can be richly symbolic, resonating with memory and meaning, with heart and soul. As Tulalip elder Hank Gobin once explained, "Food is medicine for both the body and the spirit. . . . If you get sick, eat your traditional foods. You have to feed your Indian. Native foods feed your body, but they also feed your spirit" (Krohn and Segrest, 9).

Food plays a central role in many Indigenous religious traditions in North America, where stories, practices, ceremonies, protocol, and ethics teach proper ways of behaving toward the plants and animals that sustain the people. But many tribal people are losing access to their traditional foods, as climate change, development, and invasive species push them toward the brink of extinction. This chapter explores the role of traditional foods in Native American religious life, considering how religious practices reinforce values such as sustainability, gratitude, and reciprocity. It also introduces the Indigenous food sovereignty movement, which uplifts the reclamation of ancestral foods as a vital piece of decolonization.

Reclaiming Access to Sacred Foods

Sacred activities associated with gathering and sharing food are woven into Indigenous lifeways: family traditions are sustained as berries, nuts, shellfish, salmon,
venison, corn, or wild rice are prepared, preserved, and shared. Perhaps more
often than at a church or ceremonial ground, it is in the kitchen where cultural
knowledge is passed on to the next generation. Foods are at the heart of Indigenous
identities as well: Anishinaabe wild rice, Coast Salish salmon, Haudenosaunee corn,
beans, and squash, Gwich'in caribou, Nuu-chah-nulth gray whale. When foodways are lost, stories, songs, prayers, language, and whole worldviews are lost with
them. Foods are a manifestation of a relationship with place shared by countless
preceding generations. When those foods are lost, the impacts are spiritually and
physically devastating.

As traditional foods have become increasingly scarce, the health of many Indigenous people has suffered. Some studies estimate that type 2 diabetes among Native Americans is 248 percent higher than in the general U.S. population. In one
community, nearly 70 percent of the population has been diagnosed with the disease (Geishirt Cantrell, 66). Cardiovascular disease has emerged as a leading cause
of death among Native people, accompanied by high cholesterol, hypertension,
smoking, and obesity. Prior to World War II, such diseases were rare in Native
North America, but since the 1950s, access to traditional foods has precipitously
declined, while they have been replaced by highly processed foods from federal
distribution programs or from growing numbers of fast food restaurants.

Historically, Indigenous people in North America were remarkably healthy,
eating a richly varied diet. For instance, the Puget Sound Traditional Foods and
Diabetes Project found archaeological evidence of food from over 170 different
species of plants and animals in common use, including tubers, berries, greens,
shellfish, birds, mammals, and over twenty different kinds of fish. Charlene Krise,
Squaxin Island tribal council member and museum director, explains:

> In the Squaxin Island Tribe of the Medicine Creek Nation, it was common for our
> people to live beyond 100 years old. Tribal elders attribute this longevity to knowl-
> edge about traditional foods and medicines that was passed down from generation
> to generation. Their powerful traditional science included understanding techniques
> for gathering, knowing when was the most potent time to harvest, and how food
> was processed for everyday use and how plants were used for ceremonial purposes.
> This knowledge was highly regarded as a sacred gift that contributed to living a long
> and fulfilling life. (Krohn and Segrest, 2)

As tribal leaders and medical professionals struggle to respond to the growing health
crisis in Native America, it is clear that addressing nutritional needs is not enough.
It also requires renewing spiritual relationships with the peoples' sacred foods.

Indigenous people face considerable barriers to accessing their traditional foods.
Many communities lost access to hunting, fishing, and gathering territories when
reservations were established. Access was further lost when treaties were violated,

or when the Dawes General Allotment Act eviscerated reservations, breaking them into small parcels and selling off "excess" land to non-Native settlers. Termination policies in the mid-twentieth century cost communities tribal status, reservation land, and treaty rights.

The boarding school system further strained the relationship between people and traditional foods. Taken from their homes, children were unable to learn the hunting, fishing, gathering, and agricultural practices of their people. Traditional ecological knowledge encoded in protocol, rituals, stories, and songs was not passed on. In schools, Indigenous foods were ridiculed as backward, while Euroamerican foods were portrayed as normative and civilized. Without access to their traditional economies and living on land unfit for agriculture, many were left with few choices: they could leave the reservation to find work, or they could stay and rely on commodity-issue foods provided by the federal government.

The federal Food Distribution Program on Indian Reservations (FDPIR) provides tribal communities with highly processed foods: canned fruit in syrup, canned vegetables, pasta, processed cheese, lard, flour, sugar. The kinds of foods provided in the FDPIR were the result of two postwar technological developments: chemical fertilizers that supported new industrial mono-crop agriculture and highly processed shelf-stable foods. As tribal communities came to rely on these processed foods, they experienced the emergence and rapid escalation of obesity, diabetes, and heart disease. Today, tribal communities are calling for changes in the FDPIR to shift funding away from processed foods and toward tribally run food sovereignty programs that empower tribal communities to grow and produce their own healthy, ecologically and culturally appropriate foods.

But accessing traditional foods is not easy. Invasive species and pollution threaten their survival. Fish and shellfish may be high in PCBs, mercury, or other toxins, limiting the amount that can be safely eaten. A veritable maze of legal restrictions can stand in the way as well: school schedules and truancy laws prevent Native students from traveling to hunt, fish, and gather during the academic year, while state and federal permitting or restricted access to private lands make accessing resources difficult. Development has also pushed some species to the brink as prairies are paved over, rivers are dammed, and suburbs expand into areas where these species had once thrived.

The response to this crisis is known as the Indigenous food sovereignty movement. Asserting Indigenous treaty rights, the movement affirms the spiritual importance of traditional foods and the sacred bond they forge between contemporary communities and their ancestors. It asserts the rights of rivers, mountains, streams, lakes, oceans, and the plant and animal people who live in them. It also asserts that the health of these living beings requires a genuine relationship with tribal people through the sacramental acts of gathering, consuming, and caring for sacred foods.

When the Center for American Indian Research and Education conducted a five-year study to develop and evaluate a diabetes-education program among Plains

Photo 5.1.   Colville women pose in ceremonial dress at the "Ceremony of tears," Kettle Falls, Washington, 1939. The event was a ceremony of mourning, commemorating the salmon and salmon habitat that would be lost when the area was flooded by the building of the Grand Coulee Dam. Left to right: Florence Quill, Sophie Paul Seymour, three unnamed women, Millie James, "Lezet" Camille Pichette, Mary Abraham, Elisha Lawson. (Joel E. Ferris Research Archives)

tribes (Pine Ridge, Rosebud, Yankton, Winnebego), researchers interviewed community members to better understand how tribal members understood traditional foods, healthy foods, and diabetes. Three main findings stood out. First, tribal members understood diabetes as an expression of mental, physical, and spiritual health. Participants argued that "stress, grief or anxiety could 'weaken' well-being and make one more vulnerable to diabetes" (Geishirt Cantrell, 70). Second, tribal members understood the disease to be tied to systemic inequality, including the lack of access to fresh, healthy foods. Researchers noted that one store on Pine Ridge offered only "three apples, one pear, and two bags of potatoes," all at prices considerably higher than the processed pasta, chips, and soda also sold there. The next-closest grocery store was twenty-five miles away—a not inconsequential obstacle in a community where gas money can be scarce. Access to traditional foods seemed nearly impossible, given that rivers, lakes, and streams were polluted. Tribal members had been told that it was dangerous to eat fish, and hunting licenses were expensive (Geishirt Cantrell, 71). Third, respondents emphasized that changes in diet needed to happen at the community level. They explained that healthy diets and lifestyles were not a matter of individual choice but of coming together as a tribe. Respondents pointed to tribal gatherings, weekly memorial dinners, open-gym nights, dances, organized walks and runs, and cooking workshops as spaces for changing diet and activity. Finally, participants saw a community-wide return to traditional foods as a key to solving the diabetes crisis. Working together to access and prepare traditional foods was part of what made them healthy: hunting, trapping, growing, gathering, and drying foods were all hard work and had always been done in the community. They praised tribal moves toward restoring bison populations—a cornerstone of traditional diets. These foods were valuable not just for their nutrition but also for their spiritual and emotional impact. The authors of the study noted:

> The whole process of a buffalo hunt was seen as physically and mentally healthy. The tribal members worked together to plan the buffalo hunt. Participation in the hunt was seen as a major responsibility. It was, accordingly, quite honorable to have a role in this major event. Hunting and harvesting the kill were physically healthy exercises." (Geishirt Cantrell, 71)

Fishing

In his book *The Fisherman's Frontier*, historian David Arnold explains that pre-colonial Indigenous communities on the northern Northwest coast could have depleted salmon runs—they had the technological ability to do so. But ethical and spiritual values passed on through story and ceremony kept consumption in check. Stories were told, songs sung, and dances performed that affirmed the personhood of fish, plants, and animals and the historical relationships that bound those other-than-human persons to the human community.

Gitxaała Ethical Relations

Among the Gitxaała in British Columbia, families fished on a massive scale, their catch numbering in the millions, yet without apparent damage to the viability of fish species. How did they manage this? Ecologically appropriate fishing gear limited and dispersed pressure on fish populations, while fishing practices were guided by the Gitxaała ethical and spiritual concept of *syt güülm goot*: "being of one heart" (Menzies, 442). This notion suggests a world that is interconnected, where humans and other-than-human persons live within a network of reciprocal relationships based on respect and trust, and where selfish actions can have dire consequences.

Syt güülm goot is expressed within Gitxaała social organization. Indigenous communities on the northern Northwest coast traditionally honored strict social protocols, with a system of three or four fixed social classes: high-ranking title holders, title holders, freeborn commoners (without hereditary rights), slaves and captives. High rank remains associated with mythic and historical encounters between ancestors and powerful spirits and is accompanied by resource rights passed

Photo 5.2.   The end of the Kwantlen First Nation salmon ceremony, where elders and community members, in ceremonial clothing, return the bones from the first fish harvest to the river. (Rjjago, Wikimedia Commons, https://commons.wikimedia.org/wiki/File:Kwantlen_First_Nation_Salmon_Ceremony.jpg)

along through matrilineal clans. Families and clans are in turn responsible for the care and maintenance of particular places. Hereditary site managers ensure that species are maintained for long-term sustained yield, with "goal oriented harvesting" spread over the course of the year. Resources were shared, and managers oversaw the trading of food, ensuring that everyone within an extended kin network had enough to eat. In his study, Charles Menzies quotes three Gitxaała elders to explain why this matters.

Clarence Innes puts it this way:

> [Hereditary site managers] walked the streams and anything harmful, they cleaned it up before the season. The chief used to go and look at his territory from time to time. They used to do a ceremonial cleansing too. They always let fish go up the river. They just took what they needed. The leader started the discussion among the tribe, got advice from the people about how many fish to take. If they saw a species was in trouble, they wouldn't make it extinct. They were responsible. (Menzies, 453)

Merle Bolton adds:

> The only way they taught you things like that, was take what you need. Get no more than that. If you get more, give it to your neighbour who doesn't have it. We never stockpiled anything. (Menzies, 455)

Colin Nelson cautions:

> You know when you have enough. You don't shoot animals you have no use for.
> If you're going to treat Nature like that she can come back on you twice as hard.
> (Menzies, 455)

When the Department of Fisheries banned Indigenous fishing techniques in 1964, many Gitxaała were forced to work in canaries, which provided Native people new economic opportunity but depleted resources and later excluded Native people from employment. In 1968, the state began to require fishing licenses— which were both expensive and difficult to acquire. Many Gitxaała families lost their livelihoods as a result: employment dropped from 100 percent to 29 percent. Contemporary Gitxaała continue to harvest traditional foods (seaweed, sea mammals, halibut, salmon, oolichan), despite such historical pressures wrought by colonialism.

Gitxaała notions of property played a key role in the tribe's successful resource management. They implied less a sense of *ownership* of a place and more a *responsibility* for a place and its resources. Clans owned and were accountable for particular rivers, streams, and fishing areas. Clan leaders in turn controlled who could fish and where and when, with the goal of ensuring long-term sustained yields. By contrast, as Arnold points out, European settlers to Alaska devised an "open access" fishery wherein anyone could fish as long as they liked and catch as much as they liked. This, along with the colonial undermining of traditional clan structures and property rights, meant the quick exhaustion of many resources. In his work on the fishing traditions of the Lummi Nation in Washington State, Daniel Boxberger makes a similar claim, asserting that traditional reef-netting techniques and a kin-based division of labor helped ensure that the catch was sustainably managed and equitably shared. But such traditions were undermined by policies that discouraged fishing and by state and provincial governments that prioritized commercial and sport fishing over Indigenous subsistence treaty rights.

Fishing Rights on the Columbia River
The Lummi, like other tribal people in the Pacific Northwest, reserved the right to fish at usual and accustomed places within their treaties. When those rights were restricted, they fought back. Throughout the 1950s and 1960s, tribal people participated in "fish-ins": public demonstrations of treaty rights that often resulted in violent suppression and arrest. As noted in chapter 4, a case went before district court judge George Boldt in 1974, who ruled that tribes have the treaty right to half the legal harvest and the responsibility to co-manage fisheries with state government. This decision led to the establishment of two intertribal agencies: the Northwest Indian Fisheries Commission and the Columbia River Inter-Tribal Fish Commission (CRITFC). Today, tribes are leaders in salmon restoration, managing tribal fisheries and hatcheries, and partnering with other stakeholders to restore salmon habitat.

One example of this are the Nimiipuu (Nez Perce), who are fighting for salmon on the Snake River. In his work with the Nimiipuu, Benedict Colombi explains, "Salmon and Nimiipuu survival are interdependent, and without salmon the Nimiipuu say their culture will die. The Nimiipuu revere salmon as a keystone species, the species that became embedded in cultural traditions and narratives." Nimiipuu elder Horace Axtell explains: "According to our spiritual way of life, everything is based on nature. Anything that grows or lives is part of our spiritual life. The most important element we have in way of life is water. The next most important element is the fish, because the fish comes from water" (Colombi, 75).

Prior to colonialism, Nimiipuu adults ate an average of five hundred pounds of fish a year: Chinook, coho, chum, sockeye, cutthroat, Dolly Varden, steelhead trout, sturgeon, suckers, lampreys, pike minnows, and various whitefish. They cultivated root crops like camas, biscuitroot, and snowdrops, replacing young bulbs, planting seed bulbs, and employing controlled burns. While roots, berries, and land mammals were very important, the Nimiipuu regarded water and salmon with particular reverence. *Kúus* (water) and *léwliks* (salmon) were among Haniyaw'aat's (Creator's) first creations. Julia Davis-Wheeler explains: "We need the salmon because it is part of our lives and part of our history. The salmon is part of us, and we are a part of it. Our children need to be able to feel what it is like to catch and eat salmon. They need to be able to experience that sense of respect that many of us have felt in past years" (Colombi, 84).

Salmon and water play a key role in ceremonies, including rites at birth, coming of age, naming, weddings, funerals, memorials, powwows, and other celebrations. "Water (*kúus*), chinook salmon (*nac'óox*), meat such as elk, deer, moose, and bison (*núukt*), roots (*qáaws*), and huckleberries (*cemíitx*)" are "gifts (*pínitini*) from the Creator, because these living beings gave up their lives so that the Nimiipuu can continue to prosper" (Colombi, 83).

Prior to the twentieth century, between ten and sixteen million salmon a year swam through the Columbia and Snake Rivers. The Snake saw more Chinook, coho, and steelhead than any other river in the world. In the twentieth century, massive hydroelectric projects, commercial fishing, habitat loss, and pollution have reduced these runs to less than 10 percent of their historic levels. To address this crisis, tribal leaders decided they needed to "think like a salmon" (Colombi, 89).

Salmon are an incredibly resilient species, having adapted to cataclysms like volcanic eruptions, floods, earthquakes, and glaciation. And so the Nimiipuu looked to salmon for lessons of resiliency. One of their keys to survival is their "independent groupings" (Colombi, 93) that enable each group to work together to survive, a strategy that some observers link to tribal identities. Another is their incredible tie to particular waterways and watersheds, connections that are passed down through generations, even when they have been separated from those waters for multiple generations. Those connections lie dormant, waiting for the opportunity to wake up. For tribal people working to reclaim and restore their homeland, this notion is rich with meaning. Such observations led to the creation of the Spirit of the Salmon Plan (Wy-kan-ush-mi Wa-kish-wit), which guides Columbia River tribes as they operate hatcheries, monitor fish, and protect critical habitat.

> Salmon are part of our spiritual and cultural identity; over a dozen longhouses and churches on the reservations and in ceded areas rely on salmon for their religious services. The annual salmon return and its celebration by our peoples assure the renewal and continuation of human and all other life. Historically, we were wealthy people because of a flourishing trade economy based on salmon; for many tribal members, fishing is still the preferred livelihood. Salmon and the rivers they use are part of our sense of place. The Creator put us here where the salmon return; we are obliged to remain and protect this place. Salmon are an indicator species: as water becomes degraded and fish populations decline, so do the elk, deer, roots, berries, and medicines that sustain us. As our primary food source for thousands of years, salmon continue to be an essential aspect of our nutritional health; because our tribal populations are growing, the needs for salmon are more important than ever. The annual return of the salmon allows the transfer of traditional values from generation to generation. Without salmon returning to our rivers and streams, we would cease to be Indian people. (Columbia River Inter-Tribal Fish Commission)

In the 2008 Columbia Basin Fish Accords, the Colville, Warm Springs, Yakama, Umatilla, and Shoshone-Bannok received $900 million to aid in habitat restoration and hatchery improvements, with funds to improve spillway weirs and screens on some dams. The Nimiipuu declined to sign the accords, as doing so would mean suspending their efforts to push for the removal of the four lower Snake River dams. Today, the Nimiipuu and other CRITFC tribes are working to secure water rights, protect endangered species, promote carbon sequestration projects, and advocate for dam removal.

First Fish Ceremonies

Throughout North America, Indigenous spiritual traditions, stories, and ceremonies honor the people's relationship with keystone species. In an origin story of the Skokomish in Washington State, an ancestor was transformed into a salmon, married into the salmon nation, and gave birth to many children. These children were eventually transformed back into human beings: forging a tie between the Skokomish people, their river, and the salmon people. Likewise, the Lummi tell the story of Mother Salmon, who each year travels upriver, offering her flesh and the life of her children so that human beings may live. As long as they are treated with honor and respect, she will allow her children to be caught. If the gift of their life is abused, Mother Salmon will call her children back, returning to the sea, no longer offering themselves as food. These relationships are honored through annual first salmon ceremonies.

First fish ceremonies provide space to tell stories that convey ethics and values for supporting sustainable populations. Found throughout the Pacific Coast, first fish ceremonies are an example of such a tradition, honoring the arrival of spawning fish as they return to natal waterways. Within such ceremonies, the first fish is brought to shore and honored like a visiting dignitary. It is ceremonially filleted, with every person receiving a single bite, a powerful symbol of the sacramental connection between the people and the fish: as long as one survives, so will the other. In many communities, the manner in which the bones are returned to the water is particularly important. For Coast Salish people, the bones travel back to the fish-people's home, where they are re-clothed with flesh, resurrected to new life.

Sturgeon

Living dinosaurs, sturgeon have inhabited their natal waters for over 136 million years. Anishinaabe oral traditions in the Great Lakes region tell of a young girl who had come of age, and entered into her seclusion. When she returned, she found that her family had been turned into sturgeon. Her grandmother-sturgeon told her: "From now on, our family will be living here as part of the sturgeon clan. Please carry me to the lake, so I can live" (LaDuke, 228). In the telling of such stories, the people remember that fish are relatives, not merely resources. But after millions of years, the sturgeon have been driven nearly to extinction. Prior to the 1880s, Anishinaabe caught 275,000 pounds each year, and sturgeon populations flourished. Commercial harvesting began in 1886, quickly exceeding one million pounds a year. Often, the massive fish were killed solely for their swim bladder (isinglass) or caviar, the rest of the fish left to go to waste. By 1925, the ancient population had collapsed to 1 percent of its original size. The Clean Air Act of the 1970s helped the sturgeon begin to recover. But recovery took work by Indigenous communities, in particular, the Rainy River First Nations, a group of seven bands of Anishinaabe near Fort Frances, Ontario, who devoted themselves to restoring sturgeon fisheries. Today they have "the strongest and most viable population of sturgeon in the world" (LaDuke, 232). In 1999, the White Earth Indian Nation sought to build on their northern neighbors' success, transporting fifty thousand sturgeon fry across the U.S.-Canada border to White Earth watersheds.

But fish recovery remains an uphill battle: sturgeon need to range for hundreds of miles. They need wild rivers. And these days, wild rivers are hard to come by. Over the past seventy-five years, the waterways of North America have been transformed. Restoring healthy fish populations thus requires radical work. It requires rethinking assumptions about rivers and waterways: rather than seeing them simply as channels through which water flows (and where one channel is as good as another), Indigenous worldviews challenge us to see rivers and watersheds as living things, and fish as relatives to whom we have obligations.

Indigenous-studies scholar Lindsey Schneider (Turtle Mountain Chippewa) argues that what makes tribal fish-restoration efforts successful is their deep connection with specific geographic regions and ecologies, knowledge that is based on long-standing relationships with and respect for the land, the water, and the other-than-human persons who live there. This particular and local knowledge stands in contrast to abstract generalizations of scientific approaches that can see only two options: exploitation or complete removal of human beings from a landscape (Schneider, 160).

Hunting

Indigenous sacred food traditions wrestle with a fundamental spiritual dilemma: How does one respect the life and personhood of animals—and also eat them? In his book *The Animals Came Dancing: Native American Sacred Ecology and Animal Kinship*, ethicist Howard Harrod explores this question as he examines Indigenous hunting traditions on the Northern Plains. Oral traditions describe how animals participated in Creation, volunteering their bodies as food for human beings. At the same time, animals existed in complex social relationships with human beings, creating kinship ties through marriage, adoption, and gifts of spiritual power. Humans' kinship with animals was recalled in stories, and embodied through song and dance. Across Native North America, hunting traditions vary as widely as the ecologies and species with which they interact. Despite this diversity, they often share a common notion: hunters do not overpower or outsmart the animals they hunt; rather, they give themselves to the hunters in an expression of the reciprocal relationship between people and animals.

Many Native cultures have a tradition of designated hunters who provide for large extended families and ceremonial gatherings. Designated hunters mentor young men through their first hunt, followed by a ceremonial meal and a giveaway. In his book *Landscape Traveled by Coyote and Crane: The World of the Schitsu'umsh*, anthropologist Rodney Frey explains that traditionally hunted foods are a source of nourishment and healing, providing "spiritual links to the Creator and the Ancestors." Hunters work in humble partnership with their animal kinsmen. A mentor explained to Frey: "The same Creator that created me created that Deer. So he's my brother. We're related. Everything is alive. Even a rock" (Frey, 181).

In Schitsu'umsh tradition, the natural world is not owned, but "lent to you by the Creator," and filled with relatives. Frey explains:

> The water potato consumed at a Powwow, the smoked meat chewed at a Memorial Giveaway, the camas eaten at the conclusion of a Jump Dance, and the small pouch of bitterroot tucked in the coffin beside a deceased relative, all reiterate an essential, perennial, and expanded kinship. In partaking of the plants and animals of the landscape, the Human Peoples reclaim their affiliation with and identity in relation to that landscape, the lakes and mountains, and the Creator and the First Peoples. Even in picking only "a handful of berries" and eating them, "you are connecting to the old people and to the spirit world of our ancestors, to my grandmother, asking for strength, and from them through the earth, through Mother Earth, to grant you those things." (Frey, 210)

"We Are Whalers. We Don't Want a Wonder Bread Culture."

Among the Nuu–chah–nulth, the name for whale is *iihtuup*: "big mystery." Gray whales are keystone species for the Nuu–chah–nulth of Vancouver Island and the Makah of northwest Washington, and are at the heart of their culture, history, economy, and spirituality. According to their origin story, the Creator formed the first man on a beach and gave him the treasures he would need for a successful life: a wife, a chisel, and a whale harpoon. The Creator taught first man and first woman to whale and so sustain themselves on their rugged shores. Whaling was so important that the Makah explicitly reserved the right to whale in their 1855 treaty. Elder Edward Claplanhoo explains that the treaty ancestors knew "the land was valuable, but it wasn't as valuable as the water. It wasn't as valuable as the ocean, which had all of the things that we needed to live on" (Reid, 278).

Whale hunting was a sacred task, undertaken with reverence. Only those who inherited the right to do so could hunt whales. A hunt required months of prayer, fasting, and spiritual cleansing. As Charlotte Cote explains, "My ancestors believed

Photo 5.3.   Makah whaler Wilson Parker holding whaling floats. Neah Bay, Washington, 1915. Photo by Edward Curtis. (University of Washington Libraries, Special Collections, NA 556)

that a whale was not caught, but with the proper rituals and utmost respect shown to the whale, it would give itself up to the whaler and to the people who had shown it the most esteem" (Cote, 32). The whale would come looking for the hunter. "They recognized each other" (Cote, 34).

But non-Native commercial whaling quickly devastated gray whale populations. Between 1880 and 1920, their number fell from thirty thousand to near zero. As historian and Snohomish tribal member Joshua Reid explains, "Makahs did not experience real trouble until non-Native forces wiped out the resource foundations for Northwest coast societies and employed regulatory power of the state to shut out Indigenous peoples from customary practices and spaces that had once made them wealthy and powerful" (Reid, 276).

Despite this, the Nuu-chah-nulth and Makah maintained their whaling traditions as best they could, keeping them alive in storytelling, songs and dances, hereditary names, artwork, and ceremonies. When the gray whale was taken off the endangered species list in the 1990s, the Makah were granted permission by the International Whaling Commission to once again hunt a gray whale. The Makah soon faced backlash from the general public, which did not understand their traditions or treaty rights, but the Makah persisted, training physically, mentally, and spiritually and preparing the traditional canoe and harpoon. In May of 1999, after months of preparation, a crew of Makah whalers successfully harpooned and brought a whale to shore. The community joyfully celebrated the hunt with song, drumming, dancing, and potlatching (ceremonial feasting). Reid describes it: "On that May morning at the close of the twentieth century, Makah whalers did more than harpoon a whale—they dramatically anchored their nation's identity to the sea, just as generations of ancestors had done. Through spiritual beliefs and customary practices such as whaling, sealing, and fishing, historic Makahs transformed the sea into sovereign space" (Reid, 272). The event had a powerful effect on the community, sparking cultural renewal, pride in its young people, and a return to traditional foods and lifestyles.

Raising Bison in the Buffalo Nation

Just as the whale is a keystone species for the Nuu-chah-nulth and Makah, bison is a keystone species for Indigenous peoples of the Northern and western Plains. Prior to the nineteenth century, bison were the largest single contributor to material culture in this region. Bison provided over one hundred different items, such as building material, clothing, food, and medicine, for Northern Plains people. As for the Lakota, the bison defined them to such a degree that they were known as the Pte Oyate, the Buffalo Nation.

With their powerful spirits, bison serve as a central symbol in Plains religious life. Bison skulls are the centerpiece of many religious altars—at the Sun Dance, the vision quest, the girls' coming-of-age ceremony, and others. White Buffalo Calf Woman is the supernatural figure who came to the people in time of great need, giving them the sacred pipe, teaching them how to pray with it, and instructing the people in their sacred ceremonies. When she departed, she turned into a white bison calf.

Bison hunting was no small matter for traditional Plains people. Every step of the hunt was marked by ritual. Hunters and their families prayed with medicine bundles and sacred pipes, offered sweetgrass, and kept iconic stones shaped like bison, offering songs and prayers in hopes of securing a successful hunt. Old bulls were referred to as "grandfather," and were humbly thanked for their sacrifice. Bison were not merely animals but understood to be other-than-human persons who could hear the prayers, gratitude, songs, and respectful words of the hunters and their families. They communicated with human beings in dreams and visions, and the people honored them in turn.

Historians and ecologists estimate that between twenty-five and thirty million bison roamed North America in the sixteenth century. By 1883 fewer than one hundred remained in the wild. By 1902, only two-dozen remained, protected within Yellowstone National Park. This near extinction was due in large part to nineteenth-century federal policies designed to subdue Plains people by exterminating bison. As one U.S. Army Commanding Officer said in 1867: "Kill every buffalo you can. Every buffalo dead is an Indian gone." Bounties were offered for bison hides and tongues, while tourists were encouraged to shoot them for sport from moving trains, leaving their carcasses behind to rot.

Today, tribal communities are working to restore bison populations and renew the peoples' spiritual relationship with them. The Intertribal Buffalo Council (IBC) was formed in 1991, bringing together Lakota, Crow, Shoshone Bannock, Gros Ventre/Assiniboine, Blackfeet, Winnebago, Oklahoma Choctaw, and Pueblo communities. By 2018, the IBC had grown to comprise 58 tribes in 19 states, tending 15,000 bison. For these communities, bison restoration is not simply an economic venture, it is a spiritual one, deeply informed by ritual, ceremony, and prayer.

"Caribou Are Not Just What We Eat; They Are Who We Are"

Northern Athabaskan Gwich'in are known as the "people of the caribou." Living in fifteen villages spread across central Alaska, the northern Yukon, and the Northwest Territories, the Gwich'in people rely on the porcupine caribou that migrate through their territory. In their origin stories it was the Creator who determined that the Gwich'in would hunt the caribou. To mark the sacred agreement between them, the Creator exchanged human and caribou hearts—linking the human community and the caribou community in a profound and timeless relationship. As one community member explained: "Many of us are named after these (caribou) herds. Our names become meaningless when the caribou do not come back" (Huntington and Watson, 55). Hence, while caribou are at the heart of their traditional diet, and their skins are used for clothing (boots, slippers, gloves, bags), and their bones as tools, their tie to the caribou is not simply one of resource and economy. Sarah James of the Gwich'in Steering Committee explains, "We are caribou people. Caribou are not just what we eat; they are who we are. They are in our stories and songs and the whole way we see the world. Caribou are our life. Without caribou we wouldn't exist" (http://ourarcticrefuge.org/about-the-gwichin/).

In 1983, Arctic Village residents issued a formal statement to the Alaska Department of Fish and Game, describing Gwich'in hunting practices and guidelines for ethical behavior toward caribou, and encouraging the state to learn from these guidelines to ensure the health of future caribou populations (http://arcticcircle .uconn.edu/ANWR/anwrgwichin1.html). Included in this document are traditional guidelines such as:

- Caribou meat must not be sold.
- Caribou meat must be butchered properly before being transported to a village, and the butchery area must be cleaned properly, covering the site with fresh snow.
- Caribou must not be fed to dogs.
- The first group of caribou appearing at a village must be allowed to pass through peacefully.

In his work, anthropologist Richard Nelson describes Athabaskan *hutłaanee* (ritual restrictions) that include guidelines such as these. At the heart of *hutłaanee*, Nelson explains, is the assumption that animals are sentient, aware, and share a common spirit or life force with human beings. Because human beings share life within a precarious world, showing respect and care for these other creatures is not simply an expression of moral nicety, but an absolute requirement for survival.

Each year, herds of porcupine caribou migrate to their birthing grounds on the northern coast of the Arctic National Wildlife Refuge (ANWR). For this reason, the Gwich'in strongly oppose the opening of ANWR to oil and gas exploration, citing the stress such development would place on new calves and mothers. The impacts of pollution, development, and oil leaks, not to mention fossil fuels' contribution to climate change, threaten caribou habitat. Damage to ANWR could devastate the porcupine caribou and in turn wreak havoc on the northern Athabaskan people, who share the same beating heart.

The Plant People

> This tree's a good teacher. . . . That's what we've always been taught. Our Indigenous herbalists say to pay attention when plants come to you; they're bringing you something you need to learn. (Kimmerer, 146, 274)

The plants, many elders say, are the first teachers. Over millennia, Indigenous farmers and gatherers worked to get to know these other-than-human neighbors. Today, they are a visceral link to the ancestors. As Rowen White (Mohawk) affirms, heirloom seeds are "witnesses to the past, encapsulated cultural memory" (LaDuke,

192). By recovering their relationship with these plants, Indigenous communities are preserving both themselves and these threatened species. Ethnobotanist Robin Wall Kimmerer writes that plants and the people mutually depend upon each other for survival. "Our elders taught that the relationship between plants and humans must be one of balance. People can take too much and exceed the capacity of the plants to share again. And yet, they also teach that we can take too little. If we allow traditions to die, relationships to fade, the land will suffer" (Kimmerer, 166).

While both industrial and Indigenous agriculture involve intensive management of plant resources, they dramatically differ in terms of ethics, worldview, and method. In his book *Enduring Seeds: Native American Agriculture and Wild Plant Cultivation*, agricultural ecologist, ethnobotanist, and Franciscan brother Gary Paul Nabhan contrasts Indigenous agriculture with industrial agriculture. While industrial agriculture works to standardize methods and regulate soil chemistry, Indigenous agriculture is adapted to local ecologies and microclimates. While Indigenous agriculture intensively manages the land (through controlled burns, thinning, and pruning), the goal is sustained, long-term yields rather than maximizing short-term profits. While industrial agriculture tries to supply produce out of season, Indigenous agriculture emphasizes eating with the seasons and reconnecting with the cycles of nature. While industrial agriculture emphasizes producing large quantities of a few products, Indigenous agriculture sees value in biodiversity, an ethos expressed in sacred stories and ritual expressions of respect. Indigenous agricultural traditions view heritage foods as teachers who offer profound spiritual and ethical lessons, as family stories, identities, and values are passed on through food cultivation, harvest, and preparation. Indigenous agriculture acknowledges the accumulation of wealth, but emphasizes that the purpose of wealth is to care for one's community, never to enrich an individual at the expense of others. Finally, Indigenous agricultural traditions emphasize the sacred nature of eating: all food requires taking a plant or animal life, and all life shares a common source and a common spirit.

Corn's Children

In his book *Eating the Landscape: American Indian Stories of Food, Identity, and Resilience*, Enrique Salmón (Rarámuri/Tarahumara) reflects on his family's food traditions and the ways in which sacred cultural knowledge is passed on through food.

> [When they] introduced me to individual plants, they also introduced my kinship to the plants and to the land from where they and we had emerged. They were introducing me to my relatives. My grandmother described the relationships the plants had with each other. She taught me that the plants were not only plants but also people. Some were Rarámuri, whereas others were Apaches and non-Indians. Recipes were shared during celebrations and whenever family came together. They are a form of knowledge reproduction and social exchange. They gave everyone something to talk and gossip about, to share, and to be proud of. . . . Whenever I partake of Eloisa's tamale recipe or my mother's way of preparing salsa, I am eating the memories and knowledge associated with those foods. The elements of the

stories, the jokes, and the intricate contextualized experience become embodied every time the eating takes place. (Salmón, 2–3, 7–9)

Salmón explains that while European and Euroamerican narratives emphasize human cultural heroes, for his Rarámuri ancestors, "the heroes are the trees, plants, animals, and children." In Rarámuri oral traditions, Onorúame (the Creator) becomes frustrated with the corruption and laziness of the humans and sends a flood. Only two children escape. But, regretting the harsh decision, the Creator consoles them, giving them seed corn. The children scatter the seeds, and corn plants began to grow. At first they look like regular plants. Then, "one day the children noticed human heads emerging from the ears. They could see the black hair on top of the heads, then the foreheads, and soon the entire heads and bodies sprung forth from the ears of corn and sprawled out onto the ground. . . . In a short time the land had been repopulated with Rarámuri. . . . Today, many Rarámuri continue to think of themselves as the children of corn" (Salmón, 14–15).

The Three Sisters

One of the most significant food traditions in Native North America is the "three sisters": corn, beans, and squash. Celebrated in stories from Haudenosaunee territory in the Northeast to the ancient farms of Pueblo people in the desert Southwest, the three sisters work in perfect symmetry and complementarity, each supporting the growth of the other, while together providing near-perfect nutrition for their human cultivators. Squash leaves provide shade, keeping the soil cool and wet. Corn stalks grow tall, providing natural trellising for beans. Beans return nitrogen to the soil, helping the other plants to grow.

As Kimmerer explains, the three sisters teach powerful lessons to those who are willing to pay attention:

There are many stories of how they came to be, but they all share the understanding of these plants as women, and sisters. Some stories tell of a long winter when the people were dropping from hunger. Three beautiful women came to their dwellings on a snowy night. One was a tall woman dressed all in yellow, with long flowing hair. The second wore green, and the third was robed in orange. The three came inside to shelter by the fire. Food was scarce, but the visiting strangers were fed generously, sharing in the little that the people had left. In gratitude for their generosity, the three sisters revealed their true identities—corn, beans, and squash— and gave themselves to the people in a bundle of seeds so that they might never go hungry again. . . . The Three Sisters offer us a new metaphor for an emerging relationship between Indigenous knowledge and Western science, both of which are rooted in the earth. I think of the corn as traditional ecological knowledge, the physical and spiritual framework that can guide the curious bean of science, which twines like a double helix. The squash creates the ethical habitat for coexistence and mutual flourishing. I envision a time when the intellectual monoculture of science will be replaced with a polyculture of complementary knowledges. (Kimmerer, 131, 134, 138)

As Kimmerer explains, the infusion of traditional ecological knowledge into contemporary agricultural practices is a radical undertaking, challenging existing notions of what it means to cultivate plants, what it means to eat, and what it means to live ethically in a place. Throughout Native North America, tribal communities are reclaiming their own version of the three sisters, recovering local heritage strains of these plants, and learning how their ancestors grew them within their particular bioregion.

Manoomin: Food That Floats on the Water

Manoomin, or wild rice, is a gift to the Anishinaabe people from the Creator, a promised sign that signaled their arrival in their new home. Centuries ago, the Creator sent the Anishinaabe a message: travel until you see food floating on the water. After a difficult journey, the people saw ducks feasting on this strange floating food. This, they knew, was the place the Creator had chosen for them. *Manoomin* is the food that defines them as a people. Each year during harvest, Anishinaabe people gathered for ceremony—feasting, prayer, dance, expressions of gratitude, and prayers for fertility—that the sacred gift of wild rice might continue, ensuring their survival as a people.

Photo 5.4.   In a September 5, 2017, photo, his canoe almost completely hidden in wild rice, Bruce Martineau poles to the shore of Deadfish Lake on the Fond du Lac Reservation in northeast Minnesota. In the late 1990s, the Fond du Lac Band began experimenting to try to make the rice grow like it used to. At Deadfish Lake, they put in a holding pond above the lake and a water control structure at the outlet. The lake is now a reliable source of wild rice. (Dan Kraker/Minnesota Public Radio via AP)

In the 1950s, the state of Minnesota began domesticating wild rice, industrializing production on diked paddies, and marketing the rice with appropriated Native images. Sam Grey and Raj Patel describe this industrially grown rice "decked with images of Indians in canoes and given Ojibway brand names" in "an obvious attempt to cash in on the consumer's choice to purchase an indigenous product" (Grey and Patel, 440). Mass production meant lower costs, which soon priced Indigenous harvesters of real wild rice out of the market.

Wild rice was further threatened by pollution. Mercury and other pollutants from upriver industrial manufacturers continue to contaminate waterways, while chemical fertilizers and pesticides drain microorganisms and weaken soil. Genetically modified seeds used in industrial rice production are also a concern: since seed can be carried by wind, water currents, or migrating waterfowl, it is difficult to isolate these modified strains. Genetically modified seeds do not only threaten the genetic integrity of heritage seed stocks, but they also put Native rice cultivators at risk of legal action from agribusinesses who own patents on modified genes. Among the Anishinaabe, the threat of genetically modified "terminator seeds" is particularly ominous. While Anishinaabe harvest ceremonies offer prayers for fertility, so-called terminator seeds produce sterile crops, thereby ensuring a steady market for new seeds each year. If such sterile seeds were to be carried into wild rice areas, the consequences could be devastating.

Anishinaabe people are working with allies to protect wild rice and to restore its place in Native people's lives. For example, when Exxon proposed a massive copper and zinc mine near the Mole Lake Reservation in 2003, the Anishinaabe joined with a broad statewide coalition of environmentalists, sport fishers, and other allies to successfully halt the project. Anishinaabe communities are currently working to buy back lands and waters held by their ancestors. By an 1867 treaty, the White Earth Reservation was 837,000 acres. Much of this land was lost to the Dawes General Allotment Act, among other legal maneuvers, and today the White Earth Nation has been left with scarcely 9 percent of their original land base: 76,000 acres. The White Earth Land Recovery Program (WELRP) works to utilize traditional wild rice, maple syrup, and bison production to support the community and to repurchase lands. Thus far they have acquired nearly two thousand acres. WELRP also works to provide community gardens, grow boxes, backyard gardens, and greenhouses to promote access to healthy foods. As WELRP executive director Winona LaDuke explains, recovering access to traditional foods is not just about diet. It is deeply tied to spirituality. "The recovery of the people is tied to the recovery of food, since food itself is medicine: not only for the body, but for the soul, for the spiritual connection to history, ancestors, and the land" (LaDuke, 210).

Green Corn

In the southeastern United States, Cherokee reverence for plants grew from a rich agricultural tradition. For centuries, Cherokee women managed large communal farms, tending fields of corn, squash, pumpkins, and beans. Each family also kept its own garden plots, providing for daily needs and particular favorites (Vick, 411). Ethnobotanist Clint Carroll has documented that the Cherokee historically used over seven hundred different plants. After the enforcement of the 1830 Removal Act, when the Cherokee, Choctaw, Chickasaw, Seminole, Muscogee, and Creek Nations were put on a forced march to present-day Oklahoma (the infamous Trail of Tears), they lost access to at least one-third of these traditional plants. Their relationship with corn, however, remained strong.

The Green Corn Dance is an important ceremony shared by tribal communities throughout the Southeast and Northeast, from Haudenosaunee territory in present-day New England to the Cherokee in Oklahoma. Held in summer to honor the new corn, the ceremony commemorates the turn of the agricultural year, providing a space for purification and renewal. Today Green Corn ceremonies are held over four days. On the first day, camp is set up and the community gathers for a large meal, finishing what remains of the previous year's harvest. This is followed by an all-night social dance. On the second day, the people fast. A special diuretic and purgative tea with high amounts of caffeine is consumed. Brush arbors are built in each of the four directions, and women dance the purifying Ribbon Dance, their legs bedecked with rattles, around a ceremonial fire at the center of the dance grounds. Offerings from the new crop are burned in the fire. Women traditionally took a coal from the fire to start a new fire in their own homes: in this way, every hearth fire was linked to this central sacred fire, which would be kept burning all year. On the third day, fasting continues. Men dance the Feather Dance for healing the community and ceremonially bathe. In the evening, the fast is broken with a feast and an all-night Stomp Dance. The fourth day provides a transition from sacred work: friendship dances are held, and teams compete in stick games before heading home.

Why does this ceremony matter, and what does it tell us about the way the people view planting? It reminds the people that growing food really matters. It reminds the people that planting and harvesting food is something done together: this is shared food, cooked over a shared fire. It teaches those present that social, spiritual, and nutritional life are inseparable. A four-day ceremony, replete with two days of fasting, causes everyone to pause, to remember how sacred food is, and to acknowledge the incredible and holy value of life given from the earth, a gift received through hard work, a cause for fasting, feasting, humility, and celebration.

Bean Sprout Stew

Chapter 3 discussed the sacred nature of water for Pueblo communities. Spider Woman, who weaves the world together, loves water and springs. Springs are guarded by snakes, symbols of fertility and immortality. Kachinas are powerful holy beings who reside on mountaintops and in rain clouds; they are spiritual manifestations of ancestors, deities, and bringers of rain. Centering on agriculture, Pueblo ceremonial life includes engagement with over four hundred kachinas, who bring rain to the dry landscape.

For many centuries, the Hopi have grown corn, beans, squash, and other medicinal and edible plants using dry-land-farming and semi-irrigation techniques.
Their traditions teach that land is alive, and animated by water, in partnership with
human beings. Their ceremonial cycle is built around an agricultural calendar:
fields are cleared in February; sweet corn is planted in the spring; ceremonies welcome the kachinas in the late spring and early summer, who are visiting from their
home in the San Francisco Peaks, bringing the rain with them. Among the Hopi,
the eight-day *Powamu* Festival welcomes the kachinas home from the mountains,
encouraging them to stay. As part of the festival, ceremonial kivas are kept hot
and humid. Beans are planted in the sandy floor to sprout during the festival. On
the eighth day, kiva societies don their sacred regalia and go from one kiva to the
next, connecting all nine of the kiva societies within the Hopi region. The kachinas
themselves arrive in the central plaza on the final morning of the ceremony, distributing gifts to children and handing out the bean sprouts grown in the ceremonial
kivas so that each home can make bean sprout stew. Served at the beginning of
the Hopi kachina ceremonial cycle, bean sprout stew is a powerful reminder—in
taste, smell, and texture—of the people's reliance on the ancestors and the kachina
spirits, coaxed into returning each year with song, dance, and the aroma of the stew
(Salmón, 62). For the next six months, the kachina spirits bring much-needed rain.
At the end of the rainy season, the Niman Kachina ceremony is held, honoring
the kachinas' imminent departure. Over sixteen days, kachinas dance in the plaza,
sprinkling cornmeal on the ground, carrying green corn stalks. Priests blow smoke
to simulate rain clouds, and gifts are once again distributed to children, while harvest baskets are distributed to the community. Finally the kachinas return to their
mountain homes in the west.

Participating in this ceremonial cycle teaches a vital lesson about the people's
spiritual and material connection with the landscape: they are a part of the landscape,
depending upon it for their lives, and when they die, their spirits will join that cycle.
When asked why Hopi farmers did not make use of modern irrigation systems, a
Hopi elder answered: "If the Hopi had irrigation, we would no longer need the
kachinas." Salmón explains: "To irrigate, for people that have always relied on and
trusted kachinas, is to deny everything that it means to be Hopi" (Salmón, 55). The
loss of traditional land management would ultimately mean the loss of ceremonies,
stories, language, and the deeply encoded ecological knowledge they contain.

Pueblo communities throughout the Southwest are addressing growing health
problems by calling the people back to traditional farming. Community leaders
have organized summer programs for youth to work alongside traditional farmers,
and helped to develop classroom curriculum about traditional foods and farming.
Community gardens and farms grow heritage foods, supplying them to elders and
school cafeterias. The Tesuque Pueblo has issued the formal "Declaration of Seed
Sovereignty," stating their opposition to the introduction of genetically modified
seed stock into their traditional lands, and expressing their determination to protect "our native seeds of crops, heritage fruits, animals, wild plants, traditions and

knowledge of our indigenous land and acequia-based communities in New Mexico for the purpose of maintaining and continuing our cultural integrity and resisting the global industrialized food system that can corrupt our lives, freedom, and culture through inappropriate food production and genetic engineering" (Salmón, 149). Their statement incudes "concepts of relationships, generational memory, embodied practices, spirituality, caring, respect, traditions, and celebration when declaring their revival and survival of their way of life" (Salmón, 150).

Conclusion

A long time ago, a young woman could not find a husband. She instructed her father to bury her, telling him that she would come back to life in a new way. In a few days, green leaves grew from the sandy soil where she had been buried. She became tobacco. In this form, she said, men would come to desire her. When the holy men smoked these leaves, clouds of smoke rose toward the sky, drawing down the rain. Soon, Tobacco Woman rose from the earth, returning to life. When she met Corn Man, she gambled with him. But when he won, she became angry. Your seeds will fall to the earth, she said, but they won't grow until the old men smoke my leaves, until they bring down the moisture from heaven to water the earth. Eventually reconciled, she married Corn Man, and together, they had a child: Bent Neck Squash, who later grew to become Saguaro. Together they taught the people how to grow tobacco, and how to smoke the leaves during special ceremonies for prayer and insight, and how to draw down the rain. They taught the people how to plant corn. And they taught the people how to harvest Saguaro, and make saguaro wine. The people learned to make the wine, and gather the tobacco for a special ceremony, the Wine Feast.

Embedded within this story—greatly abbreviated here—is a wealth of O'odham agricultural knowledge and a ceremonial cycle that accompanies planting and harvest. Amadeo Rea explains:

The Piman [O'odham] view of history and economic activity is circular and cyclic, not linear. A harvested plant that is smoked produces wind, which makes clouds, which drop the rain that makes plant growth possible. Squash Baby became the Saguaro whose fruit produces the essential ingredient for the Wine Feast, which brings the rain clouds that water the earth to grow crops and ensure that the Saguaros will produce fruit the following year. The People are not passive participants in this cycle: both as a community and as individuals, they must play an active role in it. [Singing] in the fields to promote the growth and development of crops was considered just as important as other farming activities—irrigating, weeding or cultivating. There were specific songs for planting, for germinating, for emerging plants, for growing plants, and for plants in flower and tassel, . . . It was always the People who were responsible for putting themselves into the cycle and turning it. They were not outside or above it, but actively within it. The individual Piman person perceived an intimate connection between himself or herself and the rest of the created world. Objectively, singing to the corn and squash plants growing in fields does not provide nourishment or other essentials to the plant. But the songs confirm and reinforce the relationship between the singer/farmer and the natural world. (Rea, 22–23)

As Rea's work helps make clear, traditional foods are at the heart of Indigenous religious life because sacred teachings, ceremonies, and practices shape, reinforce, and affirm the relationships between human beings and the plant and animal people upon whom they depend.

In her book *Yakama Rising*, sociologist and Yakama tribal member Michelle Jacob introduces her readers to X̱wayamamí Ishích, a nonprofit organization based on the Yakama Reservation and cofounded by Greg and Jessica Sutterlict. X̱wayamamí Ishích offers "seasonal workshops that bring elders and youth together to teach community members about traditional food gathering and preservation" (83). These teachings highlight the relational nature of traditional foods.

> You cannot use harsh words over a food product in our culture. 'Cause whoever is going to eat that is probably going to get those vibes or they may get ill or something. If you look at our culture, if you're in one or our churches, and in the kitchen, if someone gets angry or sad, they need to leave the kitchen. Cooking and working with our foods, is an important attitude thing. And if we feel sad or mean or mad, we might as well just leave the kitchen because you are going to hurt somebody. . . . And that's what our elders taught us. . . . Today we learn how to care for food as a gift from the Creator, and in doing so, we will understand how much we depend on the sun (áan) and the wind (hulí). These are the lessons of our ancestors. We are fortunate that elders have carried these lessons and are ready to share them with us. (Jacob, 79)

As Jacob explains, "A main lesson is that spirits of people and our foods are interconnected. . . . By teaching youth these important cultural lessons, the youth learn to respect the foods as sacred gifts, they respect each other, and perhaps most importantly, they respect themselves as they realize their spirits matter and are interconnected with others" (Jacob, 97). Indigenous religious traditions teach that all things have spirit, and all things are connected: even the attitude you bring with you into the kitchen. Cultivated in stories, songs, prayers, and ceremonies, this awareness inspires humility and gratitude.

For Kimmerer, such profound spiritual teachings are contained even within a single patch of wild strawberries.

> Finding a patch of wild strawberries still touches me with a sensation of surprise, a feeling of unworthiness and gratitude for the generosity and kindness that comes with an unexpected gift all wrapped in red and green. . . . After fifty years they still raise the question of how to respond to their generosity. Sometimes it feels like a silly question with a very simple answer: eat them. (Kimmerer, 23)

But seeing food as a gift is not so simple. In fact, "it changes everything." This reclamation of gratitude for a generous earth transforms us, calling us to something greater. As Kimmerer contends:

A gift creates ongoing relationship. . . . What would it be like, I wondered, to live with that heightened sensitivity to the lives given for ours? To consider the tree in the Kleenex, the algae in the toothpaste, the oaks in the floor, the grapes in the wine; to follow back the thread of life in everything and pay it respect? Once you start, it's hard to stop, and you begin to feel yourself awash in gifts. (Kimmerer, 26, 154)

How does one respond to a gift? Kimmerer suggests the answer is reciprocity: to give back. Expressions of gratitude might be prayer or ceremony, or they might take the form of ecological stewardship. Simply put, food is sacred stuff. And one's relationship to it matters deeply, shaping how we see ourselves, our Creator, and our place in a living world.

References and Recommendations

Arnold, David. *The Fisherman's Frontier: People and Salmon in Southeast Alaska*. Seattle: University of Washington Press, 2008.

Boxberger, Daniel. *To Fish in Common: Ethnohistory of Lummi Indian Fishing*. Seattle: University of Washington Press, 1989.

Carroll, Clint. *Roots of Our Renewal: Ethnobotany and Cherokee Environmental Governance*. St. Paul: University of Minnesota Press, 2015.

Clews Parsons, Elsie. *Pueblo Indian Religion*. Chicago: University of Chicago Press, 1939.

Colombi, Benedict. "Salmon and the Adaptive Capacity of Nimiipuu (Nez Perce) Culture to Cope with Change," *American Indian Quarterly* Vol. 36 No. 1 (2012): 75–97.

Cote, Charlotte. *Spirits of Our Whaling Ancestors: Revitalizing Makah and Nuu-chah-nulth Traditions*. Seattle: University of Washington Press, 2010.

Frey, Rodney. *Landscape Traveled by Coyote and Crane: The World of the Schitsu'umsh*. Seattle: University of Washington Press, 2001.

Geishirt Cantrell, Betty. "Access and Barriers to Food Items and Food Preparation among Plains Indians," *Wicazo Sa Review* Vol. 16 No. 1 (2001): 65–74.

Grey, Sam, and Raj Patel. "Food Sovereignty as Decolonization: Some Contributions from Indigenous Movements to Food System and Development Politics," *Journal of Agriculture, Food and Human Values Society* Vol. 32 No. 3 (2015): 431–44.

Harrod, Howard. *The Animals Come Dancing: Native American Sacred Ecology and Animal Kinship*. Tucson: University of Arizona Press, 2000.

Jacob, Michelle. *Yakama Rising: Indigenous Cultural Revitalization, Activism, and Healing*. Tucson: University of Arizona Press, 2013.

Kimmerer, Robin Wall. *Braiding Sweetgrass: Scientific Knowledge and the Wisdom of Plants*. Minneapolis: Milkweed, 2013.

Krech, Shepard, III. "Ecology, Conservation and the Buffalo Jump," in *Stars Above Earth Below: American Indians and Nature*, edited by Marsha Bol. Lanham, MD: Robert Rinehart Publishers, 1998.

Krohn, Elise, and Valerie Segrest. *Feeding the People, Feeding the Spirit: Revitalizing Northwest Coastal Indian Food Culture*. Bellingham, WA: Northwest Indian College Press, 2010.

LaDuke, Winona. "Namewag: Sturgeon and People in the Great Lakes Region," in *Recovering the Sacred: The Power of Naming and Claiming*. Boston: South End Press, 2005.

Menzies, Charles. "Returning to Selective Fishing through Indigenous Fisheries Knowledge: The Example of K'moda, Gitxaala Territory," *American Indian Quarterly* Vol. 31 No. 3 (2007): 441–46.

Nabhan, Gary Paul. *Enduring Seeds: Native American Agriculture and Wild Plant Cultivation.* Tucson: University of Arizona Press, 2002.

Nelson, Richard. *Make Prayers to the Raven: A Koyukon View of the Northern Forest.* Chicago: University of Chicago Press, 1983.

Ortiz, Alfonso. *The Tewa World: Space, Time, Being and Becoming in a Pueblo Society.* Chicago: University of Chicago Press, 1972.

Rea, Amadeo. *At the Desert's Green Edge: An Ethnobotany of the Gila River Pima.* Tucson: University of Arizona Press, 1997.

Rea, Amadeo. "Corn Man and Tobacco Woman," in *Stars Above Earth Below: American Indians and Nature*, edited by Marsha Bol. Lanham, MD: Robert Rinehart Publishers, 1998.

Reid, Joshua. *The Sea Is My Country: The Maritime World of the Makahs.* New Haven: Yale University Press, 2015.

Salmón, Enrique. *Eating the Landscape: American Indian Stories of Food, Identity, and Resilience.* Tucson: University of Arizona Press, 2012.

Schneider, Lindsey. "There's Something in the Water: Salmon Runs and Settler Colonialism on the Columbia River," *American Indian Culture and Research Journal* Vol. 37 No. 2 (2013): 149–64.

Sherman, Sean, and Beth Dooley. *The Sioux Chef's Indigenous Kitchen.* St. Paul: University of Minnesota Press, 2017.

Vick, R. Alfred. "Cherokee Adaptation to the Landscape of the West and Overcoming the Loss of Culturally Significant Plants," *American Indian Quarterly* Vol. 35 No. 3 (2011): 394–417.

Walsh, David. "The Nature of Food: Indigenous Dene Foodways and Ontologies in the Era of Climate Change," *Scripta Instituti Donneriani Aboensis* No. 26 (2015): 225–49.

Walsh, David. "Feeding the Fire: Food and Reciprocity among the Dene," *Religious Studies and Theology*, Vol. 35 No. 2 (2016): 123–30.

Zogry, Michael, and Michelene Pesantubbee, eds. *Native American Foodways.* SUNY, 2020.

Websites and Films

Columbia River Inter-Tribal Fish Commission. "Spirit of the Salmon Plan." http://plan.critfc.org

Gwich'in Steering Committee. "About the Caribou." http://ourarcticrefuge.org/about-the-gwichin/

Gwich'in Steering Committee. "Gwich'in Traditional Management Practices." http://arcticcircle.uconn.edu/ANWR/anwrgwichin1.html

Hoover, Elizabeth. "From Garden Warriors to Good Seeds: Indigenizing the Local Food Movement." https://gardenwarriorsgoodseeds.com/

Sherman, Sean. "Sean Sherman at 2018 World of Flavors." https://www.youtube.com/watch?time_continue=3&v=loRoy608LWA

Sherman, Sean. "The Sioux Chef." http://sioux-chef.com/

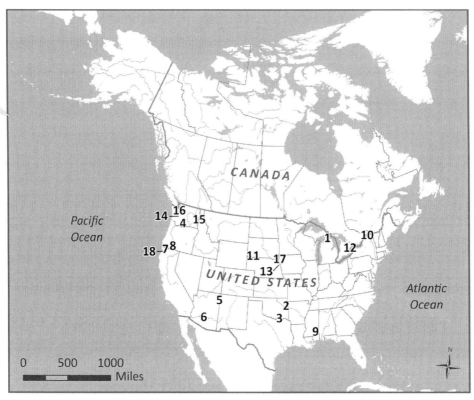

1 Anishinaabe Territories

2 Cherokee Nation

3 Choctaw Nation

4 Confederated Tribes of the Yakama Nation

5 Diné (Navajo) Nation

6 Gila River Indian Community

7 Karuk Tribe

8 Klamath Tribe

9 Mississippi Band of Choctaw Indians

10 Mohawk Nation

11 Oglala Lakota Territories

12 Ojibwe (Anishinaabe) Territories

13 Omaha Tribe of Nebraska

14 Puyallup Indian Tribe

15 Schitsu'umsh (Coeur d'Alene) Tribe

16 Suquamish Tribe

17 Winnebago Tribe of Nebraska

18 Yurok Tribe

Map 6.1. Map of North America locating the tribal communities, nations, and cultural groups mentioned in this chapter. Basemap data made with Natural Earth. (Liz O'Dea Springborn)

Medicine   6

WHEN A YOUNG MOTHER was diagnosed with cancer, she consulted with the specialist at her local hospital, and agreed to begin treatment. She wanted to be there for her children, she explained, and would do whatever it took to be well. But before that treatment could begin, she first had to see her family's doctor—a traditional healer known and respected by her Indigenous community. The hospital could treat the cancer cells in her body, she acknowledged, but if she didn't deal with the spiritual cause of the illness, it may only come back in some other form. She needed to regain balance in all areas of her life, and doing that wouldn't be easy. She was going to need help.

According to the National Congress of the American Indian and U.S. Department of Health and Human Services, Native Americans are six times more likely to have tuberculosis, five times more likely to suffer from alcoholism, and more than twice as likely to have diabetes than the general population. The infant mortality rate of Indigenous communities is twice that of white populations. Native Americans are 2.5 times more likely to suffer from serious psychological distress, and Indigenous youth have the highest suicide rates of any other ethnic group in the United States: twice as high as the national average among 14- to 24-year-olds, and three times the national average among 5- to 10-year-olds. Such horrifying statistics can only be understood in light of North American colonial history. This is a history where disease was used a means of coercion and control; where Indigenous healing practices were actively suppressed, ridiculed, and outlawed; and where Native people have been denied access to care. This chapter explores Indigenous understandings of and approaches to healing, showing how contemporary communities are drawing upon these traditions to address the physical, mental, and spiritual wounds of colonialism.

Illness, Medicine, and Healthcare

Historians estimate that between five and eighteen million people lived in North America prior to the arrival of European explorers. By 1800, that Indigenous population had dropped to 600,000. By 1890, it was 250,000. Most of these premature deaths can be attributed to imported diseases. Smallpox, the plague, cholera, influenza, diphtheria, malaria, scarlet fever, typhoid, tuberculosis, pertussis, syphilis, and gonorrhea wreaked havoc on Indigenous communities that lacked acquired immunity to these settler diseases.

Disease was also employed as a tool of conquest. Historian Barbara Mann argues that smallpox blankets, poison, and other forms of germ warfare were used to subdue Native people. Mann notes the 1763 introduction of smallpox blankets at Fort Pitt that contaminated the Odawa, Ojibwe, Lenape, and Shawnee. At the time, Lord Jeffrey Amherst wrote to his field commanders: "You will do well to try to inoculate the Indians by means of blankets as well as to try every other method that can serve to extirpate this exorable race." They replied: "Out of regard for them [i.e., two Indian chiefs] we gave them two blankets and a handkerchief out of the smallpox hospital. I hope it will have the desired effect" (Mann, 69). The "desired effect" was achieved: smallpox epidemics spread throughout the Indigenous communities of the Northeast, infecting thousands. A similar incident occurred in 1832, when the United States Army forcibly relocated a Choctaw community into a known cholera epidemic. They were denied access to immunizations, despite protests from the Choctaw, local physicians, and other humanitarian advocates. And in 1837, Mann notes an incident in which hemorrhagic smallpox was again intentionally introduced among upper–Missouri River tribes, killing 90 percent of Mandan, 70 percent of Hidatsa, and 50 percent of Arikara people.

The threat of illness was also an effective colonial tool. In 1811, fear of smallpox was used to induce cooperation from the Chinook along the Columbia River. In a story often repeated by future generations of settlers, Fort Astor official Duncan McDougal gathered tribal leaders together. "The white men among you are few in number, it is true," he told them. "But they are mighty in medicine." He pulled out a small vial and held it up for all to see. "In this bottle I hold smallpox all corked up; I have but to draw the cork and let loose the pestilence to sweep man, woman, and child from the face of the earth" (Crawford-O'Brien, 54). These moments in history remain vivid within the memories of many Indigenous people, evidence of the use of disease in the colonization of the continent, and the militarization of healthcare.

Obstacles to Care

Treaties signed in the 1850s defined reservation borders and promised access to health care. But medical care was slow to arrive and difficult to access: by 1875, physicians could be found in only half of Indian agencies (and there, a single physician might need to travel hundreds of miles to care for thousands of people, many of whom may not speak English). The first hospital for Native people was not built until the 1880s. Established in Oklahoma, it was primarily a tuberculosis sanitarium. The great majority of Native people lacked access to medical care until well into the twentieth century.

An additional bitter irony is that, while tribal communities were denied access to Euroamerican physicians, they were also restricted from practicing or passing on their own healing traditions and practices. The 1883 Religious Crimes Code banned the practice of Indigenous ceremonies—including healing practices, and the work of traditional healers.

> The usual practices of so-called "medicine-men" shall be considered "Indian of-fenses" cognizable by the Court of Indian Offenses, and whenever it shall be proven to the satisfaction of the court that the influence or practice of a so-called "medicine-man" operates as a hindrance to the civilization of a tribe, or that said "medicine-man" resorts to any artifice or device to keep the Indians under his influ-ence, or shall adopt any means to prevent the attendance of children at the agency schools, or shall use any of the arts of a conjurer to prevent the Indians from aban-doning their heathenish rites and customs, he shall be adjudged guilty of an Indian offense, and upon conviction of any one or more of these specified practices, or, any other, in the opinion of the court, of an equally anti-progressive nature, shall be confined in the agency prison for a term not less than ten days, or until such time as he shall produce evidence satisfactory to the court, and approved by the agent, that he will forever abandon all practices styled Indian offenses under this rule. (Rule Six of the Rules Governing The Court of Indian Offenses, Department of the Interior, Office of Indian Affairs, Washington, DC, March 30, 1883)

Under threat of incarceration and suspension of rations, families and communities were forced to limit their care to herbal remedies, employed in private or without the use of accompanying ceremony, or to hold such ceremonies in secret.

The knowledge of traditional modes of healing was further compromised by the imposition of the boarding school system. Removed from their homes and communities, children lost opportunities to be trained in traditional healing meth-odologies. Instead, they were taught to ridicule Indigenous practices while rever-ing turn-of-the-century biomedicine. The horrible irony is that mortality rates at boarding schools were staggeringly high. Influenza, tuberculosis, whooping cough, scarlet fever, and other ailments spread quickly in the residential schools, which lacked proper sanitation, nutrition, insulation, or medical care.

Residential schools threatened children's mental health as well: conditions were poor, and treatment harsh. Children suffered from depression, homesickness, and shame. Sexual and physical abuse pervaded many of the schools, scarring young people and leaving a legacy that continues to this day. In 1921, Congress directed Lewis Meriam to lead a team of researchers to investigate the conditions of Native Americans across the United States. The resulting Meriam Report issued a damn-ing account of residential schools, documenting appalling conditions, outdated and inappropriate curriculum, inadequately prepared instructors, and poor conditions. The recommendations of the Meriam Report were not put into action until the

1934 Indian Reorganization Act (also known as the Indian New Deal). Led by John Collier, the act provided for investments in health care, funded studies to create health care that was culturally appropriate, and called for phasing out boarding schools and investing instead in local education.

The Indian Health Service

The Indian Health Service (IHS) was created in 1955, and funding was provided for the construction of large, regional facilities. Funding increased twelvefold between 1955 and 1983, and the IHS found some success targeting issues like communicable diseases, tuberculosis, and infant mortality. During the1960s, funding improved, providing better staffing and infrastructure improvements. In 1968, the Community Health Representative Program began employing community members to work in rural locations, helping tribes begin to take ownership of their care. In 1967, the IHS was reorganized to include some urban Indian communities, and it made efforts to hire more Native people as community medics.

Despite this significant investment, however, many Native people were still unable to access care: centralized hospitals were difficult to reach, and growing populations meant the ratio of doctors to patients actually decreased during these years from 1,220 to 1,500 per physician. By way of context, the United Nations considers 1 doctor per 1,000 people to be the low-threshold required to maintain adequate health, while the United States average for the general population is 1 physician per 390 patients. The patient-to-physician ratio in Cuba is 155 to 1.

In 1982, Everett Rhoades, a Kiowa physician, took over the IHS. Rhoades pushed for culturally integrated care and promoted a variety of reforms. But under the Reagan administration, the IHS lost funding and despite Rhoades's best efforts was still providing just one physician per 1,500 patients. Tasked with tackling communicative diseases and infant mortality, the IHS struggled to address rising concerns like diabetes, mental health, sexually transmitted diseases, or addiction.

Self-Determination and Healthcare

Foundations for reform were laid with the 1976 American Indian Self-Determination and Education Assistance Act. Under this act, tribes could contract with the federal government to provide their own care, building tribally run health clinics, hospitals, and wellness centers. In 1976, the Puyallup Nation in Washington State became the first to enter into such a contract, founding the Puyallup Tribal Health Authority and opening its first clinic. In 1993, the Puyallup built the Takopid Health Center, its mission to provide care in a "culturally appropriate manner." The Puyallup Tribal Treatment Center provides chemical-dependency treatment and includes the Spirit House, where patients and their families can hold traditional ceremonies. The Puyallup continued their commitment to health care, opening the Salish Integrative Oncology Care Center in 2015, the first tribally owned cancer care center in the nation. Following this example, the shift toward tribal control of care has continued

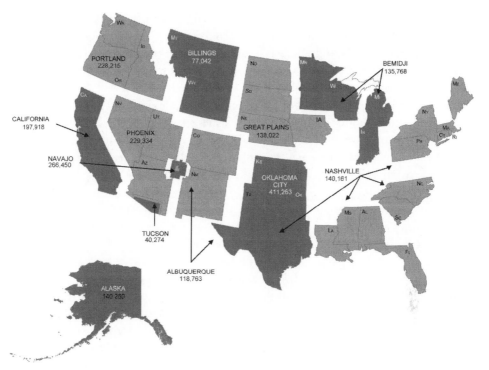

Figure 6.1.   Indian Health Service Patient Population by Area, Calendar Year 2014. (U.S. Government Accountability Office, Indian Health Service. AP Photo/Jason Wise)

to gain ground. More and more tribes now contract with the federal government to manage their own health care, and Native communities are increasingly able to direct the kind of culturally appropriate care they want to receive, integrating Indigenous approaches into healing as they build their own local wellness centers.

Despite this, many Native people still remain unable to access healthcare. According 2016 census data, 20.7 percent of United States citizens who identify solely as American Indian or Alaskan Native lack health insurance, compared to 9.4 percent for the nation as a whole. Most Native people live in urban communities and so do not have access to reservation-based health care systems, while some may not be federally enrolled, or may belong to tribal communities that are not federally recognized. Native people may also be reluctant to receive care from a biomedical doctor. Some express resistance to biomedicine, given a history steeped in assimilation; suppression of traditional healers, spirituality and ways of life; and a medical culture that promoted passivity and dependency. Others suggest that biomedicine only treats the symptoms of illness, rather than the root cause—which may be spiritual, or have its roots in the soul wounds of colonialism.

Indeed, the great majority of ailments Native people face stem from this history of colonial oppression. The loss of land, the suppression of religion and culture, the abusive nature of boarding schools, neglect, and generational trauma all contribute to illness. Systemic inequalities are at play as well: Indigenous people remain the poorest ethnic group in North America: 28.3 percent of single-race-identified American Indians and Native Alaskan households are in poverty, nearly double the national average. On the most economically disadvantaged reservations, poverty rates are closer to 50 percent, with over 80 percent unemployment. Native people are far more likely to live without telephone or cell phone service (54 percent of Native households, compared to 5 percent of the general public), indoor plumbing (20 percent, compared to 1 percent), or adequate sewage (18 percent, compared to 1 percent). No effective approach to healing and wellness among Indigenous communities can ignore the violence of colonialism or the continued impoverishment and political suppression of Native people today.

This context is important for understanding Indigenous approaches to healing because these traditions argue that genuine healing is not just about removing a pathogen or setting a broken bone. Indigenous understandings of healing are about restoring the whole person within community. That means restoring physical, mental, spiritual, emotional, and relational wholeness. It means bringing individuals into right relationship with families, communities, ancestors, and homelands. It means addressing political and economic justice. With this in mind, tribally directed wellness centers and hospitals often take a holistic approach to care, integrating allopathic medicine, Indigenous traditions, and social services.

Since Indigenous communities understand the source of their most common ailments to be found in colonialism, wellness centers often see their work as being part of the process of decolonization. For instance, in her book *Potent Mana: Lessons in Power and Healing*, Wende Elizabeth Marshall explores Native Hawaiian community health centers, arguing that important work of decolonization is being done here, as Native Hawaiians are returned to physical and mental health by reconnecting to their Indigenous identity and their ancestral heritage. Such treatment centers and clinics make the process of remembering traditions and reclaiming histories an integral part of personal renewal. As Marshall contends, health requires personal wholeness, political sovereignty, and cultural integrity.

Diabetes

One of the most powerful examples of the decolonizing potential of culturally appropriate care can be seen in tribal responses to diabetes. Between 1994 and 2004, the rate of type 2 diabetes among Native American children doubled. In some communities, it has become nearly endemic, seen as an inevitable fate. On one reservation, 48 percent of children as young as 6 show signs of being at risk, and over 80 percent of those over 45 already have the disease. As was discussed in chapter 5, the origin of the diabetes epidemic lies in the loss of land, poverty, high rates of unemployment, poor access to traditional foods, and easy access to junk food. But it is also important to note that diabetes is a relatively new disease, virtually unheard of in Indigenous communities just three generations ago. Seeing this, communities take heart: if cultural changes caused the disease, then traditional culture can fight it.

Professor of family and community medicine Jennie Joe (Diné) and professor of clinical medicine Robert Young call this work "leveraging their cultural capital." Cultural capital includes tribal language, rhetoric, storytelling traditions, symbols, foodways, traditional modes of exercise and activity, and spiritual teachings that restore the connection between mind, body, spirit, community, and land. "In this line of reasoning, health promotion strategies are effective only if they are closely tied to a community's broader value systems, behavioral norms, and perceptions of health" (Joe and Young, 19).

While typical biomedical approaches to diabetes emphasize personal choice and individual lifestyle, tribally led programs focus on what works best for the entire community. Communities insist that successful changes in diet, access to care, physical activity, and mental and spiritual health happen at the tribal level, and from the ground up. Effective community-based models do not just address personal agency and individual choice but also the social, economic, and political systems that prevent access to traditional foods and healthy lifestyles.

As Paula Allen, coordinator of the Food Is Good Medicine program at United Indian Health Services says, "We need to be eating food that represents our values" (Smith-Morris 2006, 177). One the biggest culprits in the diabetes epidemic has been the loss of access to traditional lands, waterways, and foods. Native people have lost hunting, gathering, fishing, and farming land to drought, development, and outright theft, and it has devastated their traditional foodways. As we learned in previous chapters, such connections to land and traditional foods are far from just nutritional; they are deeply spiritual, emblematic of a people's identity and belonging to a place and to one another. Tribal diabetes programs thus emphasize a return to Indigenous foodways and the lifestyle that accompanied them. Traditional foods are both physically and spiritually powerful, and gathering such foods is considered sacred work.

Winnebago

Lorelei DeCora (Winnebago) founded the Native American Diabetes Project to address what had become an epidemic: more than 80 percent of adults on the reservation had diabetes, and 10 percent of them regularly sought hospital treatment. Traditional foods like bison, native roots, and berries are high in nutritional value and low in saturated fat and sugar, but after World War II, the Winnebago had been added to a federal-commodities food program: surplus foods from farms were processed, preserved, and distributed at low cost. Canned meats, canned fruits packed in syrup, pasta, and processed cheese became the norm in Winnebago homes, school lunches, senior centers. DeCora also notes the impact of HUD housing, which arrived on the reservation in the mid-1970s, when far-flung homes and farms were replaced with clustered developments. As families moved from small farms to small communities, they gained access to services, but they lost the means to grow their own food and became far less likely to walk any distance to visit friends or relatives, leading to increasingly sedentary lives.

Photo 6.1. Gerard Kisto, a traditional practitioner, holds a hand-rolled tobacco cigarette toward the sky as an offering to the Creator, who is referred to as "Grandfather Sun" in his culture, June 30, 2001, near Sacaton, Arizona. Traditional prayers and teachings are a key part of the tribe's response to the high rate of diabetes experienced on the Gila River Indian Reservation, forty miles southeast of Phoenix. (AP Photo/Jason Wise)

Responding to the current health crisis, the Winnebago have planted a dozen community gardens emphasizing traditional foods and ways of gardening. DeCora herself led the creation of a curriculum for "diabetes talking circles." Meeting throughout the year at four different locations on the reservation, talking circles open with a prayer and a traditional story. Diabetes and its impacts are discussed in an open way. Medical staff then share information related to nutrition, exercise, and medical care. For DeCora, the path to overcoming diabetes is a spiritual and a relational one. "For Indian ancestors, food was physical and spiritual medicine. The buffalo, deer, corn, squash, beans, wild turnips, berries, and other traditional foods provide the nourishment needed by the bodies of Indian people. The foods were their allies. When they have been invited back to the table, the most significant step in eliminating the enemy diabetes will have been taken" (DeCora, 14).

Gila River

As discussed in chapter 3, between 1870 and 1903, the Gila River Indian Community lost the rights to their river and their ability to farm. By 1904, the people were starving, forced to leave their ancient foodways behind. This began to change in 1963, when a court decision affirmed their right to the Gila River, which took shape in 2004 as the Gila River Indian Community Water Settlement Act, and restored their water rights. By that time, traditional agriculture had virtually collapsed, and lifestyles had dramatically changed: the Gila River community had some of the highest diabetes and obesity rates in the world.

For tribal leaders, the answer lay in returning to traditional foods, which were high in fiber and protein and low in sugar and fat. They recognized that diabetes was not simply about individual eating choices but was the result of colonialism, and that the solution to diabetes required collective healing and renewal. Beginning in the 1990s, the tribe voted to invest in prevention and care, funding community-based field nursing, exercise and fitness resources, and new facilities for diabetes management. They trained and employed tribal members as case managers, and promoted tribal education programs that emphasized farming and gardening.

Yakama

One in five Yakama tribal members have been diagnosed with type 2 diabetes. For Indigenous Studies professor Michelle Jacob (Yakama), overcoming diabetes means healing the soul wounds of colonialism: recovering traditional teachings about food, gender, community responsibility, and care. For Jacob, some of the cultural capital that Yakama people bring to the fight for wellness lies in women's traditional roles as food providers:

> Traditional cultural teachings place women in a position of power, as they control an important source of wealth: the food supply of the people. Today, women are reclaiming this position of power as they resist widely available convenience and fast foods to nurture their families and provide for a healthier next generation on the reservation. In doing so, our people are able to resist the hegemony of the capitalist food system, which supplies most of the food on the reservation. (Jacob 2011, 69)

But as Jacob acknowledges, "poor women generally, and Native women in particular, often have very little 'choice' when one considers the challenges of being marginalized within a society that has rigid hierarchies of class, race, and gender" (Jacob 2011, 74).

In her work as a scholar and as a tribal member, Jacob explores "structural and personal barriers to wellness" (Jacob 2011, 70). On a reservation where unemployment is close to 60 percent, and 65 percent of households with young children are below the poverty level, addressing diabetes requires political, economic, and social change. Jacob explains:

> I argue that capitalist state-based policies and practices that undermine Indigenous self-determination have a direct relationship to our people's poor health outcomes

and the loss of traditional culture. . . . Non-Indian people taking control of the food economy on the reservation [results] in poor quality commodity foods from the US government, the "unhealthy" public school lunch offerings to reservation children and the omnipresence of companies such as Pepsi and McDonald's in daily reservation life. Lifestyle changes on the reservation have led to intense social and health problems. . . . The steady stream of junk food dumped into the reservation is an essential part of the assimilation process that seeks to create dispensable bodies used for profit. (Jacob 2011, 75–79)

The Yakama elders guiding Jacob's work emphasize that cultural and physical health are deeply intertwined. Traditional foods, and salmon in particular, hold the key to their well-being as a people.

But in the 1950s, Yakama fishing economies were nearly destroyed by the construction of hydroelectric dams. The families and elders with whom Jacob spoke lament the loss of traditions: hunting, gathering, fishing, ceremonies, and language. They argue that recovering these traditions is a path toward wellness. Reclaiming these traditions happens in ceremonies, and it also happens in summer track meets, where community members promote healthy eating, diabetes awareness, and pride in their culture. As Jacob explains, "Quitting or reducing their soda drinking habits and instead drinking more water not only promote better physical health, but also can help our people reclaim the importance of water as a sacred gift from the Creator" (Jacob 2011, 86).

Mental Health, Spiritual Health

In his work, Native American Studies professor Lawrence Gross (Anishinaabe) coined the term *post-apocalyptic stress syndrome* (PASS) to better explain the ways that colonialism traumatizes tribal communities. Gross argues that when human cultures experience such earth-shattering disruptions, they react in similar ways. He makes parallels to the plagues of medieval Europe to show that these reactions are not unique to Native North America. The symptoms of PASS make up a list of reactions to earth-shaking trauma: abandonment of productive employment; an increase in substance abuse, violence (especially domestic violence), and suicide and mental illness; the replacement of established religious practices with fanatical forms of religion; a loss of hope; a general sense of despair; survivor's guilt; and the collapse or weakening of family structures, government institutions, educational institutions and processes, established religious institutions, and health-care-delivery systems. Gross makes the case that restoring relationships lies at the heart of recovering from PASS. Because colonialism fundamentally fractured family structures and relationships, restoring those relationships is key to healing. Among those elements of PASS described above, two in particular concern us here: suicide and substance abuse. Addressing these crises in Native North America begins with understanding the historical roots of colonial trauma.

Suicide and Addiction

One study in a tribal community in the Pacific Northwest drew upon community wisdom to seek out solutions to the high suicide and addiction rates among Indigenous youth. Community members, parents, and elders agreed that holding family together, maintaining cultural values, and healing intergenerational trauma were all essential to preventing suicide and substance abuse. They pointed to their tribally directed wellness center, which provided culturally appropriate mental health services, drug and alcohol counseling, an active elder program, and community health nursing services, as the space where this occurs. They also pointed to the role of traditional religion and culture in addressing the impacts of historical trauma. One individual noted:

> Well my brother in law was sexually abused in boarding school. He had a lot of anger. He is abusive. He has family and he never goes to see them because he was in boarding school, so he doesn't have that family bond. He had an alcohol problem. He does not know how to vent. He holds things in. I don't remember ever being hugged. My mother never said, "I love you." I don't remember ever hearing "I love you." I don't remember that at all. No one showed me, and I was never affectionate. I did that with my kids. I mean I can't go up and hold them or hug them. If you are crying you are weak. All that goes back to don't let the White Man see you hurt. Some are afraid that if we start crying, we may not be able to stop. (Strickland, Walsh, and Cooper, 9)

Participants in this study pointed to sources of healing that included traditional foods, weaving, drum making, learning one's language, passing on stories, participating in winter ceremonies, and reconnecting with one's ancestral homeland. They noted that sacred waters and relationships with a spiritually endowed landscape offer solace and a connection with one's ancestors.

> We were taught you go down to the river when you are stressed. Use your cedar to help you heal . . . and some of us in our age group still do that. But the younger ones . . . no one is teaching them. You know like putting cedar in your house and above your door. I was taught by the elders that when you are blue or sad to go to the river and let the river draw that sadness out of you. (Strickland, Walsh, and Cooper, 9)

Others pointed to the social care and management that happens in traditional ceremonial spaces where elders can correct inappropriate behavior. As one participant explained, "There was a big gathering and my brothers and uncles were misbehaving. So my mom got them in the big house. She called witness and put them right out in the middle of the floor and she put all them alcohol bottles on the floor . . . and made it clear that this had better not happen again" (Strickland, Walsh, and Cooper, 9).

Another region-wide study based in British Columbia concluded that well-being is directly tied to a sense of "personal persistence," which was defined as an awareness of how one's individual identity relates to the past, and how it carries forward into the future. For First Nations youth in British Columbia, a sense of personal persistence was directly tied to engagement in cultural activities. Remarkably, the study found a one-to-one correlation between the degree of youth involvement in cultural programs and suicide rates. "Failures to warrant self-continuity were strongly associated with increased suicide risk. Efforts to preserve and promote Aboriginal culture related to dramatic reductions in youth suicide" (Chandler et al.).

American Indian and Alaska Native youth have higher rates of drug and alcohol abuse than any other group, with direct links to depression, dropping out of school, injuries, poverty, and suicide. Indigenous communities continue to point to spirituality, traditional cultural knowledge, and participating in ceremonies as the key to mental and spiritual health. Indeed, multiple studies have found that Native American, Alaska Native, and First Nations people are more likely to identify spirituality as an important factor in their well-being than any other ethnicity in North America.

The Omaha Nation Community Response Team

An example of successful tribal responses to suicide, violence, and substance abuse among youth can be seen in the Omaha Nation Community Response Team (ONCRT). The 2000 census found that 23 percent of Omaha families were living below the poverty line, 84 percent of deaths on the reservation involved alcohol, 42 percent of families were led by a single parent, and violent crime rates on the reservation were twice the state's average. Omaha youth struggled with high rates of substance abuse, suicide, and dropping out of school. The community responded by forming the ONCRT. While current approaches employed in schools and by social workers had emphasized individual choice, the community felt such approaches were not adequately guided by Omaha traditions and values. Instructed by elders and drawing on community input, the ONCRT determined that engaging with their traditional culture and religion would best help young people stay in school, while preventing substance abuse, violence, and suicide.

The goal of the ONCRT is that "every child will recognize, understand, and take their place in the great tribal Circle. Every child will make their way across the Four Hills of Life in a sacred manner. Every child will recognize and focus on their Spirit's innate strengths, abilities, and potential within" (Penn, Doll, and Grandgenett, 52–53). The ONCRT invites young people to take part in ceremonial activities like Native American Church services, sweat lodges, Sun Dances, tobacco offerings, burning cedar, and sobriety powwows. It teaches young people about Wakondá (Creator), Huthuga (the sacred circle), and traditional Omaha clan structure, which helped to ensure everyone a place within the community, and within which "each clan had duties, roles and responsibilities along with taboos and restrictions" (Penn, Doll, and Grandgenett, 46). The ONCRT works to help young people find their calling, the role they are meant to serve for their people. Young people join field trips and summer camps to see wildlife, or learn traditional arts like quilting, beading, drumming, and leatherwork. Working with

White Bison, Inc., ONCRT has trained one hundred community members using the "Wellbriety" model of addiction recovery.

The ONCRT also plays a role in corrective discipline. When several high school students were involved in an altercation, tribal police immediately took the young people into custody and notified their parents. The youth were held at the tribal jail for four days. Each day, with support from the ONCRT, they were required to participate in community service, a sweat lodge, and talking circles (some including their parents). Volunteer tutors worked with students in the evenings so that they would not fall behind in school. Before bed each night, students participated in a cedaring ceremony, where cedar is burned and the smoke is blown over someone as prayers are said or songs sung to purify the person and their surroundings. At the conclusion of the four days, a Native American Church ceremony was held. The response was remarkable. "Across the community everyone was impressed with the systematic, rapid, and extensive response to this violence-based incident, which included a collaborative response from virtually every leadership sector of the reservation community" (Penn, Doll, and Grandgenett, 57). After three years, the ONCRT had become a remarkable success. Participation in the program had doubled, and dropout rates had gone from 32.5 percent to 8 percent. While young people had been virtually absent from cultural and spiritual events before the ONCRT was put into place, young people were now attending in growing numbers.

Healing of the Canoe

The Healing of the Canoe curriculum is another program based on traditional cultures and values, aiming to reconnect young people with their Indigenous culture and identity and promote mental health. A partnership between the University of Washington Alcohol and Drug Abuse Institute and the Suquamish and Port Gamble S'Klallam tribes, the program is inspired by the tribal canoe journey, and asks the question: How can one navigate life without being pulled off course? The curriculum employs elders who teach about traditional values, beliefs, stories, and practices. At the conclusion, youth are honored for their individual achievements and participate in a ceremony, giving away the traditional gifts they have created throughout the program, honoring the mentors who have helped them. The curriculum is revised in each tribal location, drawing on local stories, teachings, and philosophies. For instance, Suquamish curriculum emphasizes a traditional concept of the four winds, tied to four aspects of the self and four stages of life, as a path to finding one's place in community. It considers the importance of storytelling—the skill of listening to others and the art of telling one's own story—and offers lessons on tribal history, the impacts of colonialism, and the way Indigenous cultures have been systematically undermined. In doing so, young people became motivated to become part of the process of cultural recovery. At the conclusion, students expressed increased hope, optimism, self-efficacy, a stronger sense of cultural identity and knowledge, and lower rates of substance use and abuse than their peers.

Wellbriety

The Wellbriety model of alcohol- and chemical-abuse recovery emerged from the White Bison Society, inspired by prophecies that a white buffalo calf would signal a time of healing and renewal among Native people. Although borrowing some techniques from Alcoholics Anonymous, the Wellbriety model employs them in culturally appropriate ways, engaging with Indigenous cultures and acknowledging the trauma of colonialism. Meetings include talking circles, drumming circles, sweats, and other opportunities to connect with Indigenous culture, language, and spirituality. Created by Don Coyhis (Mohican Nation), Wellbriety emphasizes not just sobriety but also thriving in a community and living a life that is balanced physically, mentally, emotionally, and spiritually. Its mission-and-belief statement emphasizes the importance of Indigenous religions and cultures to the process of recovery, explaining that Mother Earth is governed by natural laws, and envisioning recovery as coming into alignment with those laws. Healing takes place through returning to traditional ways, applying cultural and spiritual knowledge, listening to elders, attending to the four directions, and the sacred circle. As Wellbriety programs emphasize, "Alcohol is a symptom, not the cause. Drugs are a symptom, not the cause. Domestic Violence is a symptom, not the cause." Colonialism is the cause, and culture is the cure.

Participants in Wellbriety programs point to the importance of understanding alcohol and drug addiction as products of colonialism, while the path toward healing lies in recovering balance and harmony. These two personal reflections from Wellbriety participants that help to illustrate this point:

> An Elder told me, "When you first picked up the bottle—when you started drinking . . . and you start staggering, you thought that was funny. A flag should have gone up *immediately*. . . people should always know if you drink or take drugs, you are out of balance. There is something wrong because we always lived in perfect balance and harmony." . . . And that was a great turning point in my life—because I got to enjoy life then . . . got to see through that alcoholic fog that won't let you experience the reality of things.
>
>   But if I go into a [sweat] lodge you know, there are Indian people around there if I did something wrong you know, or somebody died or something—that's how I'd let my feelings out in the lodge . . . it's dark and no one is judging you . . . you just go in there and stay and it's safe. There ain't nobody going out and going around the reservation and saying "This guy was crying . . . or this . . ." You *know* you are not supposed to do that. . . . I'd go to a sweat before I'd go to an AA meeting. (Matamonasa-Bennett, 44)

Indigenous Healing Traditions

The second half of this chapter pivots to focus on traditional Native North American understandings of illness and approaches to healing. Before colonialism, the most common health maladies in much of Native North America appear to have been gastrointestinal problems, coughs and fevers, eye irritations, skin problems, insect or snake bites; injuries such as burns, bone fractures, or sprains; problems associated with childbirth; or the aches and pains associated with aging, such as those from arthritis (King, 175). The most common causes of premature death appear to have been childbirth, hunting or fishing accidents, or violent conflict.

Generally speaking—and of course particular traditions and modes of treatment varied widely from community to community—non-injury-related illnesses were often understood to have spiritual origins: spiritual imbalance, witchcraft, contact with the dead, or disrupted relationships with other people or with spiritual entities. After colonialism, another category of illness was introduced: white man's disease. This latter category included ailments introduced by settlers such as infectious diseases, and the consequences of colonial trauma: addiction, domestic and sexual violence, obesity, heart disease, diabetes.

An Interconnected Self

These various understandings of the origins of disease are informed by Indigenous views of the self. In Indigenous cultures and traditions, healing is not only about removing disease or recovery from injury. It is also about restoring the whole self in community. Contemporary communities seeking to bridge the gap between biomedicine and Indigenous healing traditions have to reclaim a different way of understanding the relationships among the body, spirit, and self. At least since the era of the Enlightenment, European and Euroamerican understandings of what it means to be a "self" have emphasized the individual, distinct and separate from its environment, its community, and even from its body. The physical body was seen as something to be tamed and controlled but ultimately separate from one's true self—which primarily existed in the mind. In this framework, healthy development was often described as a process of "individuation": becoming an independent, self-sufficient individual. But in Native North American cultures, such self-sufficiency would more likely be seen as pathological. In Indigenous philosophies, a healthy self is far more likely to be described as existing within balanced and harmonious relationships between the person and their human, other-than-human, and ancestral communities. A healthy person is defined by one's place within a web of relationships.

This intertwining of body, mind, and spirit can be seen within Indigenous healing and spiritual practices, where physical actions can be mentally and spiritually transforming, and where spiritual change can manifest physically. Among the Yurok of Northern California, religious life begins with intense physical training. Running up steep hillsides, chopping wood, fasting, bathing in icy water, and sweating all function to build the physical and mental stamina necessary for future spiritual work. Religious practitioners travel to hard-to-reach places for meditation and prayer and need to be strong enough to endure fasting or participating in long and arduous ceremonies. Mental training cultivates focus and clarity of purpose, the ability to work with an open mind and a good heart, and the ability to avoid destructive ways of thinking.

By their very nature, ceremonial traditions assume an important link between the physical and the spiritual. They rest on the notion that what you do physically

Photo 6.2.   In this October 14, 2017, photo, Herman Davis of the L'ooknax.adi clan wears the Raven Barbecuing Hat, which dates to around 1800, while he is wheeled around the floor during a repatriation ceremony as part of a conference in Sitka, Alaska. The hat was one of seven historic Tlingit pieces that were in East Coast museums for decades that were returned to southeast Alaska. The sacred pieces were brought back to Alaska through the efforts of the Central Council of Tlingit and Haida Indian Tribes of Alaska, and represent people's ongoing connection with their ancestors. (James Poulson/*The Daily Sitka Sentinel* via AP)

will affect who you are spiritually. Another example of this notion is found within Tlingit communities of southeast Alaska. In his work with the Tlingit, Sergei Kan explains that Tlingit notions of the *self* include an immortal spirit, the reincarnated spirit of one's ancestor, a ghost, as well as an inherited name and its accompanying regalia, totem, and crest. The self is complex—not simply "I," it also includes your *shagoon*: your heritage and destiny as inherited from your maternal ancestors. One's *shagoon* is performed at ceremonies and potlatches, when one dons inherited regalia and performs the songs and dances passed on from previous generations. In that moment, the "self" is not a finite creature, but a link in a chain that includes one's ancestors and one's future descendants.

A Spiritually Connected World
The illusion of an independent self can sneak up on us, especially in the individualistic society of contemporary North America. But participating in ceremonies, donning ancient regalia, moving through steps, and giving breath to songs that have belonged to those who came before you disrupts that illusion. It reminds participants that they do not exist apart from a greater continuity of life and creation.

Indigenous ritual and ceremony continually reorients the individual, locating them within a network of relationships with the natural world: with plants, animals, fish, mountains, rivers, winds, and stars. In ceremony, the body is the potent point of connection, the locus where things intersect. Because the body and spirit are intertwined, performing a physical act can have spiritual repercussions. Rituals and ceremonies work to call attention to the body, as every action and expression becomes infused with powerful symbolic meaning. Ritual actions transform one's mental outlook and one's spiritual condition

For this reason, ritual suffering plays a vital role in many Indigenous traditions and can be a necessary part of healing. Black Elk, a famous Lakota medicine man and Catholic catechist, explained that rituals such as the sweat lodge (*inipi*), Sun Dance (*wiwanke wachipi*), and vision quest (*hanblečeya*) induce a state of *unsiká*: being pitiable before the spirits, the Creator, and one's ancestors. Suffering through extremes of heat or cold or abstaining from food or water could strengthen the mind and the spirit and evoke the aid of powerful spiritual beings. Because the self is interconnected with one's human and spiritual communities, one's own suffering can also be transformative for others. This is a notion of suffering on behalf of others, suffering so that one's community will not have to suffer, suffering so that those who are sick can be well, those who are imprisoned will be free, and those who are misguided will find their way home. In some traditions, physical suffering becomes a path for spiritual enlightenment, spiritual power, and spiritual help for others.

While healing traditions vary widely by culture and by tribal community, several commonalities emerge throughout Native North America, where traditional approaches to healing tend to fall into four categories. The first is plant medicine. Herbalists maintain a vast store of plant knowledge—knowing plants both as *materia medica* and as spiritual beings living in relationship with human communities. The second is stories. Communities hold a wealth of traditional stories that speak to a wide array of situations and circumstances, providing individuals with guidance, inspiration, correction, and encouragement. Ceremonial work constitutes a third category of healing. Ceremonies are usually led by spiritual practitioners who have undergone extensive training and apprenticeship, and often include common elements like rites of cleansing and purification, rites of retrieving lost or wayward souls, rites for removing a disease-causing object or spirit, rites of protection and renewal, and rites of blessing, counseling, and prayer. Healing ceremonies might be private—with only a practitioner and patient. Or such ceremonies might be important community affairs, with the patient surrounded by extended family and community gathered in support. Such larger healing ceremonies require enormous amounts of time, resources, and energy, thus demonstrating care and support for the ailing individual. Finally, healing can take the form of various activities that heal relationships—between individuals, between people and the natural world, or between people and the spiritual world. All of these modes of healing were practiced in pre-colonial cultures and have been adapted to address the particular ailments of today, often working in collaboration with biomedical practitioners.

Working with Plants

Why do we get sick? A very old Cherokee story provides one answer. Long, long ago, human beings were only just getting started. They were just figuring things out: how to live, how to behave. At the Creator's request, the animal people shared their wisdom, showing this new species the right way to behave. The animals agreed to be food, but in turn demanded that human beings treat their remains with care, that they never waste anything, and that they refrain from hunting mothers with new babies. But human beings forgot. They killed nursing mothers and babies. They gorged themselves, and afterward they wasted what was left, tossing it on a garbage pile, laughing at the dead things. They stopped being thankful.

The animals got mad. They got together to see what could be done. They decided to create something new, something that would show these humans a thing or two. They made disease. Each animal devised a sickness to afflict the people. The people started to die in terrible ways. Their nursing mothers. Their children. They cried out in their grief.

But plants took pity on them. Every tree, herb, and shrub, even the grass and the moss, agreed to become a cure for one of those diseases. Every plant has a purpose, is medicine for something, and has a spirit that can teach human beings how it should be used.

As this story suggests, Indigenous herbalists tend to emphasize that, while the chemical properties within plants are important, the healing potential of plants is not reducible to those chemical properties. Part of the healing quality of plants comes from their spirit. Plants are not objects, but fellow persons. They have sentience and awareness. In mythic times, they made a decision to offer themselves to people—a gesture of generosity and self-sacrifice. Indigenous herbalists often contend that working with plants is not about simply drinking some tea: it is about years of listening to and getting to know the plants. As living beings older than the human species, plants are the first teachers and elders. One Coast Salish herbalist explained:

> The key to these medicinal plants is prayer, listening with love in your heart. . . . All of these plants have a spirit. That's the medicine. Prayer. Listening. . . . We need to be still. Learn to be still. To listen. Medicines and herbs will teach us what to use, and how to use it. . . . Be still, listen, let that one plant choose you, and let you get to know it. Other medicines will come because they'll like your spirit, they'll come to you because you're willing, because you're wanting to learn. Medicines are revealed from prayer. Medicines are prayed for, and they reveal themselves to a person's spirit. It's their spirit that makes them effective. (Crawford-O'Brien, 183)

Such beliefs guide herbalists' interaction with plants, whether gathered for food or for medicine. The process begins with a prayer of gratitude, and an offering to the plant that might include a sprinkling of tobacco or water, or a gift of labor such as pulling invasive weeds, cultivating the soil, removing trash, or even political advocacy to protect and preserve a space. In the Southwest, Hopi agricultural traditions of respect and care for plants reflect a similar ethos:

Hopi believe that all life is one and that each living thing also has another home where it exists in human form. Thus, when a Hopi goes out to collect a certain kind of plant, the first plant is spared and offered a sacrifice so that it may convey the message of need to other plant people. Obviously, while this is a spiritual belief, it is also sound ecology, ensuring that at least a few plants are left to repopulate an area. (King, 168)

Walking with Stories

When Kathleen Westcott suffered a brain injury, she sought care from a biomedical physician. She also sought the support of her Anishinaabe religious traditions. In particular, she turned to a story. "I've been walking with this story for twenty-five years," she told author and friend Eva Garroutte (Garroutte and Westcott, 169). In the story, a young widow is overcome with grief. She leaves her community and spends many days sitting under a birch tree, going deep into her sadness. Her community supported her in this, caring for her children and making sure she was safe. After a long time, she heard the tree speak to her. It taught her how to take its bark and make the first birch bark baskets.

For Westcott, this story is much more than the origin of birch bark baskets. It is a trail guide, a means of navigating her experience with illness. Just as the young woman in the story allowed herself time to process her grief, Westcott needed time. And just as the woman was eventually able to return to her community having learned a life-changing lesson, Westcott was able to return to her community with hard-earned wisdom. The story was the medicine. In an example like this, the line between one's personal story and a traditional story can be blurred. As people walk with a story, it becomes their own, a narrative through which they can process and make meaning of their own journeys.

After decades of deep friendship, partnership, and collaboration with Coeur d'Alene and Crow elders and teachers, anthropologist Rodney Frey was diagnosed with non-Hodgkin's lymphoma. His friends and adopted family rallied around him, praying for him, and holding a healing ceremony in his honor, dancing all night as he endured long treatments. And they gave him a story. In this story, a young boy falls into the fire, burning his face. Burnt Face leaves his community, going deep into the mountains, where he encounters the Little People, powerful spiritual beings who heal him and give him great spiritual gifts. Burnt Face returns to his community, transformed.

For Frey, the steps of the story likewise became his trail markers, guiding him through the storm of a bone marrow transplant and the painful process of recovery. Like Burnt Face, Frey had to leave the community behind as he suffered with his ailment. He felt the pain of healing. (It's easy to forget that healing can hurt more than the initial injury.) He felt the solitude. And he felt the support of the spiritual world. Frey took comfort in the story—because while Burnt Face had to go up the mountain to pray, he also got to come back. And Frey was also able to come back, recovering, returning to his community, and continuing the work and service to that community that he has undertaken for so many years.

Another example of the healing power in stories is found in the Toronto-based Native Diabetes Program (NDP). Founded thirty years ago in consultation with Ojibwe elders, the NDP relies on Ojibwe/Anishinaabe/Algonquian stories of the Windigo to help their community make sense of diabetes. The Windigo is a spirit of hunger, who devours human beings, and exemplifies the dangers of famine. One woman explains: "Some of the older Ojibway from northern areas intuitively classified diabetes as out-of-balance or *Windigo* disease. *Windigo* is starvation personified" (Howard, 55). The program also produced publications such as "Nanabush and the Stranger," drawing on trickster narratives to find ways of coping with diabetes. Nanabush, or Nanabozho, is a culture hero, creator, and trickster figure found in many Anishinaabe stories. Elder Joe Sylvester was invited to share traditional stories such as Nanabozho's battle with corn, an Anishinaabe migration story where the people find rice and cranberries, and the story of the discovery of maple syrup (Howard, 57–58). Such stories teach about the deep and abiding importance of traditional foods, suggesting different ways of being in relationship with them.

Healing Through Ceremonies

Indigenous communities also crafted ceremonies and rituals for healing, which vary widely from brief spontaneous prayers to multiday ceremonial complexes that might take up to a year of planning and preparation. In her work about Wellbriety and recovery from alcohol addiction among Lakota communities, Beatrice Medicine (Sihasapa and Minneconjou Lakota) gives special attention to the role of the revitalization of Sun Dance ceremonies, and the important role they play in recovery. Sun Dances are four-day ceremonies of sacrifice, discipline, suffering, and prayer. A wide network of families and community members provide the necessary infrastructure for such events, preparing camp areas, maintaining sanitation, providing food and clean drinking water, and building the dance arena and arbor. Dancers pledge to fast from food and water, enduring prayerful dancing in the blazing heat of the sun. Participants may dance on behalf of others, or they may be dancing through their own healing journeys, making commitments to sobriety, suffering through the trials of recovery so that they can better serve their communities.

Another example of a healing ceremony in Northern California is the Yurok, Karuk, and Hupa Brush Dance, where female doctors work to heal a sick child. Today, such ceremonies are likely to take place in the summer over a long weekend. On Wednesday, the healer, patient, and the patient's family gather at the ceremonial site. Extended family and community members might arrive the following day, staying Thursday to Sunday. Social dances and events take place Thursday and Friday, culminating in an all-night healing ceremony Saturday evening into Sunday morning. Male and female singers, all of whom don family-heirloom regalia, support the healer. Such regalia are imbued with the powerful spirit of human ancestors and the white deer and woodpecker from which they're made.

In writing about her work as a healer, Mavis McCoy (Karuk/Yurok) described her decades of training for such work, including vision quests in the mountains.

> I would be someplace and all at once something would start talking to me. There are special high-country places, like Doctor Rock and Chimney Rock that are known to everyone as being medicine places, places where medicine people go to get their powerful gifts. Then there are other places that don't look special or distinct. For instance, there is a place here on this property. And I have learned that these places are the crossroads where the spirit world can come into this world and we can go into the spirit world. These are the places that talked to me. Down the hill from here there was a place that talked, so evidently there was a crossroads there, a spiritual place. When the places talk to you, you have gone into a spirit space. The experience was just like someone was talking to me. It was like being talked to by the medicine women. The voices just told me little things. (McCovey and Salter)

Native American Church

An important ceremony of healing is also found within the Native American Church (NAC). While the current form of the NAC is a modern creation, its roots are in ancient Indigenous practices of northwest Mexico. During all-night prayer services in a specially constructed tipi, participants are seated around a sacred fire and earth altar. At sundown the Road Man (a religious practitioner directing the services) sets the altar and offers an opening prayer. Peyote (*Lophophora williamsii*) is then shared. The night passes in drumming, the singing of peyote songs, prayer, and speaking from one's heart as concerns and hopes are offered up. One elder reflected on the role of the Native American Church in his path toward sobriety.

> My child who took care of the fire spoke to God, but he is speaking to me, too, of my past drinking and behavior. He asked God to provide him with a father whom he would be proud of and the father that he always wish to have. I understand what he means. I love him very much and I heard his words and know what he is asking for from me. I am very proud of him. I never asked him something that he didn't do for me. I value his words. He also has never asked me anything that I didn't do for him. He has come back to help me out. (Garrity, 530–31)

At midnight, water is brought into the tipi, and an eagle whistle is blown toward the four directions. Prayers and songs continue until dawn, when a woman arrives with fresh water. Participants exit to greet the sun and enjoy a shared breakfast.

Peyote is considered to be a living thing with a powerful spirit, a teacher sent to Native people from the Creator. As an envoy and expression of the Creator, peyote sees into the hearts of men and women and helps to guide their actions. In his work, medical anthropologist Thomas Calabrese describes peyote as a medicinal herb endowed with God-given properties, an omniscient and helpful spirit. As one consultant told him, "I guess the physical description would be an herb. And as far as what I see Peyote as, it's a very powerful spirit, a holy being. . . . It's the opportunity to have the ability to communicate with the Creator, to ask him for the spiritual guidance that you need to solve a situation" (Calabrese, 102). Considered a benevolent guardian or messenger spirit, peyote allows prayerful participants to communicate with the divine. Some consider it a manifestation of the Holy Spirit, others see it as a sacrament on par with the bread and wine of the Eucharist, and others make a comparison with Catholic saints. While there are many ways of describing peyote, Native American Church members emphasize that it is not a drug and, while its use should be regulated, it should not be classified as such. One college student described her experience and how outsiders often misperceive it: "I could see that they [other students] didn't understand the way it is—its spirituality. They didn't think of it the way as you would think of the Catholic religion, how they have spirits. They just thought of it basically as a drug. They didn't think of what it means to the Native American people or what it does for them as a religious belief" (Calabrese, 89).

Peyote is powerful medicine. Mescaline within the spiny cactus works to heighten suggestibility, imprint memories, and make participants particularly open to guidance, insight, and social correction. Together with the focusing element of song, drum, and fire, participants experience a profound sense of heightened awareness and focus. Calabrese observes:

> Ingestion of Peyote alters suggestibility and openness to social messages. . . . Chief among these messages in the context of the Native American Church are the family values of honoring one's relatives and avoiding alcohol. In addition, communal Peyote ingestion (and use of tobacco) provides positive role modeling of a controlled and respectful pattern of use of sacred psychoactive substances by adults. Most importantly, perhaps, Peyote is seen not only as a sacred medicinal herb, but also as an omniscient spiritual entity. If socialization is successful, the omnipresent gaze of the Peyote Spirit will become a constant companion of the young NAC member, preventing the child from alcohol consumption and other sins even when the parents are absent. (Calabrese, 152)

Navajo Adolescent Treatment Center

The Navajo Adolescent Treatment Center (NATC) incorporates biomedical approaches alongside traditional Indigenous modes of healing, including intertribal practices like those of the Native American Church, Christian guidance, and Wellbriety programs. Drawing on this wealth of resources, clinicians are able to provide medical, psychological, and spiritual support to meet a patient's individual needs. When Calabrese worked with the NATC, it had five Medicine People on staff, representing the traditional Navajo religion, the Native American Church, and Lakota-influenced intertribal spirituality like the Sun Dance. They offered sweat lodges, talking circles, powwow drumming and singing, tipi building, storytelling, and Christian counseling. Patients were invited to attend Native American Church ceremonies, Christian church services, or Navajo chantways (Calabrese, 177). Costs associated with ceremonies were covered by insurance. Prior to taking this multicultural and multispiritual approach, the NATC had had a 54 percent completion rate, with 33 percent of parents visiting their children while at the facility. After integrating these methods, 80 percent of patients completed the program and 92 percent of parents visited and participated in their child's treatment (Calabrese, 180).

For Native youth struggling with severe addictions, Calabrese found participation in Native American Church meetings remarkably helpful. In part, this was because of the powerful ritual nature of the ceremonies, and their communal nature, which stood in contrast to the hyper-rational one-on-one conversations typical in psychotherapy sessions. He noted in particular the role of "education meetings" in the Native American Church: all-night prayer services held to send young people off to school with the guidance and support of their community, family, and Creator. One student explained:

> Every year in August or September we'd have an education meeting—even when I was in grade school and high school. . . . [When I went to college] I partied my first semester and got bad grades. But toward the end of my first semester, I began my second semester, and I thought about the prayer services that were being done for me. And so I decided to turn my life around because of that strong bond with my parents. . . . Those ideals and morals that they taught us. You could hear all the words of wisdom that the elders spoke about. And I really didn't understand at the time but it came through. (Calabrese, 169)

Another ceremony held upon students' return from school helps to reorient them to their tradition and community.

> [It] was like a cleaning time for me because I've been away for too long. And it was a time for me to be able to re-gather my thoughts. Get my mind in focus again. Like starting all over—a clean slate—because I just feel so rejuvenated. I think what it has done for me every time, my belief in the religion itself is so strong because I have experienced how it feels being away from home and going back and going into a meeting. It just makes me feel like I wasn't that far. I wasn't as far as I thought I was from home. It kind of brings me back. (Calabrese, 170)

Through education meetings such as these, peyote functions as a "spiritual guardian," helping young people avoid risky behaviors and make good decisions.

Despite its value and efficacy in supporting mental health, the Native American Church has been aggressively suppressed by missionaries, local authorities, and state and federal governments. The legal debate over the ceremonial use of peyote culminated in the *Oregon v. Smith* (1990) case. The case began when Alfred Smith (Klamath) was fired from his job as a drug- and alcohol-abuse counselor because of his participation in Native American Church ceremony. "One Friday afternoon, my supervisor called me into his office and asked if I was a member of the Native American Church. I said I was, and he asked if I used the drug, Peyote. I said, 'No, but I do take the holy sacrament.' He told me not to, that it was illegal, and then checked up on me on Monday, asking if I had taken the drug during the Saturday night ceremony. Again, I said no, but that I had partaken of the sacrament. He said I left him no alternative but to fire me" (Niezen, Burgess, and Begay, 147). When Smith's claims for unemployment were denied, he sued. The Oregon Court of Appeals ruled he was entitled to benefits, and when the state's attorney general challenged the ruling, it was upheld in the Oregon Supreme Court. The U.S. Supreme Court, however, vacated the judgment. Justice Anthony Scalia described religious freedom as a "luxury" that society could not afford in an increasingly diverse society.

The Smith ruling illustrated the way such judicial decisions can reinforce colonial power structures, ignoring worldviews that fall outside the accepted norm. "Religion" was here defined as freedom to *believe*, not to *practice* one's religion. Scalia wrote: "The free exercise of religion means, first and foremost, the right to believe and profess whatever religious doctrine one desires" (Calabrese, 97). Such an interpretation fits well with a predominantly Protestant Christian tradition that emphasizes faith, but fails to consider the dominant role that shared practice holds for most of the world's other religious traditions, and Indigenous traditions in particular. In response to the Smith case, Congress passed the 1994 amendment to the American Indian Religious Freedom Act, clarifying that the use of peyote is legal for documented members of the Native American Church and its affiliates.

Diné Chantways

A central focus of Diné (Navajo) religious life is healing, and it includes a wide array of herbal, material, and ritual approaches to health and wellness. Diagnosticians work as ritual specialists who discern the spiritual origin of an individual's ailment. Herbalists are steeped in the knowledge of the plants and minerals of the Navajo homeland. Ceremonial leaders train for decades in order to conduct complex chantways.

Ceremonial chantways are built upon an understanding of the world found in Diné creation accounts, a collection of stories that reveal the web of relationships that bind the world together. Within the Diné creation account, Changing Woman formed the first people. The daughter of Father Sky and Mother Earth, Changing Woman gathered together soil, minerals, and cornmeal from the four directions, mixed them with her saliva and her own skin, and shaped them into male and female figures. In some accounts of the story, Changing Woman took a small piece from each and placed it within the genitalia of the other: the foundation of sexual desire and attraction.

These figures lacked life, however, until they were animated by *niłch'i* (holy winds), which arrived from the four directions, entering the body at swirls on the skin at fingertips, toes, ears, nostrils, the top of the head. Holy winds animated the creatures, bringing them sentience and awareness. Not simply the movement of air, these holy winds themselves are alive and aware, manifestations of a conscious world. The winds continue to enter and exit the body, tying each person to the landscape and keeping them alive. However, the winds can become agitated and may be driven to withdraw from the body by unethical, imbalanced, or disrespectful behavior, thoughts, or speech. Because one's health depends on the balanced, harmonious flow of holy wind, it likewise depends on living a balanced, harmonious life. This is what Diné tradition refers to as *sa'ąh naagháí bik'eh hózhó*.

Restoring those relationships, restoring the flow of holy wind, may require a chantway. Chantways vary in duration from one to eight days and can include fasting, prayer, herbal remedies, ritual bathing or sweating, and most famously, the construction of elaborate sandpaintings on the floor of the ceremonial hogan. At the heart of every chantway is a story: the tale of a hero in the midst of crisis, who goes on a journey, encounters a holy person, and returns to their community with new teachings, songs, prayers, and medicine. Through oratory, songs, and prayers, the patient is identified as the hero, and through the ceremony, the patient repeats that journey, encountering the holy person, and returning with a new path toward wellness. Right ways of speech, thought, and action are renewed, and relationships restored. The sandpainting provides an illustration of the story, representing and evoking the presence of ancestors and holy people, as the patient is quite literally seated within the story, on top of the painting.

Chantways also work to protect patients from malevolent forces or sources of disharmony and evoke the presence of *ye'ii* (holy people) who can offer their help, support, and guidance. The goal of such ceremonies is to restore the patient to a state of *hózhó*—balance, beauty and harmony—through restoring relationships between the patient and their spiritual, natural, and human worlds.

While a biomedical physician might see the origin of disease in cancer cells, for instance, Diné tradition sees vulnerability to illness in negative psychological states, a life out of balance, or contact with dangerous things. Chantways are based on the premise that the human body mirrors the cosmos, acting as a microcosm of the macrocosm. The boundaries of the individual extend beyond that person into the world outside. Because of this, health and wellness require bringing the individual into a state of balance with the external cosmos, restoring relationships with human, natural, and spiritual beings.

Photo 6.3.   Diné (Navajo) ceremonial experts work on a sandpainting, probably in Arizona. Woven blankets and rugs are displayed nearby. (Western History and Genealogy Dept., Denver Public Library)

Coast Salish Soul Retrieval Ceremonies

Moving from the deserts of the Southwest to the rainforests of the Pacific Northwest, we find remarkably different cultures with distinct ways of understanding the source of illness and how to go about restoring a person to wholeness. Among the Coast Salish, a key ceremonial healing practice concerns the retrieval of lost souls. Coast Salish healers conduct private ceremonies, engaging in prayer, song, and meditation to retrieve a person's soul that has wandered too far on the path to the land of the dead. A historical ceremonial complex known as the Spirit Canoe ceremony or Soul Recovery ceremony provided a means of retrieving souls in particularly dire straits. Here, a healer and his or her team of assistants travel in a metaphorical canoe to the land of the dead. In a three-day ceremony, supported by extended family and the broader community, they travel in song and spirit, overcoming great obstacles to retrieve the wayward soul.

The spiritual canoe is accompanied by specially carved paddles and sacred images representing the spirit helpers of the healers. For Charlene Krise (Squaxin), the symbolism is potent. As canoe journeys are revitalizing tribal cultures around the region, supporting individuals on their path toward spiritual growth, sobriety, and healing, the canoe continues to represent a means of transformation and renewal in one's journey through life and into the spirit.

Conclusion

While restoring individuals to wellness is clearly important, healing traditions in Native North America also include practices and traditions that heal broader communities and relationships. First foods ceremonies (such as those discussed in chapter 5) are healing ceremonies, because they work to restore healthy relationships among human, plant, and animal communities, renewing commitments to care for, protect, and preserve the land and its resources. Other rites and ceremonies that create and affirm relationships between families and individuals can also work as healing rites. These ceremonies include rites of adoption or peace making. In such traditions, individuals or groups of people are brought within the fold of a family or tribe, and the bonds of filial commitment are affirmed. Such rites vary widely, but often include some common features, such as giving or exchanging gifts and bestowing a new name.

If we understand healing to be restoring individuals or communities to wholeness, enabling them to live in balanced, harmonious relationships, then many ritual and ceremonial activities can be seen as rites of healing. Ceremonies of reconciliation (where parties acknowledge wrongs done, provide compensation, and restore broken ties) are healing ceremonies. Rites of political protest can be healing ceremonies. When elders and children stand at a blockade, drumming and singing, blocking access to forests slated for clear-cutting, they are engaging in rites of healing and renewal. When water protectors walk prayerfully for hundreds of miles along a river, galvanizing support for living, sacred water, they are also healers, working to renew the world.

As this chapter shows, the risks to Indigenous lives and well-being have their roots in colonialism. Because of this, healing is necessarily decolonizing work. This includes challenging the "self" portrayed in settler-colonial culture. It requires re-claiming a holistic view of the self: mind, body, and spirit, within community. It means healing relationships within families and tribal communities, among human beings, the natural world, and the spiritual world. It means regaining a spirituality of kinship, which demands respect, care, and kindness. It means acknowledging relationship and interdependency, and realizing that when those relations are dis-rupted, illness can occur.

In 1862, the Dakota ancestors of Waziyatawin (Angela Wilson) were forcibly removed from their home. The men were held at Camp McClellan in Davenport, Iowa, while the women and children were removed to Fort Snelling and then to a desolate reservation. Many of them perished. The wounds from that trauma are still felt today. But in recent years, the community has begun holding commemorative marches, ceremonially retracing the steps of their ancestors, reclaiming their stories, memories, and lands. For Wilson, these weeks-long walks are healing medicine, re-connecting them with Minisota Makoce and healing rifts between themselves and the descendants of the Euroamerican communities who displaced them. Facing raw emotion and historical pain, they reconnect with relatives and discover spiritual and physical strength they did not know they had. They are forced to wrestle with the choices their ancestors had to make: resist? conform? convert? stand strong in tradition? Or maybe, find a way of doing all of these things at once. On that walk, in that wrestling, there is another kind of healing.

References and Recommendations

Anderson, Kim. *Life Stages and Native Women: Memory, Teachings, and Story Medicine.* Win-nipeg: University of Manitoba Press, 2011.

Buckley, Thomas. *Standing Ground: Yurok Indian Spirituality 1850–1990.* Berkeley: Univer-sity of California Press, 2002.

Calabrese, Joseph. *A Different Medicine: Postcolonial Healing in the Native American Church.* Oxford: Oxford University Press, 2013.

Chandler, Michael, et al. "Personal Persistence, Identity Development, and Suicide: A Study of Native and Non-Native North American Adolescents," *Monographs of the Society for Research in Child Development* Vol. 68 No. 2 (2003): vii–138.

Cordova, Felina, et al. "Using a Community-Based Participatory Research Approach to Collect Hopi Breast Cancer Survivors' Stories," *American Indian Culture and Research Journal* Vol. 39 No. 2 (2015): 97–109.

Crawford-O'Brien, Suzanne. *Coming Full Circle: Spirituality and Wellness among Native Com-munities in the Pacific Northwest.* Lincoln: University of Nebraska Press, 2014.

Crawford-O'Brien, Suzanne. *Religion and Healing in Native America: Pathways for Renewal.* Santa Barbara: Praeger, 2008.

DeCora, Lorelei. "The Diabetic Plague in Indian Country: Legacy of Displacement," *Wicazo Sa Review* Vol. 16 No. 1 (2001): 9–15.

DeJong, David. *If You Knew the Conditions: A Chronicle of the Indian Medical Service and American Indian Health Care, 1908–1955.* Lanham, MD: Lexington Books, 2008.

DeJong, David. *Plagues Politics and Policy: A Chronicle of the Indian Health Service 1955–2008.* Lanham, MD: Lexington Books, 2010.

Donovan, Dennis, et al. "Healing of the Canoe: Preliminary Results of a Culturally Grounded Intervention to Prevent Substance Abuse and Promote Tribal Identity for Native Youth in Two Pacific Northwest Tribes," *American Indian & Alaska Native Mental Health Research: The Journal of the National Center* Vol. 22 (2015): 42–76.

Dupuis, Anita, and Cheryl Ritenbaugh. "Preventing Cardiovascular Disease in Native Communities: The Traditional Living Challenge," *American Indian Culture and Research Journal* Vol. 38 No. 1 (2014): 101–122.

Frey, Rodney. "If All These Stories Were Told, Great Stories Will Come!" in *Religion and Healing in Native America: Pathways for Renewal,* edited by Suzanne Crawford O'Brien. Santa Barbara: Praeger, 2008.

Garrity, G. F. "Jesus, Peyote, and the Holy People: Alcohol Abuse and the Ethos of Power in Navajo Healing," *Medical Anthropology Quarterly* Vol. 14 No. 4 (2000): 521–542.

Garroutte, Eva, and Delores Westcott. "The Stories Are Very Powerful: A Native American Perspective on Health, Illness, and Narrative," in *Religion and Healing in Native America: Pathways for Renewal,* edited by Suzanne Crawford O'Brien. Santa Barbara: Praeger, 2008.

Gross, Lawrence. "Cultural Sovereignty and Native American Hermeneutics in the Interpretation of the Sacred Stories of the Anishinaabe," *Wicazo Sa Review* Vol. 18 No. 2 (2003): 127–34.

Howard, Heather. "Politics of Culture in Urban Indigenous Community-Based Diabetes Programs," *American Indian Culture and Research Journal* Vol. 38 No. 1 (2014): 49–72.

Jacob, Michelle. "This Path Will Heal Our People: Healing the Soul Wound of Diabetes," in *Religion and Healing in Native America: Pathways for Renewal,* edited by Suzanne Crawford O'Brien. Santa Barbara: Praeger, 2008.

Jacob, Michelle. "Claiming Health and Culture as Human Rights: Yakama Feminism in Daily Practice," in *New Directions in Feminism and Human Rights,* edited by Dana Collins, Sylvanna M. Falcon, Sharmila Lodhia, and Molly Talcott. Abingdon, UK: Routledge: 2011.

Joe, Jennie. "Promoting Cultural Capital in a Medical Camp for American Indian Youth with Diabetes," *American Indian Culture and Research Journal* Vol. 38 No. 1 (2014): 123–44.

Joe, Jennie, and Robert Young. "Introduction: Diabetes Programs and the Need for Cultural Capital," *American Indian Culture and Research Journal* Vol. 38 No. 1 (2014): 11–18.

Kan, Sergei. *Symbolic Immortality: The Tlingit Potlatch of the Nineteenth Century.* Washington, DC: Smithsonian Press, 1999.

Kelley, Dennis. "Traditional Identity and Community Health: Religion and Well-Being in Indian Country," in *Tradition, Performance and Religion in Native America.* Abingdon, UK: Routledge, 2014.

King, Frances. "American Indian Plant Use," in *Stars Above Earth Below: American Indians and Nature,* edited by Marsha Bol. Lanham, MD: Robert Rinehart Publishers, 1998.

Mann, Barbara. *The Tainted Gift: Disease Method of Frontier Expansion.* Santa Barbara: ABC-CLIO/Praeger, 2009.

Marshall, Wende Elizabeth. *Potent Mana: Lessons in Power and Healing.* Albany: SUNY Press, 2011.

Matamonasa-Bennett, Arieahn. "Until People Are Given the Right to Be Human Again: Voices of American Indian Men on Domestic Violence and Traditional Values," *American Indian Culture and Research Journal* Vol. 37 No. 4 (2013): 25–52.

Mays, Vickie M., et al. "Expanding the Circle: Decreasing American Indian Mental Health Disparities through Culturally Competent Teaching about American Indian Mental Health," *American Indian Culture and Research Journal* Vol. 33 No. 3 (2009): 61–83.

McCovey, Mavis, and John Salter. *Medicine Trails: A Life in Many Worlds.* Berkeley: Heyday Books, 2009.

McNeley, James Kale. *Holy Wind in Navajo Philosophy.* Tucson: University of Arizona Press, 1981.

Medicine, Beatrice. *Drinking and Sobriety among the Lakota Sioux.* Walnut Creek, CA: Alta-Mira, 2006.

Miller, Jay. *Lushootseed Culture and the Shamanic Odyssey: An Anchored Radiance.* Lincoln: University of Nebraska Press, 1999.

Million, Dian. *Therapeutic Nations: Healing in an Age of Indigenous Rights.* Tucson: University of Arizona Press, 2013.

Mooney, James. *Myths of the Cherokee.* Washington, DC: Smithsonian, 1900.

Niezen, Ronald, Kim Burgess, and Manley Begay. *Spirit Wars: Native North American Religions in an Age of Nation Building.* Berkeley: University of California Press, 2000.

Penn, John, Joy Doll, and Neal Grandgenett. "Culture as Prevention: Assisting High Risk Youth in the Omaha Nation," *Wicazo Sa Review* Vol. 23 No. 2 (2008): 43–61.

Rules Governing The Court of Indian Offenses, Department of the Interior, Office of Indian Affairs, Washington, DC, (March 30, 1883).

Sarris, Greg. *Mabel McKay: Weaving the Dream.* Berkeley: University of California Press, 2013.

Smith-Morris, Carolyn. *Diabetes among the Pima: Stories of Survival.* Tucson: University of Arizona Press, 2005.

Smith-Morris, Carolyn. "Community Participation in Tribal Diabetes Programs," *American Indian Culture and Research Journal* Vol. 30 No. 2 (2006): 85–110.

Smith-Morris, Carolyn, and Jenny Epstein. "Beyond Cultural Competency: Skill, Reflexivity, and Structure in Successful Tribal Health Care," *American Indian Culture and Research Journal* Vol. 38 No. 1 (2014): 29–48.

Strickland, C. June, Elaine Walsh, and Michelle Cooper. "Healing Fractured Families: Parents' and Elders' Perspectives on the Impact of Colonization and Youth Suicide Prevention in a Pacific Northwest American Indian Tribe," *Journal of Transcultural Nursing* (2006): 5–12.

Thompson, Nile Robert, and C. Dale Stoat, "The Use of Oral Literature to Provide Community Health Education on the Southern Northwest Coast," *American Indian Culture and Research Journal* Vol. 28 No. 3 (2004): 1–28.

Trudelle Schwarz, Maureen. *Molded in the Image of Changing Woman.* Tucson: University of Arizona Press, 1997.

Trudelle Schwarz, Maureen. *Blood and Voice: Navajo Women Ceremonial Practitioners.* Tucson: University of Arizona Press, 2003.

Trudelle Schwarz, Maureen. *I Choose Life: Contemporary Medical and Religious Practices in the Navajo World.* Norman: University of Oklahoma Press, 2008.

Waziyatawin, Angela Wilson. *In the Footsteps of Our Ancestors: The Dakota Commemorative Marches of the 21st Century.* St. Paul: Living Justice Press, 2006.

Weiner, Diane, and Mary Canales. "It Is Not Just Diabetes: Engaging Ethnographic Voices to Develop Culturally Appropriate Health Promotion Efforts," *American Indian Culture and Research Journal* Vol. 38 No. 1 (2014): 73–100.

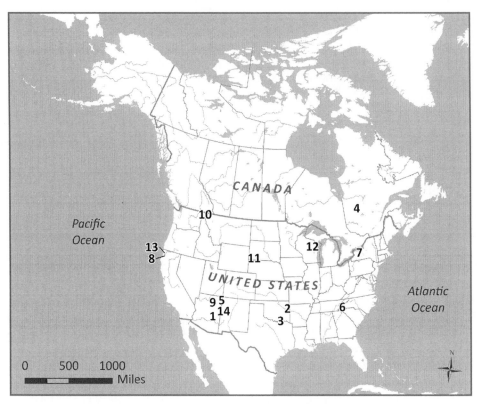

1 Apache Territories
2 Cherokee Nation
3 Choctaw Nation of Oklahoma
4 Cree First Nation
5 Diné (Navajo) Nation
6 Eastern Band Of Cherokee Indians
7 Haudenosaunee (Iroquois) Territory

8 Hoopa Valley Tribe
9 Hopi Tribe
10 Kootenai (Ktunaxa) Nation
11 Lakota Territories
12 Menominee Indian Tribe
13 Yurok Tribe
14 Pueblo of Zuñi

Map 7.1. Map of North America locating the tribal communities, nations, and cultural groups mentioned in this chapter. Basemap data made with Natural Earth. (Liz O'Dea Springborn)

Gender and Sexuality 7

IN JANUARY OF 2017, women across the country joined in the first annual Women's March. Hundreds of thousands of women—with children and partners in tow—brought signs and voices as they demanded attention to a range of issues: environmental protection, sexual harassment, and equality. In Seattle, Indigenous women led the march. Those of us who lined the streets were invited to stand in silence as Native women led the way, drumming, singing, and calling attention to their concerns. They were there to raise awareness of the high rates of murdered and missing Indigenous women and girls, threats to tribal sovereignty, and the impacts of climate change. Their place at the front of the march was a moving gesture of respect, acknowledging them as the first people of Seattle.

Months later, the Urban Indian Health Institute of Seattle released the results of a study: 94 percent of Native women surveyed reported having been raped or coerced into sex. Sixty-nine percent said they had experienced street harassment, while 86 percent said they experienced historical trauma—the violence of colonialism passed down from one generation to the next. It ought to be difficult to align such statistics with the symbolic role that Native people play in Seattle's more public image. The city is named after an Indigenous leader. Native art is highlighted and celebrated throughout the city. And Indigenous tribal and cultural leaders often serve important ceremonial roles, as they are called upon to mark important events. But such gestures of respect must be held up against a broader context of colonialism that justifies the appropriation and exploitation of Indigenous culture and people—even while at times celebrating, honoring, and uplifting them.

Native women encounter the highest rates of domestic violence and sexual assault of any ethnic group in North America. This is the product of a colonial history that stripped them of traditional authority within kinship and social structures, stereotyped them as sexualized maidens or mindless drudges, and imposed a heteronormative patriarchy upon them that undermined traditional reverence for women and those who fell outside of gender binaries.

Photo 7.1.   Demonstrators with the Missing and Murdered Indigenous Women Washington group, E. Pine St., Seattle, Washington, January 20, 2018. The text on signs reads: "'Nookoox' Geraldine Hendrickson 'Morning Star,' murdered downtown Seattle June 1998, Northern Arapaho and Yurok." The Missing and Murdered Indigenous Women Washington group raises awareness about Indigenous women, girls, and LGBT individuals who have been murdered, raped, trafficked, or gone missing. Indigenous women are affected by these issues at a much higher rate than average, and MMIWW advocates for those individuals and their families. (University of Washington Libraries, Special Collections. Photo by Kinsey, Kristin, MAR3427)

Despite this legacy of colonialism, tribal communities are turning to their cultures, reclaiming tools, traditions, and sacred teachings to heal and empower women. They are also reclaiming Indigenous ways of knowing, arguing that Indigenous women in pre-colonial cultures had considerable authority within their communities, holding the power to shape marriages, initiate divorce, and control the products of their labor. Religious and political leaders explain that gender nonconformity was acknowledged and often honored in pre-colonial cultures. Since the 1990s, the term *Two Spirit* has emerged as an inclusive term to refer to gay, lesbian, transgender, and nonbinary individuals within the Indigenous community. The colonial imposition of heteronormativity and patriarchy challenged these ancient traditions, but Two Spirit people are reclaiming Indigenous beliefs and practices, uplifting a time when sexual and gender diversity were celebrated and honored.

Violence against Indigenous Women and Children

Native American and First Nations women are five times more likely to be victims of homicide and up to four times more likely to raped or sexually assaulted than the general population. In the great majority of cases, their perpetrators are not Native.

Such staggering violence requires that we consider the gendered impacts of colonialism. For women, colonialism meant the loss of traditional political, economic, and social power, and it meant being subject to settler violence. In their work, Venida Chenault and Andrea Smith have both argued that pre-colonial gender roles provided women with power and safety, but Euroamerican colonialism deposed matriarchal and egalitarian societies, introducing misogyny and homophobia. Devaluing Native women legitimized assault.

In 1991, First Nations women of Vancouver, British Columbia, held the first Women's Memorial March, an expression of grief and anger that followed the murder of a Coast Salish woman. Now held every Valentine's Day in more than twenty-two communities across Canada, the Memorial March honors murdered and missing First Nations women, calling for action. In 2016, the Canadian government began an investigation to determine the systemic causes of violence against First Nations women, girls, and Two Spirit people. While the investigation has been criticized for poor organization, funding, and communication (http://www.mmiwg-ffada.ca), it has helped to raise visibility of concerns that First Nations have voiced for years: Indigenous women are vulnerable to assault and such crimes are left uninvestigated.

Just as Native women are disproportionately subjected to violence, so are Native children. Instances of child sexual abuse can be much higher in Indigenous communities. Statistics of child sexual abuse among Indigenous communities vary widely, from 0.8 percent to 66 percent for boys, and from 7 percent to 96 percent for girls, depending on the community (Barsalou-Verge, 69). One study found child sexual assault in a particular Canadian First Nations reserve to be *ten times* the national average, while other tribal communities had rates that were actually lower than that of the general population. Despite such variations, one thing remains consistent: on average, 80 percent of victims are female.

Child sexual abuse can devastate physical and psychological health, making victims far more vulnerable to post-traumatic stress disorder, drug and alcohol abuse, depression, and anxiety disorders. Symptoms such as headaches, weight loss, uncontrollable crying, sleep disturbance, and sexual dysfunction may also manifest later in life. Young-adult victims are far more likely to run away from home, drop out, or be suspended from school, be arrested, engage in early sexual activity, struggle with forming healthy relationships, or attempt suicide.

It can be particularly difficult to hold perpetrators responsible within Indigenous communities. Native abusers may be protected by community codes of silence, or by mistrust of police who have historically been slow to respond and quick to blame the victim. Most perpetrators, however, are non-Native, and it can be difficult to prosecute non–tribal members within the tribal system. Jurisdictional lines are often complex and convoluted as well: it may be unclear whether federal, state, county, city, or tribal police are responsible to intervene (Barsalou-Verge, 72).

Such challenges are compounded by Native women's lack of access to care and services. While Native women are more likely to need mental and physical health care, they are among the least likely to have access to it, or to become medical practitioners themselves. They continue to have the lowest mammogram rates, and are less likely to receive routine screening or follow-up care than other ethnic groups. Until recent decades, Native women were blocked from participating in the healing professions: traditional healing practices were suppressed, and Native women were excluded from universities and medical schools.

There are many reasons for Native women's lack of faith in institutionalized medicine, but one of the most devastating has been the forced sterilization of Native women. Historian Jane Lawrence has reconstructed this tragic era, documenting how 25 to 50 percent of Native women in the United States were sterilized by Indian Health Service physicians in the 1960s and 1970s. Lawrence found evidence that patients were commonly misinformed about the procedure, coerced into signing consent forms, given vague or misleading consent forms, or not granted a mandatory waiting period after signing consent forms (Lawrence, 400). For instance, out of 54 cases examined at the Phoenix Indian Medical Center, at least 19 were deemed by a government investigation to be questionable. A study by Choctaw physician Connie Pinkerton-Uri likewise found evidence of coercion. She found that "Indian women generally agreed to sterilization when they were threatened with the loss of their children and/or their welfare benefits, that most of them gave consent when they were heavily sedated during a Caesarian section or when they were in a great deal of pain during labor, and that the women could not understand the consent forms because they were written in English at the twelfth-grade level" (Lawrence, 412). The impact of these coercive policies is striking: between 1970 and 1980, Native women's average birthrate fell from 3.29 to 1.3.

Tradition as a Path Toward Healing

Colonialism is inherently violent, and it impacts women in particularly virulent ways, stripping them of traditional access to social, political, and economic power. Because of this, an essential piece of decolonizing—of healing from colonialism—is reclaiming traditional teachings about gender and sexuality. In her book *Choctaw Women in a Chaotic World: The Clash of Cultures in the Colonial Southwest*, Michelene Pesantubbee (Choctaw) provides context for contemporary Native women's struggles by considering their origins in colonial history. In her examination of the changing role of Choctaw women between 1699 and 1763, Pesantubbee shows how French colonizers curtailed women's positions of leadership and suppressed Indigenous religious life—the Green Corn ceremony in particular. The Green Corn ceremony celebrated Corn Woman, a mythic figure who sacrificed her life to provide food for the people. As the ceremony fell out of practice, Choctaw women's economic, spiritual, and political power likewise declined. Eighteenth-century Christianity demanded women's silence and required the suppression of women's ceremonial responsibilities in, for example, the Green Corn ceremony or their directing of mourning rites. As the church replaced such rites with its own (led by men), women lost access to important avenues for honor, status, and spiritual leadership.

Throughout the Southeast, women's control of agriculture had ensured them a voice in politics and diplomacy. But Euroamerican rule removed women from this position of power, breaking down traditional matrilineal structures. In Euroamerican society, men owned land, and men controlled agriculture. As a result, Choctaw and Cherokee women lost their economic and political influence, becoming vulnerable to violence, exploitation, and even enslavement.

As tribal communities respond to this legacy of violence, they emphasize the colonial nature of such trauma, teaching the lesson that violence against women and children is not Indigenous or traditional, but a product of colonialism. Community leaders emphasize that prior to colonialism, domestic and sexual violence appears to have been far more rare, and when such violence did occur, it was effectively dealt with: small-scale communities, extended families, and community policing meant that perpetrators could be identified and quickly sanctioned. The work of David Levinson appears to support such claims. In his comparative ethnographic analysis of dozens of different communities, Levinson identifies five characteristics common in low-violence communities that would have been found in many traditional Native North American settings: "(a) shared decision-making; (b) equal control over family resources; (c) no premarital sexual double standard; (d) peaceful conflict resolution within and outside the home; and (e) social sanctions and accountability for domestic violence" (Matamonasa-Bennett, 29).

Sacred stories and spiritual teachings taught the sacredness of women, emphasizing their distinctive worth and the consequences of abuse. Cultural experts also point out that women controlled certain areas of Indigenous economies, owned the products of their labor, and held positions within social and political decision making, all of which helped to ensure their safety, voice, and influence. Knowing this, successful violence-prevention programs often focus on reclaiming traditional cultures, restoring extended kin networks, and are guided by Indigenous culture and spiritual teachings. Consider for instance that the National Indigenous Women's Resource Center has titled their handbook on domestic violence "Violence Against Native Women Is Not Traditional" and that the motto of the Native Women's Society of the Great Plains (NWSGP) is "Reclaiming Our Sacredness."

In a study conducted by the NWSGP, Lakota elders were asked to identify the origins of domestic violence. They agreed that "violence against women was learned from white people," emphasized "their grandparents' relationships of respect and equality, and expressed their belief that violence is not traditional among Lakota people" (Native Women's Society of the Great Plains). Elders agreed:

> The solution to the problem of violence against women will be found in regaining spiritual balance and remembering culture and traditional values. Men need to understand the sacredness and power of the woman and their responsibilities in caring for her and the children. . . . Women have forgotten their sacredness and need to re-examine their responsibilities and refocus on their rights.

In her work, professor of clinical psychology Arieahn Matamonasa-Bennett interviewed Native men with a history of domestic violence. The men with whom she spoke all agreed that alcohol was the biggest contributing factor to violence; they described alcohol as a "foreign invasion" that "takes over," preventing them from being "human beings." Alcohol is "a poison that has ruined the Nation." By contrast, the men agreed that following one's culture was a source of true strength and that having begun to do so, they now felt a responsibility to live according to those traditional values (Matamonasa-Bennett, 37). As one of her collaborators explained: "When you pick up the values of the outside people, you also pick up their diseases. And this [domestic violence] is a disease that is frequently associated with the dominant society. When you go back and look at our old society, you didn't have them issues. It was dealt with firmly and swiftly . . . the clan and family members would take measures to immediately stop that . . . we lived in a safe society" (Matamonasa-Bennett, 39). Traditional society called upon men to protect their families and communities, the men explained, not to hurt them.

As Matamonasa-Bennett makes clear, traditional values and spirituality are the foundation for recovery.

> What was most striking is that all of these men envision a pre-contact past when violence against women was rare and socially unacceptable, which provides a foundation from which to build a nonviolent future. They believe that as individuals, they have the power to change their community by becoming more "traditional." Additionally, they believe that the community has the answers and keys for change—if given the freedom and autonomy to be "true Great Lakes tribal people," and "the right to be human again." (Matamonasa-Bennett, 47)

As her work makes clear, addressing the violence of colonialism means reclaiming traditional values and roles for men and women that are based on balanced, healthy, equitable relationships.

For scholar Patricia Gonzales, one of the important spaces for reclaiming tradition is in women's ceremonies of childbirth. Gonzales uplifts the work of women like Lucila Contreras (Apache/Nahua), who are reclaiming Indigenous ceremonies of childbirth and healing, renewing relationships with traditional plants, and emphasizing how the sacred feminine is woven throughout family stories and personal healing journeys so that women can renew their connection to land, ancestors, and spirit. Reclaiming Indigenous approaches to gender and sexuality is seen as bound up with healing from historical trauma, undoing systemic inequalities, and renewing Indigenous knowledge.

Gender and Sexuality in Indigenous Cultures

Early settlers were often shocked by the social and political influence of Indigenous women. Many Native communities were matrilocal (married couples lived with the bride's family) and matrilineal (children traced their primary affiliation through their mother's ancestry). In virtually all Native North American cultures, women and men had equitable and complementary political, economic, and social obligations. Women held significant authority and power that served as a check and balance to male authority.

Northern Plains

Indigenous cultures on the Northern Plains have typically been stereotyped as the most patriarchal in North America. But stereotypes belie the fact that women in the Northern Plains occupied complementary and highly valued social roles. The difficulties of surviving in the relatively harsh terrain of the Northern Plains meant that groups had to range widely, hunting across hundreds of miles in order to sustain themselves. Bison hunting was dangerous, and the risks of conflict with neighboring tribes increased those risks. Demonstrations of skill and spiritual power could mean being inducted into warrior societies, which were tasked with policing and protecting communities. Such societies were nearly exclusively male, and were accompanied by ritual restrictions and ceremonial obligations. But the risks of the warrior were seen as parallel to those of childbirth, and women who survived and reared healthy children gained prestige similar to that of warriors. Women were responsible for most domestic work, but they also owned their homes and controlled household resources. Women were not the property of men. Rather, they retained ownership of themselves, their children, and domestic property. Important moments in women's lives were sacralized by ritual and ceremony. Rites and ceremonies accompanied menarche, childbirth, naming, and an infant's first steps, and women played key roles in mourning ceremonies, directing the rites that release a spirit from the bonds of grief.

Northeast and Southeast

For the matrilineal Haudenosaunee (Iroquoian) cultures of the northeastern United States and southeastern Canada, economic and political life was traditionally divided along gendered lines: women farmed, while men were hunters, fishers, and warriors. Because agriculture formed the foundation of economic life, women held considerable social and political power. While women maintained primary authority over land use, they regularly ventured outside of this role, acting in trade, diplomacy, and warfare. Clan mothers chose and deposed male chiefs. They had a voice in councils and held authority within longhouses. Historian Nancy Shoemaker has demonstrated that Haudenosaunee women maintained control over their land, property, and marriage rights through the nineteenth century, continuing to insist that women maintain rights over economic resources equal to men.

Southeastern agricultural communities like the Cherokee were also matrilineal and matrilocal, with women holding authority within their multigenerational households. Women's responsibility for home and agriculture ensured them a strong political voice. But, as Pesantubbee argued, gender roles among Indigenous communities on the East Coast began changing as early as the eighteenth century.

Influenced by Christian missionaries and settler economics, Indigenous women lost much of their influence.

However, women in these communities still retained covert forms of influence and social authority. Clan mothers remained the bearers of culture, continuing millennia-old traditions of planting, medicine, and storytelling, and continued to exert influence within extended families and religious communities. They maintained planting and harvesting traditions, and the Green Corn ceremony survived the colonial onslaught.

Columbia Plateau

Among Indigenous communities on the Columbia Plateau in the interior of the Northwest, gender roles continue to be defined by complementarity and equity, even as they have been challenged by settler culture. Lillian Ackerman has made the case that Plateau men and women had access to different roles, but equal access to social, economic, and religious power (Ackerman, 78). As discussed in chapter 5, sacred foods form the foundation of Indigenous religious life on the Plateau. As Michelle Jacob has argued, women controlled access to and distribution of food. Notably, first foods are divided equally between the sexes: men are responsible for venison and fish, women for roots and berries. In first foods ceremonies, all of these are honored and held in equal regard. Only water—a gender-neutral element—takes precedence.

Because Plateau women maintained most plant knowledge, they mediated access to medicine and the materials necessary for men's work, such as salmon weirs and nets, hunting implements, and clothing. Women also processed and preserved the meat and fish that men provided, and in doing so gained control over food resources, determining when and by whom food would be eaten. Women built, maintained, and owned their homes. Because women owned the products of their labor, they were ensured economic, social, and political influence. Economic life is intertwined with religious life: the spiritual work of cultivating and harvesting plants is imbued with prayers, stories, and sacred teachings.

Ackerman also notes that women on the Plateau could live independently of men. Because she owned the home, a woman could initiate divorce: all she needed to do was place her husband's possessions outside the door, indicating he was no longer welcome. Women were the chief authority within the home, and elder women had almost unquestioned authority to mediate disputes. Woman also had access to typically male vocations, should they have the gift to undertake them. Historical accounts affirm that some women joined war parties and served as chiefs and were honored because of their unusual gifts and strengths.

Perhaps most importantly, Plateau religious traditions afforded equal opportunity for women and men. Historically and today, both genders vision quest and have the same access to dreams and visions. Both are able to offer the wisdom gleaned from such spiritual work back to the community, and both are heeded and respected when they do. Women and men alike can serve as healers and spiritual

leaders; they can both access spiritual power associated with gambling and participate in single-gender sweat lodges. They share the same restrictions as well: both
abstain from sex before hunting or gathering, and both mothers and fathers observe
the same dietary restrictions during pregnancy and immediately after birth.

Jacob explores the importance of reclaiming traditional women's roles within
the revitalization of Plateau religious, cultural, and linguistic life. Patriarchy, she
argues, is a tool of settler colonialism, undermining Indigenous values, spirituality,
knowledge, and social cohesion. Hierarchical worldviews reduce the landscape to
a collection of objects, occluding the sentience, subjectivity, and inherent spiritual
value of the natural world. For Jacob, reclaiming the sacred role of women is inherently intertwined with healing from colonialism and reclaiming their lands.

Southwest

Pueblo, Diné, and Apache cultures in the Southwest are matrilineal and matrilocal.
Within matrilocal communities, one's primary identification is with one's maternal
grandmother's clan and their land. Broadly speaking, women hold primary ownership and authority within domestic spheres of life, while men are responsible for
those tasks that take them away from home: warfare, politics, hunting. Men are
more likely to be ceremonial leaders and singers, and among Pueblo communities,
men's sacred societies appear to dominate religious life. But women are also trained
as singers, spiritual mentors, and healers, and women maintain separate ritual and
ceremonial practices that honor the female cycle of life.

Among Pueblo agricultural communities like the Hopi, the ceremonial year is
divided between men's and women's responsibilities: men's ceremonies are held
during the first half of the year: the time of planting and rain. Women's ceremonies are held during the second half of the year: the time of harvest. This gendered
organization of time and society is vital to their cosmology, which emphasizes a
harmonious balance between the masculine and the feminine.

Enrique Salmón discusses Hopi agriculture in his book *Eating the Landscape*,
describing a time when he brought his students to visit with a Hopi family. When
several of the young men offered to help in the kitchen, they were given a lesson
in Hopi culture. Jane, the family's matriarch,

> quickly and assertively told the young men that offered to help that their place was
> with the other men in the living and dining rooms. To Jane, the kitchen was the
> realm of women with little room for men. This was not a conservative antifeminist
> stance, but one that reflected centuries of Hopi gender roles. In most American In-
> dian communities, traditional women's roles are viewed as equal to and sometimes
> more important than those of men. At Hopi, women reflect the core Hopi base
> metaphor, which is that corn is mother. Mothers and women are the foundation
> of Hopi life, and everything that is done. At Hopi, the clan system remains vibrant
> due to a matrilineal system that passes down knowledge and kinship through the
> mother's side of the family. (Salmón, 61)

The Sacred Feminine in Native American Traditions

Economics, social organization, and the demands of the land all help to account for the relatively egalitarian complementary gender roles of traditional Indigenous cultures. Respect and reverence for women are also guided by stories and ceremonies that honor the sacred feminine. Throughout Native North American oral traditions, female holy people, creators, saviors, and spiritual beings shape the world, form human beings out of clay, and teach the humans how to live.

Throughout Native North America, one finds stories of Father Sky and Mother Earth. While the stories differ in their particulars, this veneration of the earth as one's mother is shared across Indigenous cultures and traditions, forming a foundational story that underpins ethics of care, reverence, and relationship with the land. It implies an earth that is not simply rock, gas, and resource, but a living being. Calling earth *mother* implies a spirit of love, care, self-sacrifice, discipline, correction, nurture, and wisdom.

Other sacred female figures are responsible for creating and shaping the world or giving life to human beings. Revered throughout many Indigenous cultures of the American Southwest, Spider Woman is a creator, weaving the world into being. Associated with water, sacred springs, and the renewal of life, Spider Woman weaves life on her loom, building the intricate patterns of an ever-becoming story. In Haudenosaunee tradition, the creation of the earth began with Sky Woman falling from the heavens. Birds flocked to slow her descent, and animals gathered to keep her aloft on the oceans covering the earth. Floating on the back of a great turtle, Sky Woman was sustained by the sea animals that provided her with food. They gathered mud for her from the bottom of the sea, and she spread it on the turtle's back, creating Turtle Island (North America). Sky Woman sowed the first plants across the great back of Turtle Island, preparing the ground for other animals that would come later. When humans came, she asked the plants to be their teachers, showing them how to live on this new land. In the Apache and Diné traditions, when Changing Woman was first discovered, she was emerging from a pool of water, covered in the brilliant gold of cattail pollen and the ochre of clay. She grew to maturity in just a few weeks, the first to experience the girls' coming-of-age ceremony that would become the basis of the Diné Kinaaldá and Apache Isanaklesh Gotal. She shaped human beings from clay and taught them how to live in the newly created world, instructing them in the use of plants for food and medicine.

Other sacred female figures brought food, new ceremonies, and wisdom that saved human beings from starvation and gave them the tools to live well. For instance, variations of the Corn Mother story are widespread throughout North America. In many iterations, Corn Mother visits a starving community and provides food for them by rubbing her skin and producing corn. In other stories, Corn Mother instructs the people to bury her near their village, predicting that a new kind of plant would spring from her grave. She tells them how to gather and plant, ensuring future harvests. A powerful story of the origin of a sacred food, it is also a meditation on the nature of life arising from death, of sacrifice, and the nature of motherhood. On the Northern Plains, one of the most important holy people is

White Buffalo Calf Woman. During a time of great famine, two young men went out hunting, hoping to find something to bring back to their people. When they saw an approaching figure, they were shocked to discover it was a beautiful young woman. One of the men tried to rape her, but a cloud descended upon him, and when it lifted, the young man had been reduced to bones. The other begged for pardon, falling on his knees and averting his eyes. The woman took pity on him and told him to return home, telling the community that she would come to help. When she arrived, the people greeted her, giving her the best of everything they had. In return, she taught them the ceremonies that lie at the heart of Lakota religious life today: one of which is the girls' coming-of-age ceremony. Finally, she gave them the White Buffalo Calf Pipe, and taught them how to pray. As she left, she was transformed into a white bison. Chief Arvol Looking Horse is the nineteenth keeper of the White Buffalo Calf Pipe, the same given to his ancestors by White Buffalo Calf Woman.

Finally, there are countless female spiritual beings, found throughout the natural world and described in oral traditions, who offer the people spiritual support and guidance. Among Coast Salish communities in the Pacific Northwest, for instance, western red cedar is known as Sequalal: Grandmother Cedar. Sequalal is endowed by the Creator with the gifts of memory, compassion, and wisdom. Her branches are burned to purify spaces and minds. The wood of her body is used to build homes, canoes, bentwood boxes, and serving dishes. Her inner bark is peeled, pounded, and used to make baskets, clothing, hats, and other adornments. Her life and spirit remains within these objects, carrying her memory, compassion, and wisdom. Carved from cedar, objects like canoes and welcome poles are living things, retaining her spirit. Old-growth cedar is one of the most important elements among Native Northwest coastal cultures, and Grandmother Cedar is a powerful spiritual entity that nurtures her people and inspires them to fight for her protection.

Gender and Ceremony

The complementary roles of women and men are reflected in rituals and ceremonial obligations. Some ritual and ceremonial activities are performed in virtually identical ways, regardless of whether the practitioners are male or female: the structure of a vision quest, a sweat lodge, or a rite of thanksgiving will be much the same. At the same time, of course, one's experience of a ritual or ceremony is shaped by personal identity and experience, which includes gender.

In other instances, men and women have separate ceremonial obligations. Girls' coming-of-age ceremonies are a particularly powerful example of this. Indigenous cultures honor the arrival of a girl's first menstrual cycle in different ways: it may be a private family matter or cause for community-wide celebration. It may call young girls into a time of quiet seclusion, or it may demand a show of public leadership. Regardless, all of these traditions share a reverence for women's ability to create new life and emphasize the sacred value of girls and women as culture bearers and leaders.

Insanaklesh Gotal

Among Apache communities, a girl's coming of age is celebrated with an eight-day *gotal* (sing). During the ceremony, the girl becomes the embodiment of Changing Woman, 'Isánaklesh, and is sung into adulthood. After a young woman has her first period, a year of preparation for the ceremony begins. She and her family gather all the necessary materials and begin creating her ceremonial regalia. Depending on her community, such regalia might be a heavy buckskin or cotton cloth covered in beadwork and metal cones. Pollen, sacred clay, and other materials are gathered. A ceremonial singer (*gutaal*) is found. Guided by her sponsor (*naaikish*), the girl trains throughout the year, running and studying the language, songs, and dances of her people.

On the first day of the ceremony, the family constructs the ceremonial tipi where the girl will stay for eight days. She is transformed through ritual bathing and dressing, her hair washed with yucca soap. Her diet is restricted, her speech and movement limited: for eight days, she will drink through a special drinking tube and use a special scratching stick. She carries a cattail-pollen bag, which she will use to offer blessings to anyone who requests it. Songs are sung as the tipi is raised, lifted up as the sun crests the horizon. The singer draws footprints in pollen, and the girl follows these steps, running to the east. For the next four days, the young woman will be secluded during the day, resting, praying, and blessing others.

In the evening, the girl listens as the singer's songs describe the creation of the world and the Apache people. From dusk until late into the night, the girl dances at the door of her tipi. The Gaahe, mountain spirits, dance as well: men don remarkable regalia and are transformed into the mountain spirits who have arrived to support the girl. The Gaahe dance around an enormous bonfire, offering her their strength, spiritual power, protection, and encouragement.

For the first three nights, the girl will dance until late into the night. On the fourth night, she will dance until dawn. Songs carry time, while also helping each individual be present in the moment. Inés Talamantez and Ann Shapiro have observed the role of music and song in this sacred ceremony, noting that "those elements which in music help mark the passage of time: pulse, repetitions, change and silence are a carefully structured part of the ceremony, and give a grace, flexibility, and logic to it, felt by participants and audience alike" (Talamantez and Shapiro, 78). Music is a powerful mnemonic device, helping to fix core teachings in the mind and the heart. At the same time, the repetition of the songs allows space where thoughts can wander. "The girl seems to be in a trance-like state as she dances back and forth, staring into the fire. The Singer instructs her to think in images about the tribe—to think, for instance of a sick grandfather, and to send his sickness over the mountain away from the tribe—images of motion and healing, in other words, against the static music of dance and movement" (Talamantez and Shapiro, 86).

On the last morning, they greet the dawn. The girl is painted with clay and covered in pollen, just as Changing Woman was when she emerged from the water. The community is blessed with clay and pollen, particularly the young, the

Photo 7.2.   On the San Carlos Apache reservation, thirteen-year-old Little Cornflower participated in her coming-of-age ceremony on April 30, 1955. She was accompanied by her sponsor, a woman appointed by her family and who had trained her in the rituals for many months. During the ceremony. initiates are the embodiment of Isánàklesh (White Painted Woman). Through the ceremony, girls learn how to live as Apache women, and the entire community is reminded of the sacred role that women play within the world. (Associated Press)

elders, and the sick. The girl is led out of the tipi and once again follows the pollen footprints on the buckskin, before running to the east. This public part of the ceremony concludes with an enormous feast and gifts to all who attended. For the girl, however, the ceremony will continue with four more days of prayerful quiet reflection in the ceremonial tipi, accompanied only by her singer, sponsor, and immediate family.

Photo 7.3.   Apache Mountain Spirit Dancers. On Thursday, November 18, 2010, Grand Canyon National Park celebrated Native American Heritage Month. In this photo, the Dishchii' Bikoh' Apache Group from Cibecue, Arizona, demonstrates the Apache Crown Dance. (NPS Photo by Michael Quinn. Wikimedia Commons, Public Domain, https://commons.wikimedia.org/wiki/File:Grand_Canyon_Native _American_Heritage_Day_0651.jpg)

Diné Kinaaldá

Like the Isanaklesh Gotal, the Diné Kinaaldá entails a year of preparation during which the girl trains, improving her physical stamina, and learns about Diné traditions, beliefs, and what is expected of traditional Diné women. Her family gathers all of the material needed for the multiday event: food, ritual objects, minerals, and corn. Her dress will be woven on a loom in the Diné tradition: perhaps from the family's own sheep, whose wool will be spun and died by hand.

Through their Kinaaldá, young women become the embodiment of Changing Woman. A source of healing, balance, harmony, and beauty, Changing Woman created and shaped human beings, bringing fertility into the world. The four-day ceremony reflects the importance of the four directions in Diné cosmology and their association with particular holy people (ye'ii), the four sacred mountains that define Diné homeland, the four clans of one's grandparents, and the four stages of one's life.

The girl will remain awake through the night in the ceremonial hogan, while the singer (hataałi) and his assistants sing the ceremonial songs. Her hair will be washed and combed, her body massaged and molded by her female mentor, shaping her into the form of Changing Woman. By the end of the fourth night, the transformation is complete: she has become Changing Woman. Each morning and evening, the girl will run to the east, going farther each time. Throughout the day, she will be sung over, special rituals will be held, and she will work, grinding cornmeal on a large flat stone to create the fine cornmeal necessary for her *alkaan*, an enormous cornmeal cake baked on the final day of the Kinaaldá. A pit oven (about four feet in diameter and one foot deep) will be lined with coals. These will be covered with earth and then with fresh cornhusks. The batter will be baked in this earthen oven, and everyone present will be given a piece of the cake, receiving the blessing that comes with it.

Northern California Flower Dance

According to a Native Northern California story, when Wespurowak (the Creator) was bringing the world into being, the Creator offered *wogey* (immortals) a choice of form: some became fish, others became animals, plants, or humans. After a time, the fish, animals, and plants began to complain. Things weren't fair, they said. Human beings ate them, causing them pain, but these humans scarcely suffered at all. Human women heard these complaints, and together they wondered what could be done. They came to a decision. The human women spoke with Wespurowak and offered to take a share of pain. They would bleed once every month in payment for the lives of deer, salmon, and acorns. So moved by their offer, Wespurowak created a lake for the women. It would be a sacred place, in the center of the sky, where women could go to bathe and pray. Yurok scholar Mary Virginia Rojas and Hupa scholar Cutcha Risling Baldy point out that this story presents a different way of thinking about menstruation. Rather than a curse for original sin (as suggested in the biblical tradition), menstruation was a choice, an offering, a sacrifice women offered up in exchange for the many gifts they received from creation.

In Native Northern California cultures, girls' first menses are greeted with a coming-of-age ceremony, the Flower Dance. The ceremony may last three, five, or ten days, during which a variety of activities take place (talking circles, fasting, bathing, steaming, and lessons in herbalism, weaving, and language), providing the young women and their community with opportunities to learn about traditional culture, values, and spirituality. Each day, initiates run along ancient trails to sacred bathing places, visiting sites where their female ancestors had prayed for millennia. They wear special regalia, such as a veil of blue jay feathers that partially obscures their vision. At each site, they offer songs and prayers and bathe in sacred pools. Throughout the night, their community gathers around them. The girls might sit quietly as women, men, and children sing and pray over them, or they might try not to laugh when they sing ribald songs or crack jokes, teasing them that laughing during one's Flower Dance could mean wrinkles when one is older.

The Flower Dance was suspended during the era of the Gold Rush, when prospectors filled the valleys and mountains of Northern California. They raided villages, assaulting, kidnapping, and forcing young girls into slavery. This meant Native Californian women and girls could no longer safely visit their sacred sites. Along with violence, settlers brought disease: epidemics swept through the region, devastating families. And later, government officials took the children away, placing them in far-off boarding schools. Under dire stressors such as these, ceremonies like the Flower Dance nearly died out. But in the 1990s, women began revitalizing their ceremonies, calling for a return to traditional ways of seeing and rearing young women.

In her book *We Are Dancing for You: Native Feminisms and the Revitalization of Women's Coming of Age Ceremonies*, Cutcha Risling Baldy describes the importance of these ceremonies for contemporary Native Northern California women.

> As I have continued to participate in Ch'ilwa:l ceremonies, it has become very clear to me that the resurgence of the Ch'ilwa:l is a tangible, physical, spiritual and communal act of healing and decolonization . . . revitalized women's ceremonies (re) write, (re)right and (re)rite the roles and status of women in our community. . . . These are the spaces that help us decolonize our bodies; they are the locations of decolonization, where we sing and dance together and where our young women embody our First People so that connection can never be severed. (Risling Baldy, 128–29, 151–52)

In her book, Risling Baldy records an interview with one mother explaining the ceremony's importance for her daughter:

> What I hoped I was doing was balancing her spirit, putting on what I characterized as a suit of armor so that in going out into the world [she would] know who she is as a Hupa person, that nobody would be able to disrupt anything. And that's held true, she's held her ground in a number of different places, in a number of different countries, in a number of different languages—that has held true. She knows who she is and can call on that strength at any given time; call on the strength that is Hupa, the land, the people, the language [and] the ancestors. (Risling Baldy, 133)

In her work, Rojas considers why young women are required to only scratch themselves using special scratching sticks (*sado'ktcuts*) during their Flower Dance. Treasured heirlooms carved from wood, bone, or shell, Rojas argues that *sado'ktcuts* provide a means of engaging in "mindful prayer." "Meditation is the moment-to-moment awareness of self within the cosmos. . . . Generations of women perfected a methodology and a technology that would permit ritual participants to have a transcendental experience . . . to be one with the 'holy'" (Rojas, 136).

The work of Alfred Kroeber, Thomas Buckley, and contemporary Indigenous scholars like Risling Baldy and Rojas have helped to recover Native Northern California menstrual practices. Traditionally, each month, menstruating women took a respite from their labors, retreating to women's houses, running to and bathing in sacred places, and engaging in prayer and meditation. During this time, the work of caring for home and children was left to older women and men. Until recently, anthropologists and historians saw this as evidence that women's biological cycles were seen as "unclean." However, early ethnographic evidence and continuing oral tradition among these communities shows this was not the case. Women were in fact seen as particularly powerful, and their monthly bleeding was understood to be a form of physical and spiritual purification. Strikingly, young men took part in parallel acts of separation and purification: running, training, praying, sweating in the men's house, and bathing in nearby streams. Women, it was understood, did not need to sweat because their bodies naturally purified themselves each month.

> The sweat house is referred to as a womb and everyone that enters or leaves it must do so backwards as we are born into this world. The same is true for the traditional houses: they must be entered and left the same way. The house and the sweat are woman. Here [*Weitchpec*] when a man sweats for a good purpose, he sweats ten nights. That is the same amount of time that a woman is relieved of household duties when she is on her moontime . . . it is because men must purify themselves artificially, where the process to do that occurs naturally in woman. That's why here, woman have no need to sweat. (Rojas, 143)

In Northern California, men and women play complementary roles within a religious life intended to maintain health and restore balance to the world. Women are most often called upon to be doctors, committing to the difficult training, fasting, purification, dreaming, dancing, and prayer that it requires. They lead healing ceremonies such as the Brush Dance, a multiday ceremony held during the summer months to heal sick children and restore community. Men in turn lead the powerful World Renewal ceremony, held during the summer to balance the world. In the girls' coming-of-age ceremony, men play a supporting role. As Risling Baldy explains, "Men are also an important part of this dance, because they are an important part of the young woman's community. . . . A man must run with the young woman on her last day as a representation of how men can support her as she moves through adulthood." In so doing, the ceremony "empowers young men to embrace Hupa epistemologies of gender balance and respect" (Risling Baldy, 145).

Isna Ti Ca Lowan

Among Siouxan cultures on the Northern Plains, a young girl's coming of age is celebrated. The Lakota Isna Ti Ca Lowan centers on four days of seclusion in a ceremonial tipi, during which a sacred altar is constructed, and a medicine man sings and prays over the young woman. Throughout this sacred time, the young woman becomes the manifestation of White Buffalo Calf Woman, and is welcomed with prayer and honor.

In one contemporary adaptation of the rite, the ceremony is led exclusively by women. In the 1990s, women on the Yankton Sioux/Ihanktonwan Oyate Reservation in South Dakota were determined to revitalize the Brave Heart Women's Society, a society of women warriors traditionally tasked with retrieving wounded warriors from the battlefield. In NPR's "Four Days, Nights," Faith Spotted Eagle, one of the founders of today's society, saw a connection. "In a way we are doing the same thing today with our modern Brave Hearts, bringing back our people from emotional death."

Within their rite of transformation, girls build their own tipi, wear handmade regalia, and receive lessons in herbalism, traditional foods, courtship, ethics, self-care, and the dangers of drugs and alcohol. The women talk openly about difficult things: violence, suicide, sexual abuse. They are fed by their mothers, aunts, and grandmothers and are forbidden to feed themselves. At the conclusion of the four days, they are presented to their communities and celebrated as powerful women and as bearers of culture and the future.

Two Spirits

This part of the chapter considers the significance of gender nonconformity and sexual diversity in the sacred traditions and cultures of Native North America. Given the high value placed on distinct gender roles, one might expect a demand for gender conformity in these communities. But Will Roscoe, Walter Williams, and Sabine Lang argued that in the vast majority of cases, Indigenous communities in North America included and honored individuals who did not fit within typically gendered identities. Roscoe argues that Two Spirit traditions can be found across Indigenous North America, noting surveys that document them throughout the continent, among all language groups, and in every kind of Indigenous community, from the Southwest, to the Plains, to the Arctic.

Two Spirit refers to Indigenous people who do not identify as heterosexual, who do not identify with typical gender roles, or who do not identify with the sex assigned them at birth. Until the 1980s, the term *berdache* was often used to refer to such individuals, but it has been widely rejected today, in part because it derives from a French term for a male slave or prostitute. Since the 1990s, *Two Spirit* has become the preferred term, referring to Indigenous spiritual teachings that such individuals are valued and important because they embody both male and female spirits.

Two Spirit individuals held particular ceremonial, ritual, and social responsibilities, mediating between men and women and having rare access to both male and female sacred responsibilities. They were able to embody in one person the complementary balance between genders—so sought after in the wider world. For instance, poet and essayist Deborah Miranda (Chumash) discusses the role Two Spirit people played in caring for the dead in Native California. Because they occupied a liminal space between genders, Two Spirit people were able to mediate experiences: between genders, and between the living and the dead. They were equipped with special training, special tools, and personal spiritual gifts that enabled them to do this important work.

In many instances, being Two Spirit was not simply tolerated, but was considered a revered spiritual calling. If it came in a dream or vision, such a calling was considered to be from the Creator or the holy people and, as such, had to be honored. Spiritual callings were accompanied by strengths that the individual would bring to his or her community. In some cases, Two Spirit people were revered as holy people, endowed with remarkable gifts and abilities, and blessed with what Williams has called "double vision," the ability to see two worlds at once.

Lozen (1840–1890)

Lozen (Chiricahua Apache) was a distinguished warrior and horsewoman. After her vision quest, she was endowed with great spiritual power and was determined never to marry. A formidable fighter, healer, prophet, horse thief, and medicine woman, she served alongside Geronimo, who guided her through years of resistance.

Kau'xuma'nupika (b. 1810)

Kau'xuma'nupika was a Ktunaxa/Kutenai prophet, healer, interpreter, and warrior, who traveled throughout the Columbia Plateau in the first half of the nineteenth century. Born a woman, she grew up and married within her Kutenai community. As a young adult, however, she became seriously ill, traveling to the land of the dead, where the spirits informed her that she would no longer be a woman but would return to life as a man. He awoke, with a new name: Kau'xuma'nupika, Gone to the Spirits. Kau'xuma'nupika went on to marry several women in succession, traveling throughout the interior of the Northwest as a guide, translator, courier, and prophet. He predicted a coming spiritual and epidemiological apocalypse, which proved to be eerily prescient. Kau'xuma'nupika was killed as he helped a group of Flathead escape a Blackfoot raid. Observers reported that he was nearly impossible to kill. His supernatural abilities seemed to protect him: bullets and knives scarcely touched him, and it was only when his heart was removed that he ceased to breathe. Observers reported that wild animals would not go near the body, and his spirit harried his attackers all the way to their home.

We'wha (Zuñi)

Born male, We'wha identified as female and was a respected expert in Zuñi arts and culture. Appointed as a delegate to represent her people in Washington, DC, in 1886, We'wha met with and was received as a woman by President Cleveland, members of the Supreme Court, senators, congressmen, and administrators at the Smithsonian.

Hastiin Klah (1867–1936)

Nadłeehi is a Diné (Navajo) term for Two Spirit individuals who are biologically male but identify as female. Nadłeehi were valued within traditional Diné society, blessed with the ability (and social sanction) to move back and forth between male and female worlds. In the Diné creation account, they played a particularly important role. In the third world, men and women fought and separated. Moving to opposite sides of a river, they refused to speak to one another. But the world was ravaged by monsters, and the people's very existence was threatened. Still they refused to compromise. It was the nadłeehi who traveled back and forth across the river, brokering a truce. The people were reunited, and so survived.[1]

Maureen Trudelle Schwarz and Gabriel Estrada have explored the Diné notion of sa'ąh naagháí bik'eh hózhó, a philosophical idea sometimes translated as "the essence of long life, peace and harmony." Schwarz and Estrada both note that the term comprises sa'ąh naagháí (male) and bik'eh hózhó (female) spiritual elements inherent in all creation. Estrada points out that Diné philosophers have described

Photo 7.4. We'wha, a Zuñi lhamana, weaving. In Zuñi culture lhamana are biological males, who adopt and live out traditionally female roles. A respected cultural ambassador, We'wha was a skilled artist and ceremonial leader, who performed in both male and female ceremonial and artistic tasks. (Smithsonian Institution. Bureau of American Ethnology)

sa'ąh naagháí as a "protective element" and *bik'eh hózhó* as a "blessing element" (Estrada 2011, 180). Health and harmony occur when these two elements are held in balance, such as when men and women work together in peaceful collaboration. Two Spirit individuals have a particular blessing, because this balance can happen within one person. As Diné scholar Wesley Thomas notes, Two Spirit people "were herbalists. They were negotiators. They were healers. They were match-makers. They counseled couples. And when children were orphaned, the *naddleeh* would become the caretakers of the children" (Estrada 2011, 171). When he was young, it was Thomas's grandmother who explained to him: "That's who you are. That's what you were born into. Nobody has the power to derail you from that, not even yourself, because that's a power that's given to you by the Holy People" (Estrada 2011, 172).

In the Diné language, there are four words for four genders, just as there are four directions, four sacred mountains, four clans, four times of day, four seasons of the year, and four times of life. The first gender, associated with the east, is "*asdzáán*, feminine woman," associated with the matrilocal and matrilineal bases of Diné culture. The second, associated with the south, is "*hastíín*, masculine man." The third gender, associated with the west, is "*nádleehí*, feminine man," one who is "born as a male person but functions in the role of girl in the early childhood and functions more in the role a woman in adulthood." The fourth gender, associated with the north, is "*dilbaa*, masculine woman," those who carry out male gender roles within a biologically female body (Estrada 2011, 172).

Hastiin Klah was one of the most famous of *nadłeehi*. He was a medicine man and artist, working with the ceremonial sandpainting tradition that is largely the purview of men. He was also a famous weaver, an art typically reserved for women. His status as *nadłeehi* allowed him to move between worlds, learning both, which he demonstrated at the 1893 World Expo in Chicago. A powerful ceremonial leader, Hastiin Klah mastered eight chantways (most ceremonialists learn one or two), and was one of the founders of the Wheelwright Museum of the American Indian in Santa Fe, New Mexico.

Challenging Homophobia

Settler colonialism undermined Indigenous Two Spirit traditions. Historian Mark Rifkin has documented the impact of heteronormativity within nineteenth-century settler imperialism as it worked to break down Indigenous worldviews, kinship, land tenure, and modes of governance, enforcing patriarchy and private property at the expense of tribe and kin. Indigenous women and Two Spirit people saw their places in traditional economies, ceremonies, and social organization undermined. As patriarchal and heteronormative worldviews came to dominate, Two Spirit people were increasingly ostracized or forced to conceal their identities. As Chris Finley has argued, "This attitude of silence has more intense consequences for Native peoples, because of the relationship of sexuality to colonial power. . . . Heterosexism and the structure of the nuclear family needs to be thought of as a colonial system of violence" (Finley, 32). Finley, along with other scholars, activists, and community members, is working to reclaim the place of Two Spirit people in Indigenous communities.

Reclaiming Erotic Sovereignty

Contemporary Two Spirit authors argue that a key element of decolonizing must include reclaiming Indigenous traditions of sexual diversity. Ritual, ceremony, and sacred stories provide spaces where this healing can occur. In such a context, gay pride parades serve as a new kind of ceremony where Two Spirit people don their regalia, dance their traditional dances, and identify as both Indigenous and queer.

The Green Country Two Spirit Society is another such space for reclaiming Two Spirit people's place in Indigenous culture. The society began as an HIV clinic for Native men, then expanded to include bisexual and transgender people and women. Eventually it became more than a clinic, offering workshops, gatherings, and opportunities where Two Spirit people could celebrate their cultures. In his work, Brian Joseph Gilley describes a Two Spirit stomp dance, transformed to meet this particular community's needs. Here Two Spirit people can move freely between gender roles, dressing in women's or men's dance regalia, leading the women's or men's dances as they prefer. Participants learn from elders and are welcomed into a sacred circle of learning. Some participants, Gilley notes, will drive up to three hours to attend bimonthly gatherings, while others might travel a thousand miles to join the annual stomp dance. An organizer explained, "The gathering is so popular because of the balance between Native and gay cultural practices. Some of these queens have never been around traditional activities and we can't shove it down their throat. We are also here to have fun and to show people how to be healthy two-spirits" (Gilley 2004, 85). At the weekend camp, participants join in a drag show, powwow, and Stomp Dance.

Gender roles are strictly defined at normative Stomp Dances. Dancers circle a ceremonial fire, while the male song leader guides the dance. Women follow men, keeping time by stomping their rattles; lines alternate, male and female. Because of its strict gender division and the lingering homophobia within many communities, Two Spirit people are rarely inclined to cross those gendered lines. At a Two Spirit Stomp Dance, however, they are free to dance in the role that fits best, wearing shells or stomp dance skirts, or alternating roles throughout the weekend. As one participant explained, "I can dance here at the gathering how the creator intended me to . . . as a two-spirit person" (Gilley 2004, 89).

As Gilley explains, the purpose of such events is not to undermine, but rather *affirm* traditional Indigenous cultures, including their role in those communities.

> At powwows around Oklahoma, Ben is usually a straight male dancer, but at this event he was fulfilling a long-held desire to powwow dance in female regalia. For Ben, this self-described "switch" culminated and resolved years of struggle to adapt his sex and gender identity to his Native culture. Ben saw his participation as a woman in the gathering powwow as a way to "take back" the years of shame he endured because of his gender identity and to honor "the child who knew what gender it wanted to be." (Gilley, 90)

The Montana Two Spirit Society provides another example of spaces where individuals can celebrate Indigenous culture, spirituality, and Two Spirit identities. Formed in 1996, today, nearly one hundred attendees travel to Montana each summer to participate in the annual multiday gathering, which has grown to include a special gathering for Two Spirit youth.

In his work as a poet and essayist, Qwo-Li Driskill argues that reclaiming Two Spirit erotic sovereignty is a vital piece of decolonization.

> My own resistance to colonization as a Cherokee Two-Spirit is intimately connected to my continuing efforts to heal from sexual assault and the manifestation of an oppressive overculture on my erotic life. . . . My own journey back to my body, and the journeys of other first nations people back to their bodies, necessarily engage historical trauma. Our erotic lives and identities have been colonized along with our homelands. . . . I have not only been removed from my homelands, I have also been removed from my erotic self and continue a journey back to my first homeland: the body. (Driskill, 51–53)

Like Driskill, poet Chrystos (Menominee) sees reclaiming her erotic identity as part of her decolonizing praxis. In "Tenderly Your," Chrystos frames eroticism as a path toward healing:

> We're in the grass of prairies our grandmothers rode
> Sweet smell of distant cookpots edges the blue
> Your kisses are a hundred years old & newly born
> [. . .]
> Flaming ride us past our rapes our pain
> past years when we stumbled lost.

Finally, one might consider the work of Cree artist Kent Monkman, which has been described as a playful subversion of classic tropes and styles (landscapes, still lifes, seated portraits) employed in ways that challenge Indigenous stereotypes, settler colonialism, and heteronormativity. In his painting *The Scream*, Monkman captures the horror of the forced removal of children as they are abducted by agents of church and state, and removed to residential schools.

It is Monkman's alter ego *Miss Chief Testickle* that usually garners the most attention. A warrior dressed in thigh-high red stiletto boots, *Miss Chief* upends stereotypes and shocks heteronormative sensibilities. In the installation *Lot's Wife*, Monkman reflects on his Cree great-grandmother's exile from her homeland. Like Lot's wife she, too, looked back. But here it is Miss Chief who claims her right to look back, embodying the visceral longing for home. Monkman explains:

> She is looking at her great-grand-mother's land; her longing is physically mani-
> fested. Miss Chief is also Lot's wife, who is punished for looking back at the "sinful"
> city of Sodom after God had told Lot's family not to look back at the city's destruc-
> tion. Lot's wife was supposedly contaminated by Sodom's depravity and is punished
> for disobeying God's edict. Similarly, Miss Chief is supposed to forget her family's
> land. But her arousal signals erotic sovereignty. The two-spirit Miss Chief cannot
> forget her place both in history and on the land. (Scuderer, 28)

Conclusion

The tactics and techniques of colonialism are gendered, impacting women, girls, and Two Spirit individuals in particular ways, and with particular violence. But elders, historians, and cultural experts attest that in pre-colonial cultures, women and Two Spirit people had access to economic, political, spiritual, and artistic power. While occupying different roles and maintaining different responsibili-ties, they nonetheless had social capital, acting as respected members within their communities. Religious traditions provided ritual and ceremonial spaces to honor women and girls, and sacred stories provided examples of female holy people who created and healed the world. Two Spirit people were honored in legends, and fulfilled sacred obligations that only they could. Under colonialism, women lost ac-cess to traditional forms of economic and political power, while Two Spirit people

Photo 7.5. *The Scream* by Kent Monkman (Cree), 2017. The painting calls attention to the forcible removal of First Nations children from their families and communities. (Denver Art Museum, courtesy of Kent Monkman)

faced denigration and ridicule at best, and brutal violence at worst. Fractured by patriarchal and heteronormative polices of settler-colonial culture, contemporary communities continue to wrestle with the impacts of those policies. Indigenous women, girls, and Two Spirit people face staggering rates of violence, homicide, and disappearance. But communities are reclaiming their traditional ways, finding in them a path toward renewing the sacred place of women and Two Spirit people, healing from the soul wounds of colonialism.

Note

1. According to some accounts, it was then that First Man and First Woman (the original holy people and parents of the people) divided up responsibilities, hoping to limit future conflicts: men would be responsible for hunting, warfare, and ceremonial life, while women would own the land and the home and have control over the agricultural and domestic matters. Contemporary female ceremonial leaders reframe this story, pointing instead to the importance of the balance between men and women, and the ways in which these roles had been transformed in recent years: men are allowed to own property and maintain leadership in agricultural matters now. So too, women should be allowed to enter into the ceremonial realm. Chantways do impose limitations on women and men that can prevent them from leading or participating in ceremonies, such as contact with blood. Men cannot attend or participate in a chantway if they have recently been hunting or engaged in warfare. Women cannot attend a ceremony or apprentice while menstruating. For this reason, many female practitioners are postmenopausal.

References and Recommendations

Ackerman, Lillian. "Gender Status in the Plateau," in *Women and Power in Native North America*, edited by Laura Klein and Lillian Ackerman. Norman: University of Oklahoma Press, 1995.

Ackerman, Lillian, and Laura Klein. *Women and Power in Native North America*. Norman: University of Oklahoma Press, 2000.

Allen, Paula Gunn. *The Sacred Hoop: Recovering the Feminine in American Indian Traditions*. Boston: Beacon Press, 1986.

Arvin, Maile, Eve Tuck, and Angie Morrill. "Decolonizing Feminism: Challenging Connections Between Settler Colonialism and Heteropatriarchy," *Feminist Formations* Vol. 25 No. 1 (2013): 8–34.

Barsalou-Verge, Xavier, et al. "Current Knowledge on Child Sexual Abuse in Indigenous Populations of Canada and the United States: A Literature Review," *American Indian Culture and Research Journal* Vol. 39 No. 3 (2015): 65–82.

Buckley, Thomas. "Menstruation and the Power of Yurok Women: Methods in Cultural Reconstruction," *American Ethnologist* Vol. 9 No. 1 (1982): 47–60.

Buckley, Thomas. *Standing Ground: Yurok Indian Spirituality 1850–1990*. Berkeley: University of California Press, 2002.

Chenault, Venida. *Weaving Strength, Weaving Power: Violence and Abuse against Indigenous Women*. Durham, NC: Carolina Academic Press, 2011.

Child, Brenda. *Holding Our World Together: Ojibwe Women and the Survival of Community*. New York: Penguin, 2013.

Chrystos. "Tenderly Your," *In Her I Am*. Vancouver: Press Gang Publishers, 1993.

Crawford O'Brien, Suzanne. "Gone to the Spirits: A Transgender Prophet on the Columbia Plateau," *Journal of Theology and Sexuality* Vol. 21 No. 2 (2015): 125–43.

Deer, Sarah. *The Beginning and End of Rape: Confronting Sexual Violence in Native America*. St. Paul: University of Minnesota Press, 2015.

Driskill, Qwo-Li. "Stolen from Our Bodies: First Nations Two Spirit/Queers and the Journey to a Sovereign Erotic," *Studies in American Indian Literatures* (Summer 2004): 50–64.

Driskill, Qwo-Li, and Daniel Heath Justice. *Sovereign Erotics: A Collection of Two Spirit Literature*. Tucson: University of Arizona Press, 2011.

Edwards, Tai. *Osage Women and Empire: Gender and Power*. Lawrence: University of Kansas Press, 2018.

Epes Brown, Joseph. *The Sacred Pipe: Black Elk's Account of the Seven Rites of the Oglala Sioux*. Norman: University of Oklahoma Press, 1989.

Estrada, Gabriel. "An Aztec Two-Spirit Cosmology: Resounding Nahuatl Masculinities, Elders, Femininities, and Youth," *Frontiers: Journal of Women Studies*, Vol. 24 No. 2/3 (2003): 10–14.

Estrada, Gabriel. "Two Spirits, Nadleeh, and LGBTQ2 Navajo Gaze," *American Indian Culture and Research Journal* Vol. 35 No. 4 (2011): 167–90.

Finley, Chris. "Decolonizing the Queer Native Body (and Recovering the Native Bull-Dyke): Bringing Sexy Back and Out of Native Studies Closet," in *Queer Indigenous Studies: Critical Interventions in Theory, Politics, and Literature*, edited by Quo-Li Driskill, Chris Finley, Brian Joseph Gilley, and Scott Lauria Morgensen. Tucson: University of Arizona Press, 2011.

Gilley, Brian Joseph. "Making Traditional Spaces: Cultural Compromise at Two-Spirit Gatherings in Oklahoma," *American Indian Culture and Research Journal* Vol. 28 No. 2 (2004): 81–95.

Gilley, Brian Joseph. *Becoming Two-Spirit: Gay Identity and Social Acceptance in Indian Country*. Norman: University of Nebraska Press, 2006.

Gonzales, Patricia. *Red Medicine: Traditional Indigenous Rites of Birthing and Healing*. Tucson: University of Arizona Press, 2012.

Harvard, Memee Lavelle. *Until Our Hearts Are on the Ground: Aboriginal Mothering, Oppression, Resistance and Rebirth*. Toronto: Demeter Press, 2006.

Jacob, Michelle. *Yakama Rising: Indigenous Cultural Revitalization, Activism, and Healing*. Tucson: University of Arizona Press, 2013.

Lang, Sabine. *Men as Women, Women as Men: Changing Gender in Native American Cultures*. Austin: University of Texas, 1998.

Lawrence, Jane. "The Indian Health Service and the Sterilization of Native American Women," *American Indian Quarterly* Vol. 24 No. 3 (2000): 400–419.

Matamonasa-Bennett, Arieahn. "Until People Are Given the Right to Be Human Again: Voices of American Indian Men on Domestic Violence and Traditional Values," *American Indian Culture and Research Journal* Vol. 37 No. 4 (2013): 25–52.

McGegney, Sam. *Masculindians: Conversations about Indigenous Manhood*. Winnipeg: University of Manitoba Press, 2014.

Miranda, Deborah. "Extermination of the Joyas: Gendercide in Spanish California," *GLQ: Journal of Lesbian and Gay Studies* Vol. 16 No. 1–2 (2010): 253–84.

Noel, Jan. "Revisiting Gender in Iroquoia," in *Gender and Sexuality in Indigenous North America*, edited by S. Slater and F. Yarbrough. Columbia: University of South Carolina Press, 2011: 54–74.

NPR, Morning Edition. "Four Days, Nights: A Girls Coming of Age Ceremony." https://www.npr.org/templates/story/story.php?storyId=129611281

Pesantubbee, Michelene. *Choctaw Women in a Chaotic World: The Clash of Cultures in the Colonial Southwest.* Albuquerque: University of New Mexico Press, 2005.

Powers, Marla. *Oglala Woman: Myth, Ritual and Reality.* Chicago: University of Chicago Press, 2010.

Rifkin, Mark. *When Did Indians Become Straight? Kinship, the History of Sexuality, and Native Sovereignty.* Oxford, 2011.

Rifkin, Mark. *The Erotics of Sovereignty: Queer Native Writing in the Era of Self-Determination.* St. Paul: University of Minnesota Press, 2012.

Risling Baldy, Cutcha. *We Are Dancing for You: Native Feminisms and the Revitalization of Women's Coming of Age Ceremonies.* Seattle: University of Washington Press, 2018.

Rojas, Mary Virginia. "She Bathes in a Sacred Place, Rites of Reciprocity, Power and Prestige in Alta California," *Wicazo Sa Review* Vol. 18 No. 1: 129–56.

Roscoe, Will. *Changing Ones: Third and Fourth Genders in Native North America.* New York: Palgrave MacMillan, 1998.

Salmón, Enrique. *Eating the Landscape: American Indian Stories of Food, Identity and Resilience.* Tucson: University of Arizona Press, 2012.

Schanche Hodge, Felica. "Breast Cancer Screening Behavior among Rural California American Indian Women" *American Indian Culture and Research Journal* Vol. 33 No. 3 (2009): 35–42.

Scuderer, June. "'Indians on Top': Kent Monkman's Sovereign Erotics," *American Indian Culture and Research Journal* Vol. 39 No. 4 (2015): 19–32.

Slater, Sarah, and Fay Yarbough. *Gender and Sexuality in Indigenous North America 1400–1850.* Columbia: University of South Carolina Press, 2011.

Stote, Karen. "Coercive Sterilization of Aboriginal Women in Canada," *American Indian Culture and Research Journal* Vol. 36 No. 3 (2012): 117–50.

Talamantez, Inés. "The Presence of Isanaklesh: The Apache Female Deity and the Path of Pollen," in *Unspoken Worlds: Women's Religious Lives,* edited by Nancy Aver Falk and Rita Gross. Seattle: Cengage Learning, 2000.

Talamantez, Inés, and Anne Dhu Shapiro. "Mescalero Girls Puberty Ceremony: The Role of Music in Structuring Ritual Time," *Yearbook for Traditional Music* Vol. 18 (1986): 77–90.

Tinker, George. "Jesus, Corn Mother and Conquest," in *Native American Religious Identity,* edited by Jace Weaver. Maryknoll, NY: Orbis Press, 1998.

Trudelle Schwarz, Maureen. *Molded in the Image of Changing Woman: Navajo Views on the Human Body and Personhood.* Tucson: University of Arizona Press, 1997.

Williams, Walter. *Spirit and the Flesh: Sexual Diversity in North America.* Boston: Beacon, 1992.

Websites and Videos

Kent Monkman. http://www.kentmonkman.com/

Montana Two Spirit Society. https://www.mttwospirit.org

National Inquiry Into Missing and Murdered Women and Girls. http://www.mmiwg-ffada.ca

National Indigenous Women's Resource Center. http://www.niwrc.org/resources

National Public Radio. "Four Days, Four Nights: A Girls' Coming of Age Ceremony." https://www.npr.org/templates/story/story.php?storyId=129611281

Native Women's Society of the Great Plains. http://www.nativewomenssociety.org

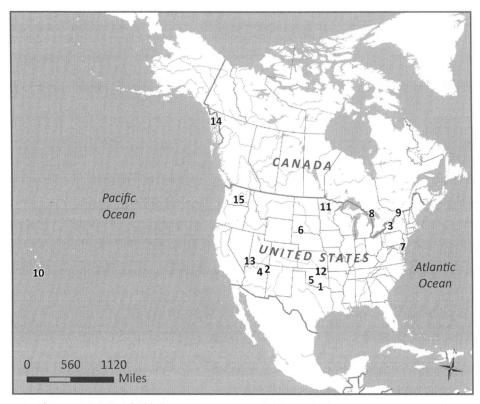

1 Choctaw Nation of Oklahoma
2 Diné (Navajo) Nation
3 Haudenosaunee (Iroquois) Territory
4 Hopi Tribe
5 Kiowa Tribe
6 Lakota Territories
7 Lenape Indian Tribe of Delaware
8 Manitoulin Island
9 Mohawk Nation
10 Native Hawaiian Territories
11 Ojibwe (Anishinaabe) Territories
12 Osage Nation
13 Paiute (Ute) Nation
14 Tlingit and Haida Tribes
15 Wanapum Indian Village

Map 8.1. Map of North America locating the tribal communities, nations, and cultural groups mentioned in this chapter. Basemap data made with Natural Earth. (Liz O'Dea Springborn)

Christianity

8

WHEN I SLIPPED INTO MY SEAT at the United Methodist Church in Apache, Oklahoma, I expected to find myself right at home. The familiar wood pew, the row of red-bound hymnals and black-bound Bibles were all old friends. Head bowed in familiar silence, I readied myself for worship. Then a voice, deep and resonant, carried through the room. My eyes opened, and I looked around, surprised. What was happening? The song was in a language I didn't recognize. No organ or piano accompanied the singer, but a rhythm sounded easy in his voice, and soon I found my knee bouncing in a steady beat. I heard words I recognized: *Jesus, Holy Spirit*, but the rest was a mystery to me. Another song followed where this one left off, then another.

I'd just had my first introduction to Indian hymn singing. Organized in 1945, the UMC Church of Apache is a community of Kiowa, Comanche, and Apache families, and a proud member of the Oklahoma Indian Missionary Conference, a coalition of Native-led churches throughout the region, celebrating Indigenous languages and cultures as gifts from the Creator and integral elements of Christian faith and spiritual life.

Native people's experience with Christianity has been fraught. The call to missionize the New World was used as a rationale for colonialism, evoked as a justification for stripping Indigenous people of their lands, their bodies, their religions, and their cultures. In much the same way that it was used to justify the evils of slavery, Christianity was also employed to justify the conquest and genocide of Indigenous Americans. The gospel was a tool of empire.

But as my experience at the UMC of Apache demonstrates, stopping there provides too simple a picture. One must also ask: What did Native people make of Christianity? How did they respond to it? Challenge it? How did they take up this tool of conquest, refashioning it for their own ends and spiritual empowerment? This chapter demonstrates that Native people engaged with Christianity on their own terms: at times, Native people resisted missionization, rejecting conversion and expelling missionaries from their midst; at others, they accommodated them, strategically incorporating elements of Christian belief and practice, finding spiritual power, healing, and inspiration, while others found ways to walk two paths at once, experiencing them as parallel avenues for spiritual growth and renewal. In this chapter, I briefly introduce the history of missions to North America before going on to consider what Native people have made of Christianity, framing this experience using three conceptual categories: pluralism, inculturation, and decolonization.

Missionization

Spanish Franciscans

The earliest missions to North America were led by the Catholic Franciscans, an arm of the Spanish colonial effort. Established in New Mexico by the 1590s, missions were an extension of Spanish settlements that included army barracks, churches, colonial housing, and plantations. Franciscans mandated church attendance, actively suppressing Indigenous religious practices. But Indigenous people of present-day New Mexico refused to abandon their traditions and continued maintaining their sacred societies and ceremonies. In 1680, the Spanish territorial governor ordered the arrest of forty-seven Pueblo religious leaders, accusing them of sorcery. Four of them were sentenced to death, and the rest were publicly flogged. Pueblo people were outraged; gathering at Santa Fe, they protested en masse, demanding the release of their revered leaders. Then, between August 10 and 21, 1680, the prophet Popé led a revolt against the Spanish. Four hundred Spaniards were killed, and the remaining two thousand fled the region. Decades would pass before Spanish colonial settlers returned to New Mexico. They would again seek to establish their missions. But they never challenged Pueblo religious leaders the same way again.

Franciscan missions were established in Spanish California between 1769 and 1833. Accompanied by military and political might, here too, missions were a tool of colonialism, providing spiritual support for colonial settlers and effective subjugation of Indigenous peoples, working to make them docile subjects and obedient laborers. Spanish militia relocated Indigenous people to closed settlements, known as *reducciones*, governed by Franciscans. Without pay, and without permission to leave, the Indigenous people of the central and southern California coast did the work of the mission: farming, building, sewing, cleaning, cooking, candle making.

Mission leaders have become notorious for the harsh punishments meted out to Native people who tried to escape or failed to comply with mission rules. Common punishments included being locked in confinement cells, public lashings and beatings, and denial of food. The conventional wisdom of the day meant that conversion entailed complete submission to church authority, and disobedience called for corporal punishment. But Indigenous parishioners in the California mission system were not merely subject to church authority, they were also confined as prisoners and slaves. Unmarried women and men were housed in separate dormitories, locked in at night to prevent unapproved socializing. Families lived under the close supervision of the Franciscan fathers. In close quarters, disease spread rapidly, resulting in devastating mortality rates.

In 2015, the Catholic Church granted sainthood to Junípero Serra. Father of the California mission system, Serra personally founded ten of its twenty-one missions. Many Native Californians were outraged: to them, Serra was a symbol of colonial brutality and genocide. How, they asked, could the church canonize a man who "physically beat the Indians, forced conversions, failed to learn their languages, denigrated their cultures, worked for the infamous Spanish Inquisition, and established what we would identify as 'concentration camps'?" (Beebe and Sancowicz, 29).

Serra's defenders cautioned against judging a historical figure by present-day ethical standards. They emphasized Serra's love for the communities he served and the lengths he went to protect them. They explained that it was Spanish law, not just Serra, that infantilized Native people, placing them under the custodial care of the church. As neophytes, California Natives were expected to submit to the church, and were subject to physical punishment if they failed to do so. At times, such discipline might be excessive. As Father Serra himself wrote in 1780, "I am willing to admit that in the infliction of the punishment we are now discussing, there may have been inequalities and excesses on the part of some of the Fathers and we are all exposed to err in that regard" (Sandos 1988, 1254–55).

Historian James A. Sandos explores the life and context of Serra and the California mission system. While agreeing that scholars must be cautious about judging historical figures by present standards, he argues that canonization is a different matter, requiring that Serra's ethics and morals transcend time and place.

> Sainthood means that his is a universal example for all Catholics to follow. . . . But, if Serra's hagiography ignores the controversy over Indian punishment, and if his missiology is today set aside, what then would Serra exemplify? Concern for the unfortunate? If so, it was concern administered with corporal punishment judged excessive at the time by both the Spanish and the Indians. Are we to believe that Serra's concern, though expressed in a manner physically damaging to Native Americans, is nevertheless to be universally exemplary because his intention was to save immortal souls? Cannot the Indian interpretation also be applied, namely, that sainthood for Serra is yet another example of white over red, of European dominance over aboriginal culture, but this time not only justified but glorified in the name of religion? (Sandos 1988, 1269)

Jesuits of New France

Another type of early missionary activity in North America came through the French colonial effort. The Jesuit missions in New France and the Great Lakes region began as early as 1608, differing greatly from their Spanish Franciscan counterparts. Jesuit missions were small and not accompanied by large-scale settlements or military escort. Instead, Jesuits traveled alone or in pairs, living alongside Native people as they gradually grew their mission. Jesuits studied Indigenous languages and cultures, recording what they learned in some of the earliest eth-nographic texts.

Despite this difference in approach, Jesuits shared the assumption that Indige-nous people were in danger of damnation, and only full conversion to the Christian faith could save their souls. Importantly, conversion was not just theological, but required an entire cultural transformation. Jesuits challenged complementary gen-der roles, insisting upon women's submission to men. They opposed Indigenous views of sexuality, calling for chastity, heterosexuality, and monogamy. In doing so, they radically undermined traditional clan structures, political and economic systems, and social organization.

Protestant Missions

The earliest Protestant missions to North America were a Puritan experiment. Between 1646 and 1675, "praying towns" were established in Massachusetts to provide sanctuary for Indigenous Christians. Here they could seek protection from the harassment of Euroamerican settlers and isolation from non-Christian relatives who did not approve of their conversion. They learned Anglo-American agricul-ture, language, and cultural expectations. By 1660, English settler John Eliot had founded six praying towns, where he preached sermons in local Native languages. By 1675, the praying towns were in decline, but they provided a model for future efforts that would share the prevailing assumptions that conversion required assimi-lation into Euroamerican cultural norms, and that Native people should—during this transitional time—be granted safe spaces where they could be removed from the worst vices of Euroamerican society.

Protestant missions gained new energy in the nineteenth century, largely as a key component of westward expansion. Missionaries were driven by the notion that Indigenous religions were little more than superstitions preventing Native people from assimilating into civilized society. By contrast, Christianity and the wonders of modernity would liberate them into the modern age. Conveniently, this would also work to open up their homelands for Euroamerican settlement.

As an expression of colonialism, nineteenth-century evangelism was inextrica-bly tied to this question of land. Closely linked to the nineteenth-century gospel was the good news of private property. Indigenous religions and cultures, with their emphasis on kinship, relationship, and reciprocity, were seen as inherently incompatible with the individualistic ideal of free market capitalism and private property. Commissioner for Indian affairs T. Hartley Crawford argued in 1838: "Common property and civilization cannot co-exist" (Craig, 9). Collectivist In-digenous cultures stood in the way of the colonial agenda.

Missionary activity arrived relatively late in the Northwest: Catholics in the 1830s, Protestants in the 1840s. Missionaries were greeted by populations wracked by disease. Protestant missionaries declared the epidemics to be divine providence, clearing the way for Euroamericans, and shifted their clerical attentions to newly arriving settlers. Catholic missionaries turned their attention to performing the last rites over dying people, baptizing them into death and into the Christian afterlife. For the most part, evangelizing to Native Americans of the Great Plains, Columbia Plateau, Great Basin, and Pacific Northwest did not see real success until the signing of treaties and the establishment of the reservation system in the 1850s.

Reservation Era

Reservations provided new opportunities: a more settled population and the opportunity to construct mission schools and to require church attendance. Proponents argued that reservations protected Indigenous people and settlers alike: Native people were protected from Euroamerican violence and vice, while settlers could freely claim land without fear of reprisal. Missionary influence over reservations increased following the Civil War, when President Ulysses S. Grant responded to widespread corruption among Bureau of Indian Affairs (BIA) agents supervising reservations. Resources intended for Native communities had gone missing; fraud and corruption were rampant. Hoping for more ethical leadership, Grant's Peace Policy divided up reservations among religious denominations. Because Native people had the legal status of children, government agents and missionaries would act as their legal guardians, making decisions and distributing resources. This gave them considerable power within these communities.

At the behest of agents and missionaries, several statutes were put into place with the intent of suppressing Indigenous religions and cultures. The Indian Religious Crimes Code of 1883 (cited in the previous chapter) effectively made it illegal to participate in Indigenous rituals, ceremonies, or healing rites. Agents and missionaries likewise advocated for the 1884 Dawes General Allotment Act, which broke up tribal lands into small individual holdings. Teaching parishioners to be "intelligently selfish," to value private property and the accumulation of wealth, was seen as necessary for their conversion to the Christian gospel.

Mission schools also played a vital part in this effort. It was widely held that successful conversion required literacy, the adaptation of the English language, and assimilation into Euroamerican culture. To accomplish this, advocates argued that Indigenous children needed to be removed from their families. Several types of schools served Native students: church-run reservation day schools and boarding schools, regional church-run residential schools, and centralized federal boarding schools, the most famous of which was the Carlisle Indian Industrial School. Schools were run with military-style structure and discipline, adhering to strict schedules, and separating students by age and gender (a source of distress for siblings and cousins). Children were separated from their families for months or years at a time, and in many cases were subject to abuse and neglect. As discussed in chapter 6, the forcible removal of Indigenous children from their families—both in the United States and in Canada—left a legacy of trauma. Boarding schools, religious-crimes codes, and the Dawes General Allotment Act all worked to undermine Indigenous religions and cultures and fracture communities, reaffirming the long-held notion that conversion to Christianity by necessity also meant whole-scale cultural assimilation.

Photo 8.1. Tom Torlino, Navajo, pictured upon entering Carlisle Indian Industrial School in 1882. (John N. Choate, Carlisle, Pennsylvania. National Archives and Records Administration. RG 75, Series 1327, box 18, folder 872)

Photo 8.2. Tom Torlino, Navajo, Carlisle Indian Industrial School student three years after his arrival. (John N. Choate, Carlisle, Pennsylvania. National Archives and Records Administration. RG 75, Series 1327, box 18, folder 872)

Russian Orthodoxy

The earliest missions to present-day Alaska were Russian Orthodox. Father John Veniaminov (1797–1879) served among the Aleuts in Unalaska for ten years before moving on to Sitka, where he served for another fifteen years. Veniaminov was consecrated bishop in 1840 and archbishop in 1850. In 1977, he was canonized as St. Innocent. Veniaminov translated hymns and services into Native languages and allowed for the modification of ceremonial activities (like funerals) to accommodate Native traditions and cultures. Veniaminov was famous for engaging in dialog with Native leaders, debating philosophy and theology. He learned several Native languages and dialects and wrote some of the first scholarly works on Native cultures, including grammars and dictionaries that are still used today.

While he and other Orthodox missions were generally tolerated by Native Alaskans, they were not at first very successful in their evangelism. That changed after 1867, when Alaska was sold to the United States. At the time, U.S. citizenship was granted only to Euroamerican Alaskans. In the 1870s and 1880s, the federal government appointed Congregationalist missionaries to govern Alaskan Native communities and schools. With political backing, these missions sought to curtail Native cultures and actively worked to suppress Indigenous religions, cultures, and languages, imposing Protestant forms of worship, marriage mores, and ways of living. Alaskan Natives responded by largely rejecting the Congregationalist missionaries who sought their conversion and turned instead to Orthodoxy. In his book *Memory Eternal: Tlingit Culture and Russian Orthodox Christianity through Two Centuries*, historian Sergei Kan documents this history and considers the way in which a distinctly Tlingit expression of Orthodoxy came about—where Tlingit language is spoken, and Tlingit culture is respected and integrated into worship and ceremonial life.

Latter-day Saints

For members of the Church of Jesus Christ of Latter-day Saints (LDS), evangelizing Native Americans has particular salience. LDS teachings express the belief that Indigenous people of North America descend from the Lamanites, descendants of ancient Israelites believed to have fled Jerusalem before its fall to the Assyrian and Babylonian Empires, and whose conversion will hasten the second coming of Christ. Early teachings were complicated by racial overtones (some taught that as Indigenous people became more godly, their skin tone would lighten), but the LDS church nonetheless felt a profound affinity for Native American people.

The LDS mission to Hawaii provides a compelling example of how this theology shaped missionary practice. In her book *A Chosen People, A Promised Land: Mormonism and Race in Hawaii*, Hokulani Aikau explores this history. The first mission to Hawaii began in 1850, led by George Q. Cannon. Cannon and his supporters found success, and soon sought to create a space where Native Hawaiian Latter-day Saints could live and practice their faith. In 1865, they founded Le'ie, a 6,000-acre settlement on the island of O'ahu. The LDS mission was remarkable for its explicit celebration of Native Hawaiian culture, in striking contrast to other Catholic and Protestant missions of the time. The settlement expanded, eventually contributing to the creation of La'ie Temple, the Brigham Young University–Hawaii campus, and the Polynesian Cultural Center. Aikau documents how community members and students saw their work in the center as both a religious and cultural obligation, celebrating Native Hawaiian culture and affirming LDS values. Cannon points to the *Iosepa*, a double-hull vessel built by BYU students and PCC staff as a telling example of this relationship. The *Iosepa*'s two hulls were described as a symbol for the strength and stability gained from two foundations: Native Hawaiian culture and the LDS faith.

The LDS Student Placement Program is another example of LDS outreach to Native Americans. Between 1956 and 1990, fifty thousand Native children were fostered by LDS families, providing them access to better public schools. Participation in the program was voluntary, but required that students be baptized into the LDS church. Studies of the Student Placement Program (most of which were conducted by sympathetic observers) report generally positive outcomes, citing some enthusiastic supporters who found valuable stability within the family setting and educational opportunities they were afforded. After his stint in the program, for instance, Jim Dandy (Diné) returned to the reservation, where he built two high schools and an elementary school, all with bilingual and bicultural programs. He also went on to become a priest in the LDS church. Since the program's end in 1990, accusations have emerged of physical and sexual abuse within some foster families, while others accused the program of suppressing Indigenous religious and cultural practices. Dandy disagrees:

> There were a lot of things said about it that were false. People accused the program of doing away with Navajo culture by removing young people from it. That is not true. A lot of the people I know who were on placement are now principals, school superintendents, and in other leadership positions. They have sought out their culture, understand it, are good Navajo speakers, and continue to learn. . . . Students who went through the program have done well in both worlds. (McPherson, Dandy, and Burak)

LDS outreach efforts contrast with earlier missionary efforts because of their appreciation for Indigenous cultures and the special place Native people hold within LDS doctrine. However, the LDS church shared with other missions a belief that salvation lay in religious conversion, and that the best way to achieve those ends lay in removing Native children from their families and communities.

Good Intentions, Cultural Genocide

In his widely quoted book *Missionary Conquest: The Gospel and Native American Cultural Genocide*, theologian George "Tink" Tinker (Osage) articulates the dangers of "good intentions," which can nonetheless lead to devastating outcomes. He cites the United Nations definition of "cultural genocide" as "the effective destruction of a people by systematically (intentionally or unintentionally in order to achieve other goals) destroying, eroding, or undermining the integrity of the culture and systems of values that define a people and give them life." For Tinker, the good intentions of historical missionaries cannot occlude the terrible havoc their actions wrought on the lives of Native people. Equating religious transformation and cultural conversion did violence to both the gospel and Indigenous communities. For Tinker, missionaries were "partners in genocide, guilty of complicity in the destruction of Indian cultures and tribal social structures. Perhaps the most fearful aspect of the missionary history of conquest and genocide is the extent to which it is a history of good intentions. None of the missionaries discussed here listed cultural genocide among his goals, yet the genocidal results are patently obvious in retrospect" (Tinker 1993, 112). Tinker's analysis has challenged a generation of historians and theologians to consider the devastating impacts of cultural genocide and colonial conquest within missionary endeavors.

Indigenous Religious Resilience

While acknowledging the destructive consequences of missionization, it is important to not reduce Indigenous people to a caricature of passive victim. One must also consider the ways that Indigenous people have demonstrated agency around religious practice, choosing to convert or not, to make strategic accommodations or not. What did Native people make of Christianity? In most instances, what we find is not a simple dualism, but rather cultural amalgams, where traditions were blended with elements of Christian practice and thought, creating something new.

Prophetic Movements

Native American prophetic movements were some of the first Indigenous responses to Christianity, providing a way of responding to the devastating consequences of colonialism. Many such movements incorporated elements borrowed from Christianity, including a monotheistic creator, a belief in an afterlife, a millenarian notion of world destruction and renewal, and in some instances, a savior. Many prophets experienced a death and rebirth, prompting powerful visions that authorized their spiritual authority. While many pre-colonial Indigenous traditions included visions and travels to the land of the dead, the presence of such an experience in the Christian narrative helped to further authenticate their claim. Prophetic movements drew on Christian theological ideas, particularly those related to sin, salvation, the afterlife, and ethics such as kindness and nonviolence (Irwin, 7). Within their diversity, Native American prophetic movements shared a resistance to settler colonialism (and its threat to Native culture, spirituality, and sovereignty) and a call for a return to Indigenous traditions. Prophetic movements reframed Indigenous religious traditions, integrating elements of the Christian tradition that enabled them to survive and better respond to the present moment. By gathering together in common prayer and ceremony, for example, the community could regain its strength, and restore harmony to their world.

Historian Willard Johnson has explored how the unifying nature of prophetic movements in the eastern woodlands created intertribal solidarity within their resistance to colonialism. For instance, the prophet Neolin (Lenape) experienced a religious vision in 1761, which inspired him to call for his people to abstain from alcohol, reclaim their culture, and cling to their traditional homelands. Tenskwataw (Shawnee), also known as Handsome Lake (1735–1815) revitalized Haudenosaunee traditions and helped shape a regional Indigenous identity in the Northeast, built on shared values and common resistance to cultural assimilation. He incorporated elements of Christianity, such as a monotheistic deity and regular worship, into the revitalized Longhouse tradition.

Similar prophetic movements would also rise in the West. Smohalla (1815–1895) was a Wanapum prophet on the Columbia Plateau who helped strengthen Plateau culture and spirituality through his integration of certain elements of the Christian tradition. In what is today known as the Waashat or Seven Drums tradition, worshippers celebrate the Creator and honor the sacred first foods. Wovoka (1856–1932) was a Paiute religious leader and prophet. In the late nineteenth century, he died and, after three days, returned to life with a powerful vision. He called followers to return to traditional lifeways, stories, dances, and songs and to pray to their ancestors. If they did so, the dead would return to life, and the world would be renewed. This movement became known as the Ghost Dance. As participants joined a circle dance, some fell into a trance, visiting with the ancestors and returning with stories, songs, ritual instructions, and guidance. The nineteenth-century expression of this movement ended in the massacre at Wounded Knee, but it was revived in the 1970s, an expression of renewed spiritual and political activism.

In 1881, Squaxin Island tribal member Squisachtun (John Slocum) died and visited with God. He returned to life during his own funeral and called for the creation of a new Indian church. Slocum preached against settler vices such as alcohol, smoking, gambling, and fighting, and encouraged his followers to care for their families and communities. His wife, Mary Slocum, introduced a new way of praying and shaking over the sick, effecting miraculous cures and inspiring spiritual renewal, in what would become known as the Indian Shaker Church. The movement spread to become a dominant expression of Indigenous religiosity from British Columbia to California, affirming Indigenous worldviews and lifeways, while integrating symbols and teachings of the Christian tradition.

A contemporary prophetic leader was Thomas Banyacya (1909–1999), who shared the Hopi prophecy, calling attention to twentieth-century threats to land and water, particularly through coal and uranium mining. The prophecy describes environmental devastation, nuclear warfare, and the earth's protests against such treatment in the form of earthquakes, volcanoes, fires, and hurricanes. While settler greed would lead to ecological destruction, Banyacya taught that a new world would emerge when humanity and the earth were once again reconciled.

Christianity in Native North America

As these prophetic leaders help to show, religious traditions do not exist in a vacuum. Religions have always been the product of cultural exchange, negotiation, and emerging responses to new challenges. One way to understand this is to consider three different means by which Indigenous people have navigated religious exchange: plurality, inculturation, and decolonization. *Plurality* suggests maintaining multiple traditions at once—even when they may seem contradictory. *Inculturation* happens when a dominant tradition incorporates aspects of colonized or subordinate culture. *Decolonization* occurs when members of the subordinate or colonized culture engage with dominant religious traditions *on their own terms*, often presenting a radical challenge to the theological and material foundations of the status quo. Here the gospel is unhitched from its colonial moorings, freed to become a means of empowering the oppressed. The gospel itself is transformed, illuminated by Indigenous teachings and experiences.

Plurality

For many Indigenous people, the legacy of settler colonialism and missionization means that they are religious *pluralists*: they maintain more than one religious tradition at a time. To better understand how this is possible, it helps to remember two things. First, claims to exclusive truth were not a part of Native North American cultures. Each community had their own stories, traditions, and practices, but none claimed theirs alone was correct. In fact, there is ample evidence that tribal communities shared and exchanged stories and traditions. Practices traveled through cultural exchange, marriage, and friendship and were even acquired through war. Second, religions in Indigenous communities are in fact *lifeways*, ways of being and managing spiritual relationships, rather than dogmatic theologies or fixed belief systems. Third, an emphasis on practice over belief also helps account for plurality: one can *practice* multiple traditions without having to wrestle through apparent contradictions in theology or doctrine.

Sociologist Eva Garroutte has noted that of the 4.1 million people identified as American Indian or Native Alaskan, between 95 and 99 percent said that religious beliefs "were at least somewhat important," a remarkable contrast to the general population where 83 to 86 percent said the same. In her own research, Garroutte found that tribal communities in the Southwest were more likely to ascribe high value to Christianity than those on the Plains, and Indigenous women in the Southwest were "significantly more likely than any of their Northern Plains counterparts—male or female—to claim Christian beliefs" (Garroutte, 493–94). Garroutte found that half of respondents assigned high salience to aboriginal beliefs, a third to Christian beliefs, and a third to the Native American Church. That this total exceeds 100 percent makes clear that many respondents identified with more than one religious tradition. This was of particular interest to Garroutte, who noted that more than one-quarter of Northern Plains people identified with more than one tradition, while more than a third did so in the Southwest. Garroutte writes: "Our findings suggest a portrait of the country's largest Indian reservations as sites of considerable religio-spiritual diversity—settings where a multiplicity of beliefs is highly salient, often in rich combination" (Garroutte, 496–97).

One way to better understand how religious plurality works is to consider it within the context of people's lived experience. On the Navajo (Diné) reservation, for instance, much work has been done to consider the role of religious traditions in healing and medical practice, with particular focus on the ways in which patients draw upon traditional Navajo religion, Native American Church ceremonies, and Christian faith healing. As discussed previously, Navajo healing techniques are composed of chantways that include prayers, song, sand painting, storytelling, herbal remedies, and other ritual objects and activities. Diagnosticians employ hand trembling, crystal gazing and star gazing to determine the proper chantway, and then a medicine man or woman performs the chantway. Chantways range in length from a few hours to eight days and require a great deal of preparation and expense. Native American Church ceremonies are all-night services conducted in a ceremonial tipi and center on the sacramental use of peyote. Services often include one's family, as well as other members of the Native American Church community. Individuals confess their struggles, speaking freely of concerns and fears. By contrast, Christian faith healing can take place virtually anywhere and typically includes prayer, confession, anointing with oil, and laying on of hands. On the Diné reservation, faith healing services occur during Pentecostal revival meetings or in charismatic Catholic prayer services, and are often in the Diné language.

For traditional Navajo healers, illness results from disrupted relationships with the human, natural, or spiritual worlds. Healing requires repairing those relationships and growing in understanding of one's proper orientation to the world. In the Native American Church, healing requires reconnecting with one's Creator and a growing sense of self-worth. Christian traditions see sin as the source of all sickness in the world and, thus, locate healing within repentance and forgiveness. Several studies have noted that the Diné draw upon multiple healing traditions at any given time, moving freely from biomedicine, to traditional Navajo chantways, to Native American Church services, to Christian faith healing. While fundamentalist Christians are the least likely to participate in other traditions, one nonetheless finds a remarkable degree of openness in these communities. One author described a Diné family where three brothers were all religious leaders, in three different traditions.

Despite their differences, the three traditions on the Diné reservation agree that illness provides an opportunity for spiritual growth, and all agree that healing occurs through the restoration of relationships, whether with the natural world, family, church family, or Creator.

> The vast majority of Navajo patients in our study utilized multiple healing systems to address their distress. Though they reported that they were cautious and often reticent in revealing their involvement in one system (for example, a religious healing system) to the healer of another system (such as another religious healer or a Western medical provider), they generally did not regard the systems as mutually exclusive. Many, perhaps most, patients regarded their religious healing involvement as an activity that had served or could have served a complementary and collaborative role with their Western medical care. (Storck, Csordas, and Strauss, 592)

All of these traditions offer spaces for "ritualized introspection and self-examination," ways of living that explicitly stress sobriety, commitment to one's family, reverence for the Creator, and the power of transformation. Formal rituals, spontaneous prayer, and the support of family and community provide the structure to begin anew. The influence of peyote in Native American Church services and the influence of the Holy Spirit within Pentecostal services both create an atmosphere of "receptivity, honesty, and insight." As one participant noted, the Christian church and the sweat lodge have much in common. Church is "like going to a sweat house. When you get out of sweathouse you feel very light and happy. That experience is like when you come out of the church, that's how you feel. It is wonderful and it makes you happy" (Garrity, 532).

According to Elizabeth Lewton and Victoria Bydone (Navajo), all three healing traditions share Diné values of balance, harmony, and right relationship, described by the Diné spiritual principle of *sa'ąh naagháí bik'eh hózhó*. Diné language does not have a word for *evil* or *sin* as understood within the Christian tradition, but its closest equivalent could be translated as "being out of control," having lost harmony and balance (Garrity, 535). "Harmony or balance requires the establishment and maintenance of proper relationships guided by principles such as respect, reverence, kindness, and cooperation" (Lewton and Bydone, 479). One reason plurality works in the Diné community is that these traditions all have common values and serve similar needs. They all offer a means of regaining control, and restoring balanced, harmonious relationships with one's extended family and the natural world. And they all emphasize shared principles of respect, reverence, kindness, and cooperation. For traditional Diné people, the ideal life is to "walk in beauty." For one Diné Christian, this very traditional value could be affirmed both in and out of the church. "When you say, 'I walk in beauty,' you live according to the Holy Spirit. . . . That's what it means, but you have to straighten out your language, how you see things, speaking positively, in everything. That's what it means to walk in beauty" (Lewton and Bydone, 490).

Inculturation

If *pluralism* describes the experience of participating in multiple religious traditions at once, *inculturation* describes those moments when a colonial religious tradition adopts elements of Indigenous culture. Such inclusion might happen through symbols, architectural styles, foods, or music. For Alberta Pualani Hopkins, who is both Native Hawaiian and Episcopalian, including Hawaiian food and symbols within the liturgy helps make the church feel like home. She explains: "The challenge of the future is to create a nurturing and accepting environment that allows me to belong to the church without having to check my cultural identity at the door of the cathedral before entering. The challenge is to create a place that people like me can call home" (Hopkins, 164). Honoring elements of Indigenous cultures can send a powerful signal of respect and inclusion for Indigenous members of the congregation. At the same time, it also has the potential to leave foundational theological, social, political, or economic assumptions of the church unchallenged.

In her study of the Church of the Immaculate Conception, a congregation serving an Anishinaabe community on Manitoulin Island, Ontario, Theresa Smith describes what could be seen as inculturation. Elements of Anishinaabe culture have been incorporated into the church design: architecture and colors evoke *midewiwin* medicine societies, and works by Anishinaabe artists suggest parallels between Indigenous imagery and biblical stories. In doing so, "the church appears to seek a fusion of spirituality that has proven to be both enlightening and sometimes confusing to Natives and non-Natives alike" (Smith, 518). Considering the church, Smith is uncertain whether such innovations are appropriate signs of conciliation

Photo 8.3.   St. Joseph's Catholic Church, Mescalero, New Mexico
(1975). The church incorporates elements of Mescalero culture,
including Mountain Spirit dancer crowns, and a representation of
Jesus as an Apache medicine man. (Wikimedia Commons, Public
Domain, https://commons.wikimedia.org/wiki/File:St._Joseph%27s_
Mescalero.jpg)

for a violent colonial past, creative spiritual synthesis, or merely another form of
colonial appropriation.

Built in the 1970s, the Church of the Immaculate Conception was modeled
after a circular Anishinaabe *midewiwin* lodge, the cross replaced with a skylight
"smokehole." The image of the sun on the doors represented the Creator (*Kitche
Manitou*) and Christ, and colors represent the four directions, the *midewiwin* society,
and Anishinaabe understandings of spiritual power. The number 4 evokes the four
directions and the four evangelists. The stations of the cross were commissioned by
a non–Christian traditionalist, Leland Bell, who drew heavily on *midewiwin* symbols
to convey shared values: purification, healing, and love.

Smith notes that many members of the Anishinaabe community are ambivalent at best about the integration of such images, insisting that the differences between traditions should not be occluded. "Anishnaabe consultants, without exception, assert that the Thunderbird and Holy Spirit are distinct entities. Many Anishnaabeg prefer to speak their spiritual symbols without translation" (Smith, 526). In the end, Smith concluded that the "Church of the Immaculate Conception speaks most clearly to the non-Native Christians who now fill the services and whose faith is informed, and seemingly enriched, by the Anishnaabe experience," but not the Anishinaabe community itself (Smith, 526).

Decolonizing Christianity

For a long time I thought I was a Catholic Indian,
but I'm beginning to see myself more as an Indian Catholic.

—JUANITA LITTLE, MESCALERO APACHE AND FRANCISCAN SISTER (LITTLE, 217)

In order to distinguish between inculturation and decolonization, it helps to ask: Who is in the position of power? Who chooses which elements of Indigenous culture will be included, and what they might mean? Are they expressions of respect and inclusion that nonetheless leave theological interpretations unchallenged? Or do they lead to beliefs, practices, and political agendas being fundamentally reconsidered? In contrast to inculturation, which runs the risk of token inclusion (or outright cultural appropriation) of Indigenous imagery by non-Native churches, Indigenous theologians and spiritual leaders call for a more radical, decolonizing approach to Christianity. Tinker writes:

> Today there can be no genuine American Indian theology that does not take our Indigenous traditions seriously. This means, of course, that our reading of the gospel and our understanding of faithfulness will represent a radical disjuncture from the theologies and histories of the Western churches of Europe and America as we pay attention to our stories and memories instead of to theirs. (Smith, 517)

When Indigenous worldviews are taken seriously, they entail a fundamental reevaluation of Christian theology, philosophy, practice, and political commitments. In Indigenous theologies, the self exists within a web of relationships, a sacramental earth is the expression of an imminent Creator, and social, political, economic, and environmental justice are nonnegotiable. By shifting attention toward Indigenous people's responses to, and reforming of, Christianity, we begin to see Indigenous agency, creativity, resiliency, and the ways in which the Christian tradition can motivate radical justice.

For example, Clara Sue Kidwell documents the ways in which nineteenth-century Choctaws employed Christianity as a tool for ensuring the survival of Choctaw community, culture, and language. In his work, Sergei Kan explores Tlingit Orthodox Christianity, which found a space for Tlingit language, culture, values, and rites of mourning and remembrance. Michael McNally considers the tools Christianity provided for Ojibwe survival, arguing against an approach that reduces Native people to victims, passive before the onslaught of colonialism and religious suppression. Instead, McNally insists that scholars consider the "historical agency of Native people," as they negotiated and renegotiated their cultural positions (McNally 2000, 837).

Beginning in the 1820s, Euroamerican missionaries and Native clergy translated thousands of hymns into the Ojibwe language. Revitalized in the 1980s, elders sing these Christian hymns at all-night wakes and at prayer societies fashioned after traditional drum societies. They share food with the sick and grieving and offer solace and song. As McNally argues, nineteenth-century missionaries did not simply convert Ojibwe people to Christianity; they provided a tool that ensured the survival of Ojibwe culture, community, and values. Today, Ojibwe singers affirm traditional values of relationship, community, and honoring ancestors, even as they ensure the survival of Ojibwe language. Ojibwe hymns and hymn singers function in a way that is distinctly Ojibwe, affirming Ojibwe ways of seeing and being in the world. For McNally, this distinction is vital.

> Students of African American religious history have long recognized that although the mission to slaves was in part an extension of a power system that upheld slavery, the Christian tradition became a resource with which African Americans tapped into sacred power; fashioned a meaningful, shared culture; and criticized the moral contradictions of a slaveholding Christian society. Why has the possibility that Native Americans could find similar resources in the Christian tradition been so consistently overlooked in the field of native religions? (McNally 2000, 845)

Ethnomusicologist Chad Hamill (Spokan) provides another compelling study of the way music translates, navigates, and builds bridges between different religions and cultures. In his work, Hamill explores a relationship between a Catholic priest, a medicine man, and an Indian hymn singer. Hamill shows how Catholic hymns become indigenized, strengthening Native communities at a time when they were struggling to survive. "Rather than Catholicizing Indians," he argues, "the hymns were themselves Indigenized—absorbed, reconstructed, and re-sung as expressions of Native identity" (Hamill, 2). Traditions are stitched together through settler harmonies and Indigenous "melodic glides" (Hamill, 51). What makes this new creation possible is the potential within music for holding and conveying spiritual power: to receive a song in a dream or vision is to receive spiritual power. To share that song in prayer or worship is to share that spiritual power for the well-being of others.

Music and song transcend theological discord, providing a way to affirm multiple traditions, enlivening each with new vision. As in the example of Indian hymn singing described at the outset of this chapter, Luke Lassiter, Clyde Ellis, and Ralph Kotay present readers with Kiowa hymns, a vital part of Native church life in southern Oklahoma. Kiowa hymns are grounded in personal experience, inspired by the spirit, sung in Kiowa, set to traditional melodies, and performed without accompaniment. Received by individuals during times of particular need, the hymns now belong to those families. Each song has a story behind it. Donna

Kotay, daughter of a Kiowa singer, explains: "Because all of a sudden, their eyes were opened and they saw God. There's a Spirit, and it just moves through them. It's just something that happens to them, and it's got to come out. And it comes out in song" (Lassiter, Ellis, and Kotay, 111–12). Each song is the encapsulation of a religious experience, of the miraculous within one's life. A community member explains: "It was her religious experience, and most of these songs are just that. They *are* miracles" (Lassiter, Ellis, and Kotay, 112). Songs do not just retell an experience; hymns bring spiritual power and transformative presence into the present, making it real and palpable each time that song is sung.

Part of what makes Native hymnody potentially decolonizing is that it affirms the equal position of Indigenous spirituality alongside the Christian tradition. Kotay explains:

> Even before the missionaries came, our people already knew God; we were a praying people already. And we prayed to the Creator. The missionaries, they brought in what the old Indians used to call the "Jesus Road." They brought us the Bible. And they brought us their songs with the English tunes, but they really didn't catch on. We had our own way of singing. Actually, our Kiowa hymns are very similar to our Ghost Dance songs from way back. It's really surprising, but many of those Ghost Dance songs say almost the same thing as the Bible. . . . Those Indians were praying to meet their relatives in heaven—just like Christians. And their Ghost Dance songs, they came to the people in the same way that our Kiowa hymns come today . . . from God, through His Spirit. (Lassiter, Ellis, and Kotay, 92–93)

Music and hymnody provide one example of decolonizing Christianity. Another example can be seen within ritual practice, such as among the Tohono O'odham in Arizona. In his book *Walking to Magdalena: Personhood and Place in Tohono O'odham*, Seth Schermerhorn argues that Spanish missionaries were unsuccessful in their attempts to convert the Tohono O'odham. Rather, "when Tohono O'odham community leaders took up the project of Christianizing themselves, they did so for their own reasons and in their own ways" (Schermerhorn, 139). Here, Christianity is not a fixed or unitary tradition, but what Schermerhorn describes as a "tradition in tension with itself," transformed by Indigenous peoples, who have "indigenized Christianity by localizing it." (Schermerhorn 141). Schermerhorn explores Indigenous theories of personhood and place within pilgrimage, songs, and material culture. As they walk from Arizona to Magdalena, Mexico, he argues, they tether Christianity to the landscape. Songs serve as a system for mapping history onto the landscape, documenting religious journeys. But as Schermerhorn notes, when Christian pilgrimage staffs—storied sticks that record previous journeys—are left inside a cave sacred to Indigenous creation accounts, Christianity both literally and symbolically enters the landscape, becoming another thread in an Indigenous tapestry.

In his work, anthropologist Richard Haly likewise challenges assumptions that Nahua traditions have been appropriated by Catholicism, suggesting it is actually the opposite: it is these Nahua who have done the appropriating, employing Christianity to resist settler colonialism. Among the Nahua people of central Mexico, local guardian spirits are associated with Catholic saints. The Heavenly Father suggests both the Christian God and the sun—the giver of maize. The cross invokes Christ and the four directions. The Virgin Mary represents both the mother of Jesus and Nahua deities who interceded on behalf of women and childbirth. "The images are living metaphors. Using the language of Roman Catholicism, Nahuas represent their relations in a world that is self-evident to all Nahuas: a world or worlds in which ancestors, the sun and earth, are the epistemological guarantors of such sense as the world makes" (Haly, 546).

Kateri Tekakwitha

In 2012, Kateri Tekakwitha became the first North American Indian canonized within the Roman Catholic Church and was declared patroness of the environment. Born in 1656 to an Algonquin mother and Mohawk father, Saint Kateri was one of a few people to survive a smallpox epidemic that decimated her home village. She converted to Catholicism at nineteen and died five years later. Previous Catholic historians and hagiographers celebrated her submissive femininity, holding her up as a model of Native conversion. But such representations obscure a more complicated story, wherein Saint Kateri herself has become the means through which Native North Americans are transforming Christianity to better meet the needs of their communities and strengthen their traditional cultures and languages. For the nearly 20 percent of American Indians and Alaskan Natives who are Catholic, Saint Kateri has become a symbol of Indigenous strength and fortitude. She is a living presence, inspiring her followers to care for the environment, build community, and reclaim the Native feminine as sacred.

In her book *Indian Pilgrims: Journeys of Activism and Healing with Saint Kateri Tekakwitha*, Michelle Jacob (Yakama) uplifts the importance of Saint Kateri for decolonizing Catholicism, even as she acknowledges the irony that this movement to celebrate "Indigenous peoples, cultures and women, takes place within the deeply patriarchal and settler colonial context of the Roman Catholic Church" (Jacob, 5). For Jacob, this irony fades when she sets aside the views of church fathers and instead prioritizes Native women's perspectives. There she learns that "Saint Kateri is at the heart of an Indigenous social movement that serves as a model for those working to honor Indigenous peoples and cultures *within* Western institutions," helping the people to "decolonize their minds, spiritualties and lives" (Jacob, 7). As Jacob insists, decolonization requires handing the interpretive reins to Native people, recognizing their authority to tell Saint Kateri's story. As Indigenous women and men take control of her story, wresting it from the hands of settler colonialism and Catholic hierarchy, Saint Kateri has new meaning, providing an alternative to Catholic master narratives.

Jacob found repeated examples where the veneration of Saint Kateri supports the revitalization of Indigenous culture, language, and values. For example, Jacob points to the way Saint Kateri provides spiritual sustenance to the Yakama community as they fight to protect *Nch'i-wána* (the Columbia River) from pollution, dams,

Photo 8.4.   Statue of Kateri Tekakwitha, Cathedral Basilica of St. Francis of Assisi, Santa Fe, New Mexico. Jemez Pueblo artist Estella Loretto was commissioned to make the sculpture of Kateri in commemoration of the Archdiocese of Santa Fe's 150th anniversary in 2003. While Kateri was Mohawk, she holds a special place in the hearts of Indigenous Catholic people around the continent, who celebrate her as the first Native American saint. (Dieterkaupp, Wikimedia Commons, https://commons.wikimedia .org/wiki/File:Statue_Kateri_Tekakwitha.jpg)

and development. This vision is represented by a quilt panel hanging over the altar of the Yakama Catholic Church: a Native woman in traditional regalia kneeling at the altar as a salmon leaps high over her head. And indeed, Saint Kateri's role as patroness of the environment is particularly important, with the potential to challenge Catholicism to protect the natural world and affirm Indigenous sovereignty.

Jacob describes a Yakama community dinner at this same church, celebrating Saint Kateri, and featuring their traditional first foods:

Our sacred foods, which have sustained us for thousands of years are a gift from the Creator [and] continue to be blessings that link our culture and spirituality with the natural world. Bringing traditional foods into the center of community gatherings is a healthy way to revitalize our culture and people. It reminds us what is sacred. From a Catholic perspective, the communion wafers at the church, purchased from an outside vendor and shipped to the mission church, are blessed and become holy, but for Yakama peoples, the elk and salmon are also holy—foods, gifts, from the Creator given to us and sustaining us as a people since "time immemorial," as our tribal elders say. . . . The food is a sacred covenant between our people and the Creator, *Tamanwiłá*. (Jacob, 87–88)

As Jacob's analysis helps to make clear, radical decolonizing work can happen in "unexpected places" because the work continues wherever Native people's "health and spirituality are interwoven and lived in daily life" (Jacob, 111). Hence, even within a patriarchal institution like the Catholic Church, an Indigenous saint can be employed to represent the resilience of Native women and matriarchal culture.

Native women, perhaps the unlikeliest of agents within the Catholic Church, are indeed active in providing an alternative narrative about Kateri and Native peoples, compared to the master narratives that have dominated history. . . . They recast land, bodies, and culture as sacred parts of their spiritual expression, placing Saint Kateri at the center of the regenerative and supportive practices that affirm Indigenous arts, representation, language, culture and land. (Jacob, 140)

The Indigenization of the church is not simply the piecemeal or superficial inclusion of signs and symbols. Instead, it entails the radical work of remaking settler-colonial institutions, reforming them into means for radical political change, honoring and protecting Native women and caring for the earth. For Ray Squi Qui/ Saʔatil Williams (Swinomish), Indigenous ceremonial life and Catholicism work together to sustain his family. "My grandmother was a very devout Catholic and, to us, she was the bridge between our spiritual ways . . . and the Church itself. She had shown us just through example that you can be at [Indigenous] ceremonies on Saturday night until 3 o'clock in the morning, and still be the first one in church on Sunday." (Jacob, 99)

Native American Theology

Native American theologians are also making space within settler-colonial institutions of textual discourse and debate, calling for the radical decolonizing of Christian theology. For Jace Weaver (Cherokee), this takes the form of what he calls a "post-colonial hermeneutic." As Weaver describes it, a post-colonial interpretation of scripture must do several things: It must be communal in character, rejecting anything that divides the community. It must demand inclusion and advocate for the corporate good. It must take land seriously, acknowledging the earth as a locus of communion with the Creator and a source of revelation. It must accept Native cultures as valid and equal. It must reject historical tendencies to colonize and dominate others, and it must work to decolonize its theology and language. When Native cultures are taken as equals within a spiritual conversation, Indigenous traditions can be understood as a path toward illumination.

In their book *Native American Theology*, George Tinker, Clara Sue Kidwell, and Homer Noley reexamine classic theological categories through an Indigenous lens. For example, "eschatology" is a key theological category that typically explores life after death or the end of time and assumes that the "real world" exists on some other spiritual plane. But Tinker, Kidwell, and Noley suggest that an American Indian eschatology would instead call for a focus on this world, on healing and sustaining life on earth, rather than pining for a heavenly afterlife. The earth gains new value in Indigenous theology; more than a brief way station, it becomes our primary means of encountering God and the Sacred. It becomes a source of life and the means through which God manifests and speaks. Indigenous theology radically challenges settler-colonial hierarchies, presenting a vision wherein human beings exist as equals within a web of creation rather than as rulers at the apex of a cosmic pecking order. If one's theology allows for the *imminence* of God (meaning that the divine is manifested and revealed in the natural world), then the other classical categories of belief might be challenged as well. For instance, they might point out that typical Christian notions of "sin" privilege individual action and individual salvation, while in Indigenous theology, wrongdoing is more likely perceived as being out of balance, the result of broken relationships, or failing to honor one's responsibilities within the community. In turn, virtue has more to do with harmony and balance through right relationships. The view of Christ is also radically challenged by an Indigenous theology. Rather than paying a debt for humanity's sin, Christ is portrayed as a healer who shares in humanity's suffering.

For Marie Archambault, reclaiming her Indigenous lifeways and worldviews alongside her Catholic faith has helped reveal new aspects of Christ.

> We must learn to subtract the chauvinism and the cultural superiority with which this Gospel was often presented to our people. We must, as one author says, "de-colonize" this Gospel, which said we must be European in order to be Christian. We have to go beyond the *white gospel* in order to perceive its truth. When we do this, we shall meet Jesus as our brother and recognize him as one who has been with us all along as the quiet servant, the one who has strengthened us through these centuries. Then we will know that the cry of Jesus Christ from the cross was the cry of our people at Wounded Knee, Sand Creek and other places of the mass death of our people. He was our companion during these years of our invisibility in this society. (Archambault 1996, 135)

In his work, Tinker reclaims an emphasis on Christ as the *Logos* found in the Gospel of John, the nongendered Word of God that is the creative, healing, and redeeming aspect of the Creator. Coexisting with God the Father at the time of Creation, the Logos preexists and is not limited to its manifestation in the historical Jesus. While Jesus is clearly the most famous embodiment of the Logos (or Christ) he is not its only manifestation. Tinker explains:

> If the Logos or the Christ is merely that aspect of God that communicates creativity and healing or salvation to human beings, then [Indigenous people] can even add to Christianity's knowledge of salvation from our own experiences and memories of

God's functioning among Indian communities throughout history. In this sense we can claim to have a history of many such experiences of the Christ and can even begin to name some of them and tell the stories that go with the naming. But this also means that we can never be trapped into saying that God has only spoken the Good News through Jesus, or that the only way to salvation is through a European or Amer-European message brought by the colonizer to the conquered. (Tinker 1998, 149)

For Tinker, Corn Mother stories exemplify the Logos, because "in all these tellings the self-sacrifice of the woman is emphatically consistent and results in the enduring fecundity of the earth and production of vegetable foods" (Tinker 1998, 150). The divine act is transformative, for "food must henceforth be considered sacred. Eating becomes . . . sacrament" (Tinker 1998, 151). When Corn Mother and other stories of the origins of people's sacred foods are taken seriously, the Christian tradition is transformed. First foods become sacraments, become relatives, and the act of eating becomes a sacred expression of communion, of relationship, and of gratitude. As Tinker explains, "Corn and all foodstuffs are our relatives. . . . Thus, eating is sacramental . . . because we are eating our relatives" (Tinker 1998, 151).

Among the Anishinaabe people of the Great Lakes, Wenabozho is a powerful spiritual figure, a spiritual helper who comes in times of trial to help the people and provide them with guidance. It was Wenabozho who gave the people their language, medicine, and spiritual traditions and taught them about the world around them. Both spiritual and corporeal, he can take many forms, emerging sometimes as a bear, a rabbit, or even a plant—whatever is required to teach the people and guide them. For Lawrence Gross (Anishinaabe), he provided a means for making sense of the Christian tradition.

> The birth story of *Wenabozho* generally states that the west wind was his father. However, one of my teachers, Thomas Shingobe, developed a different take on *Wenabozho's* heritage. He taught that *Wenabozho*, along with Jesus Christ, was the son of God. He held that God sent Jesus to teach the white people, and He sent *Wenabozho* to teach the Indians . . . having *Wenabozho* equal to Jesus Christ translates into the notion that Anishinaabe religious teaching, which is thought to have originated with *Wenabozho*, stands on a par with Christian religious teachings. Again, no ground is given to colonial forces, and the *Anishinaabe* remain strong and independent in their religion. (Gross 2003, 131)

Here, Wenabozho is not another (presumably inferior) manifestation of the Logos. Rather, he retains his difference and even predates Jesus. As Christ's older brother, Wenabozho holds an authoritative position.

Conclusion

The renowned Lakota medicine man and Catholic catechist Nicholas Black Elk (1863–1950) was nine years old when he received his great vision. Thunder Beings took him to meet the six Grandfathers. At the center of a vast hoop, he saw a great flowering tree that sheltered all the children of humanity. His visionary experience led him to become a renowned medicine man and healer, revered by his people for his knowledge of Lakota traditions. When he was forty years old, Black Elk converted to Catholicism, was baptized, and went on to raise his children as Catholics. He eventually served his community as a lay leader and catechist, even as he continued to pray with the sacred pipe and worked to keep alive Lakota teachings and ceremonies.

Black Elk's life has been read in many ways. For some, his conversion is a sign of the subversion of Indigenous religions by the Christian church. For others, he is an example of religious pluralism, a man who managed to hold two traditions, separately and at the same time. For others, he is an example of inculturation, as the Christian church appropriates Native symbols and stories, using the tale of his conversion for their own ends. And for yet others, Black Elk's life story is a powerful example decolonization, of the ways in which Native people and traditions can indigenize and transform Christianity. Because Black Elk was a devout Catholic even as he insisted that the Indigenous teachings of his people be afforded equal value and respect, his life and teachings provide a path toward transforming the gospel and Catholic theology. Black Elk himself argued:

> We have been told that God sent to men his son, who would restore order and peace upon the earth; and we have been told that Jesus the Christ was crucified, but that he shall come again at the Last Judgment. . . . This I understand and know that it is true, but the white men should know that for the red people too, it was the will of Wakan-Tanka, the Great Spirit, that an animal turn itself into a two-legged person in order to bring the most holy pipe to His people; and we too were taught that this White Buffalo Cow Woman who brought our sacred pipe will appear again at the end of this world, a coming which we Indians know is now not very far off. (Brown, xix–xx)

Archambault explains: "If Black Elk, a follower of Christ, left us an example, it is of understanding two traditions and rejecting neither. In his life, he brought unity to them in himself. Black Elk lived these two ancient traditions" (Jacob, 95, quoting Archambault 1998, 98). For Archambault, it was Black Elk's vision that provided her a way for affirming her Indigenous heritage while also entering into holy orders in the Catholic Church.

In his vision, the holy flowering tree at the center of the sacred hoop was occupied by a man. Black Elk explained:

> Then they led me to the center of the circle where once more I saw a holy tree all full of leaves and blossoming. Against the tree there was a man standing with arms held wide in front of him. I looked hard at him, and I could not tell what people he came from. He was not a *wasichu* [white man] and he was not an Indian. His hair was long and hanging loose, and on the left side of his head he wore an eagle feather. His body was strong and good to see, and it was painted red. . . . He was a very fine looking man. While I was staring hard at him, his body began to change and became very beautiful with all colors of light, and around him there was light. He spoke like singing: "My life is such that all earthly beings and growing things

belong to me. Your father, the Great Spirit, has said this. You too must say this." (Neihardt, 153–54)

Black Elk's life exemplifies the complexity of Native North Americans' relationships with Christianity. He is revered for his work in revitalizing and preserving Lakota religious traditions. At the same time, he was a devoted catechist in the Catholic Church. While writers in both camps have sought to claim him, the complex reality remains elusive.

As this chapter has shown, the Christian tradition was a tool of colonialism, as many missionaries directly tied their work to the destruction of Native cultures and the assimilation of Native people. But as Michelle Jacob points out in her discussion of Saint Kateri, decolonization happens in unexpected places, even in the bastions of colonial power. As Native prophets, congregants, and theologians bring Indigenous spiritual traditions into conversation with Christianity, the results can take us by surprise—like an Indian hymn sung with joy and faith during a Sunday morning service at the United Methodist Church of Apache. These new interpretations and practices are reasons for hope, challenging all Christian people to honor the earth and to seek justice for Indigenous communities for whom it has so long been denied.

References and Recommendations

Aikau, Hokulani. *A Chosen People, A Promised Land: Mormonism and Race in Hawaii.* St. Paul: University of Minnesota Press, 2012.

Anderson, Karen. *Chain Her By One Foot: The Subjugation of Women in Seventeenth-Century New France.* Abingdon, UK: Routledge 1993.

Archambault, Marie Thérèse. "Native Americans and Evangelization," in *Native and Christian: Indigenous Voices on Religious Identity in the United States and Canada*, edited by James Treat. Abingdon, UK: Routledge, 1996.

Archambault, Marie Thérèse, Mark G. Thiel, and Christopher Vecsey, eds. The *Crossing of Two Roads: Being Catholic and Native in the United States.* Maryknoll, NY: Orbis, 2003.

Barnett, Homer G. *Indian Shakers: A Messianic Cult of the Pacific Northwest.* Carbondale: Southern Illinois University Press, 1972.

Beebe, Rose Marie, and Robert M. Senkewicz. *Junípero Serra: California, Indians, and the Transformation of a Missionary.* Norman: University of Oklahoma Press, 2015.

Bradford, Tolly, and Chelsea Horton. *Mixed Blessings: Indigenous Encounters with Christianity in Canada.* Vancouver: University of British Columbia Press, 2016.

Brown, Joseph Eppes. *The Sacred Pipe: Black Elk's Account of the Seven Rites of the Oglala Sioux.* Norman: University of Oklahoma Press, 1989.

Craig, Robert. "Christianity and Empire: A Case Study of American Protestant Colonialism and Native Americans," *American Indian Culture and Research Journal* Vol. 21 No. 2 (1997): 1–41.

DeMallie, Raymond J., ed. *The Sixth Grandfather: Black Elk's Teachings Given to John G. Neihardt.* Lincoln: University of Nebraska Press, 1985.

Farmer, Jared. *On Zion's Mount: Mormons, Indians and the American Landscape.* Cambridge: Harvard University Press, 2008.

Garrity, John. "Jesus, Peyote and the Holy People: Alcohol Abuse and the Ethos of Power in Navajo Healing," *Medical Anthropology Quarterly* Vol. 14 No. 4 (2000): 521–42.

Garroutte, Eva, et al. "Religiosity and Spiritual Engagement in Two American Indian Populations," *Journal for the Scientific Study of Religion* Vol. 48 No. 3 (2009): 480–500.

Graber, Jennifer. *The Gods of Indian Country: Religion and the Struggle for the American West.* Oxford: Oxford University Press, 2018.

Gross, Lawrence. "Cultural Sovereignty and Native American Hermeneutics in the Interpretation of the Sacred Stories of the Anishinaabe," *Wicazo Sa Review* Vol. 18 No. 2, (2003): 127–34.

Haly, Richard. "Upon This Rock: Nahuas and National Culture, A Contest of Appropriations," *American Indian Quarterly* Vol. 20 No. 3–4 (1996): 527–63.

Hamill, Chad. *Songs of Power and Prayer in the Columbia Plateau: The Jesuit, the Medicine Man, and the Indian Hymn Singer.* Corvallis: Oregon State University, 2012.

Hopkins, Alberta Pualani. "The Challenge of the Future: Creating a Place Called Home," in *Native and Christian: Indigenous Voices on Religious Identity in the United States and Canada*, edited by James Treat. Abingdon, UK: Routledge, 1996.

Irwin, Lee. *Coming Down from Above: Prophecy, Resistance, and Renewal in American Indian Religions.* Norman: University of Oklahoma, 2008.

Jacob, Michelle. *Indian Pilgrims: Journeys of Activism and Healing with Saint Kateri Tekakwitha.* Tucson: University of Arizona Press, 2017.

Johnson, Willard. "Contemporary Native American Prophecy in Historical Perspective," *Journal of the American Academy of Religion* Vol. 64 No. 3 (1996): 575–612.

Kan, Sergei. *Memory Eternal: Tlingit Culture and Russian Orthodox Christianity.* Seattle: University of Washington Press, 2014.

Kelley, Dennis. "Jesus as the 'Ultimate Sun Dancer,' On Being Native and Christian in the City," in *Tradition, Performance and Religion in Native America: Ancestral Ways, Modern Selves.* Abingdon, UK: Routledge, 2014.

Kidwell, Clara. *Choctaws and Missionaries in Mississippi, 1818–1918.* Norman: University of Oklahoma Press, 1995.

Kidwell, Clara, Homer Noley, and George Tinker. *American Indian Theology.* Maryknoll, NY: Orbis, 2001.

Knaut, Andrew. *The Pueblo Revolt of 1680: Conquest and Resistance in Seventeenth-Century New Mexico.* Norman: University of Oklahoma Press, 1995.

Lassiter, Luke, Clyde Ellis, and Ralph Kotay. *The Jesus Road: Kiowas, Christianity, and Indian Hymns.* Lincoln: University of Nebraska Press, 2002.

Lewton, Elizabeth, and Victoria Bydone. "Identity and Healing in Three Navajo Religious Traditions: Sa'ah Naaghai Bikeh Hozho," *Medical Anthropology Quarterly* Vol. 14 No. 4 (2000): 476–97.

Little, Juanita. "The Story and Faith Journey of a Native Catechist," in *Native and Christian: Indigenous Voices on Religious Identity in the United States and Canada*, edited by James Treat. Abingdon, UK: Routledge, 1996.

Martin, Joel, and Mark Nicholas. *Native Americans, Christianity, and the Reshaping of the American Landscape.* Durham: University of North Carolina, 2010.

McNally, Michael. *Ojibwe Singers: Hymns, Grief, and a Native Culture in Motion.* Oxford: Oxford University Press, 2000.

McNally, Michael. "The Practice of Native American Christianity," *Church History* Vol. 69 No. 4 (2000): 834–59.

McPherson, Robert, Jim Dandy, and Sarah Burak. *Navajo Tradition, Mormon Life: The Autobiography and Teachings of Jim Dandy.* Salt Lake City: University of Utah Press, 2012.

Neihardt, John G. *Black Elk Speaks.* Lincoln, NE: Bison Books, 2014.

Rivera, Luis. *A Violent Evangelism: The Political and Religious Conquest of the Americas.* Louisville, KY: Westminster John Knox Press, 1992.

Sandos, James A. "Junipero Serra's Canonization and the Historical Record," *American Historical Review* Vol. 93 No. 5 (1988): 1253–69.

Sandos, James A. *Converting California: Indians and Franciscans in the Missions.* New Haven: Yale University Press, 2004.

Schermerhorn, Seth. *Walking to Magdalena: Personhood and Place in Tohono O'odham.* Lincoln: University of Nebraska Press, 2019.

Smith, Theresa. "The Church of the Immaculate Conception: Inculturation and Identity among the Anishnaabeg of Manitoulin Island," *American Indian Quarterly* Vol. 20 No. 3–4 (1996): 515–26.

Stockel, Henrietta. *On the Bloody Road to Jesus: Christianity and the Chiricahua Apache.* Albuquerque: University of New Mexico Press, 2004.

Storck, Michael, Thomas Csordas, and Milton Strauss. "Depressive Illness and Navajo Healing," *Medical Anthropology Quarterly* Vol. 14 No. 4 (2000): 571–97.

Thomas, Robert, Jr. "Thomas Banyacya, 89, Teller of Hopi Prophecy to the World," *New York Times* (February 15, 1999). https://www.nytimes.com/1999/02/15/us/thomas-banyacya-89-teller-of-hopi-prophecy-to-world.html

Tinker, George. *Missionary Conquest: The Gospel and Native American Cultural Genocide.* Minneapolis: Fortress, 1993.

Tinker, George. "Jesus, Corn Mother, and Conquest: Christology and Colonialism," in *Native American Religious Identity: Unforgotten Gods,* edited by Jace Weaver. Maryknoll, NY: Orbis, 1998.

Tinker, George. *American Indian Liberation: A Theology of Sovereignty.* Maryknoll, NY: Orbis Books, 2008.

Treat, James. *Native and Christian: Indigenous Voices on Religious Identity in the United States and Canada.* Abingdon, UK: Routledge, 1996.

True, Micah. *Masters and Students: Jesuit Mission Ethnography in Seventeenth-Century New France.* Montreal: McGill-Queens University Press, 2015.

Weaver, Jace. "From I-Hermeneutics to We-Hermeneutics: Native Americans and the Post-Colonial," *Semeia* Vol. 75 (1996): 153–76.

Weaver, Jace. *Native American Religious Identity: Unforgotten Gods.* Maryknoll, NY: Orbis, 1998.

Websites and Films

Sacred Land Film Project, "Hopi Messenger Thomas Banyacya Sr (1909–1999)." https://www.youtube.com/watch?v=3igP8udqfaw

Conclusion

Lessons Learned

When the First Peoples of the Columbia River volunteered to be a voice for salmon—as we learned in the story that opens this book—they probably didn't realize how hard that task was going to be. They did not know about the industrial dams that would someday block the river, or that the Hanford Nuclear Site (which has been called the most toxic site in America) would be built along its shores. They did not know about commercial fishing, the impacts of climate change, ocean acidification, or any of the other factors that have made life desperate for salmon. But they did know that they had agreed to a sacred obligation, one based on the very sources of life itself: food and water. And that sacred obligation has not changed.

That story helps us get a sense of how sacred work and spiritual engagement in Native North America is not just something that happens in a church or formal ceremony. It happens in a fishing boat, or during a political protest. When writing this book, we had to ask right away: What do we mean by "religion"? Would that word even work here? As we discussed in chapter 1, in Indigenous traditions, there is no clear line between the sacred and the profane, between the natural and the supernatural, between spirit and matter. The spiritual world infuses the material world, and the heart of spiritual life is the negotiation and affirmation of relationships with that living world: ancestors, plant people, animal people, forces of nature, the Creator. Because it is all about these relationships, "religious" life happens just about everywhere: in salmon hatcheries, health clinics, kitchens, and community gardens. Wanting to upset the familiar understanding of religion, this book moved away from the classic categories that academics tend to use, instead focusing on those issues of concern to tribal communities themselves—climate change; deforestation; water rights; health care; traditional foods; the well-being of women, children, and Two Spirit people; and the church.

This book also called attention to our colonial history and how it has shaped the religious experience of Native North America. As the previous chapters show, colonialism is not a relic of the past. It did not end in the nineteenth century. Rather, it is alive within the ongoing experiences of Native people today. Its consequences continue to play out in religious life, and make clear that genuine healing and renewal necessitate genuine decolonization.

To that end, this book began with reflections on listening, on the importance of learning how to be *quiet* and heed the lessons that the natural world has to offer. Such listening might take place in prayer, in meditation, or in fasting and long solitude in sacred places. But it can also happen through scientific study or artistic work. Indigenous traditions cultivate this gift of heeding the lessons the natural world has to teach, and Native elders are calling on Native and non-Native folks alike to listen a little more closely. This book encourages members of the settler-colonial culture to try something new: to choose the periphery instead of the center, to *listen* to those communities that have historically been silenced, or talked over, or talked around, to quiet those voices that have enjoyed history's privileged position, and instead heed what Indigenous people have to say, the stories they have to tell. Because these stories can call us all to a radically different way of seeing the world.

This listening begins with the earth, the ground beneath our feet, the source of life. Instead of inert matter, religions and cultures of Native North America point to a spiritually endowed landscape, one that is sentient and aware. We find an earth called Mother, or Grandmother. We find a community of other persons, bound by kinship. We find that all living things are relations, or relatives, with obligations to one another. And we find that life is filled with incredible surprises, not a world filled with resources to be extracted and exploited, but gifts to be savored, like a ripe berry on a perfect summer day. And as Robin Wall Kimmerer reminded us in chapter 1, receiving a gift should evoke gratitude and a desire to return the favor.

In this spiritually endowed world, it is difficult, if not impossible, to draw the line between sacred and profane. But Indigenous traditions do distinguish between places that are more powerful, more sacred than others. As we learned in chapter 2, places acquire this particular potency for a variety of reasons: they may be the location of events that occurred in the mythic past; they may commemorate historical events of ancestors, where someone encountered powerful spiritual beings; or they may be locations of ancient and ongoing ceremony. They may be more sacred because of the nature of spiritual beings that dwell there, who may be powerful, terrible, healing, or endangered. Some of these most sacred sites are high places, mountaintops, hillsides, geological oddities with broad vistas, and places of remote purity and spiritual power. And yet many of these high places, and others, are at risk of being destroyed, compromised, or lost. Proposed ski developments, telescopes, tourism, mining, or other resource extraction threaten these places. Two centuries of the systematic removal of Native people from their lands, through violence, through coercion, and through broken treaties and poor federal policy have left these powerful places without protection. But where these places *have* been protected, the success often rests on the shoulders of collaborative conservation, where Native people have joined in partnership with other stakeholders. Worldviews and religious commitments may differ, but ranchers, Native people, and urban conservationists have found common ground around their love for the land.

This living earth is threatened in a new and terrible way by the consequences of climate change. For Indigenous people, the threat is particularly dire. Their ancient ties to places and to the species that have evolved alongside them in those places are threatened by rising seas, warming seasons, and changing weather patterns. The ability of people to access their sacred foods and medicines and to simply survive in their territories is at risk. Their ceremonies, cultural traditions, and very identity hang in the balance. Climate change is a *religious* concern because it is fundamentally an ethical one, and because it is fundamentally about the relationships between human beings, their Creator, and the other-than-human persons who also inhabit our earth. The global crisis is, at Richard Atleo puts it, "one of relational disharmony" (Atleo 2012, 37). At the same time, Indigenous cultures and teachings offer vital wisdom for addressing climate change and other forms of environmental destruction. Traditional Ecological Knowledge (TEK), encoded in stories, songs, and ceremonies, provides deep knowledge of ecosystems, how those systems have changed over time, and provides guidance for how to heal places and species at risk. TEK bridges the gap between Western notions of science and religion, integrating sacred teachings and spiritual awareness with careful observation, experimentation, and systematic analysis.

Traditional teachings also offer guidance when we consider the vital importance of water and the growing threat to our waterways. Indigenous communities are more likely to lack access to safe, clean drinking water than any other groups in North America. But this is an issue that concerns us all. Water is not merely a biological necessity. Indigenous traditions remind us that water is the source of life. And water is alive, infused with spiritual power to renew, restore, purify, and heal. Water is home to powerful other-than-human persons with whom we live in an interdependent web of life. Water heals in ceremony and purification rites. Water also heals through activism: transforming lives through ceremonies of protest that remind Indigenous people of their cultural foundations and their reciprocal responsibilities to the earth.

Considering this idea of religion and culture in Native North America also calls us to a radically different way of thinking about our food. In many origin stories, a people are defined by a particular food that was given to them by the Creator at the time that they became a people. Their relationship with this food makes them who they are. Like the Gwich'in who exchanged hearts with the caribou, or the Anishinaabe whose ancestors turned into sturgeon, their bond is *ontological*—meaning that it lies at the core of their very being. Elders remind the people that Creator sent plants and animals to be our first teachers, to guide us in ethical ways of living, and to instruct us in balance, harmony, reciprocity, gratitude, and respect. Abusing those resources or failing to show respect and gratitude can have dire consequences. Colonialism radically disrupted traditional foodways, fracturing these relationships and identities. But today, Indigenous communities are devoting remarkable spiritual and material resources to the restoration of traditional food-ways. Through food sovereignty movements, communities are claiming the right to access and care for healthy, traditional, and culturally appropriate foods, on their own land and on their own terms. As communities revitalize these foods, they find a key to renewing their cultures, languages, communities, and economies. Across the continent, revitalized first foods ceremonies, community gardens, and food sovereignty workshops affirm and honor these sacred relationships between Native people and their keystone species. But these traditions challenge *all* people to remember that eating is sacred work. Every meal we consume involves the giving (or the taking) of life, and in that gift lies some of the most profound of truths. We are reminded that we depend upon other beings for our life and well-being, that what and how we eat matters, and that we have a sacred obligation to care for the things that feed us.

This renewal of Indigenous peoples' relationships with sacred places and sacred foods is not just nice: it is a matter of life and death. Native people face enormous challenges to physical, mental, and spiritual health. The soul wounds of colonialism have impacted Indigenous people in devastating ways, leaving them struggling with high rates of diabetes, heart disease, substance abuse, mental illness, violence, and suicide. Colonialism is the cause of these ailments, but culture is the cure. As Indigenous people return to their traditional foods, medicines, and healing traditions, they find pathways toward recovery from generational trauma.

We have also argued that this trauma is often gendered. Colonialism upended traditional gender roles, which had ensured women access to complementary economic, political, social, and religious power. Under colonialism, Native women became newly vulnerable and found themselves in a system that targeted them for abuse. The Canadian government has launched an inquiry into the high rates of murdered and missing First Nations women, albeit with limited success thus far. But the United States continues to lag behind on this issue. Within tribal communities, cultural leaders argue that reclaiming traditional gender roles for women, through revitalizing ceremony, language, and tradition, holds promise for creating safe spaces for women and children.

Sexual diversity had once been an integral part of Indigenous communities. Two Spirit people crossed gender lines to negotiate a truce, explore artistic expressions, or go to war. But settler colonialism introduced new ways of thinking about gender and sexuality and severely punished those who failed to conform to the heteronormative standard. Only in the last three decades have Two Spirit people begun to actively reclaim their place in their communities. Decolonization takes place through the reaffirmation of the sacred feminine in girls' coming-of-age ceremonies, and in the celebration of the creative healing potential of Two Spirit gatherings.

Of course, religion and culture in Native North America is not just about reclaiming pre-colonial traditions. Christianity has become deeply imbedded in the fabric of Indigenous communities, and for the majority of Indigenous people, it serves as a source of profound spiritual inspiration, comfort, and guidance. But this new tradition came at a great cost. For centuries, the prevailing assumption had been that the gospel required complete and utter cultural assimilation into Euroamerican ways of being. Conversion to Christianity required abandoning Indigenous lifeways, relationships with the natural world, languages, foods, economies, philosophies, and social organization. It required a complete transformation, leaving the Indian behind, to become the Christian. This tragic assumption directly contributed to the cultural genocide of Native people.

Thankfully, this genocidal impulse was not successful. Prophetic movements arose throughout Native North America, calling people to retain their Indigenous identities and traditions, even as they incorporated certain elements of Christianity. By the twentieth century, Christianity had been integrated into much of Indigenous life. Sometimes it existed alongside family traditions, seemingly without conflict. Other communities found ways to integrate these two religious worldviews, bringing them into conversation, accommodation, and compromise. Others

Photo 9.1. Church, Pueblo de Taos, by Ansel Adams (1941). The Taos Pueblo church sits within the traditional community, which honors both Catholic teachings and traditional Taos practices and beliefs. (Wikimedia Commons, Public Domain, https://commons.wikimedia .org/wiki/File:Ansel_Adams_-_National_Archives_79 -AA-Q01_restored.jpg)

have entered into the church but are demanding that Indigenous worldviews and experiences be brought into the Christian conversation, and in doing so, they have transformed the face of the faith. At the Taos Pueblo in New Mexico, the church opens onto the central plaza, where traditional ceremonies are held on feast days throughout the year. Behind the church's altar is the Blessed Virgin. During a recent tour, the young man showing us around nodded toward the Virgin. "You might wonder why Jesus is in the back of the church, and the Virgin is here at the front? We Taos people honor Mother Earth, you see. So the mother is here, at the altar. We like to keep her front and center."

How to Be a Good Neighbor, and a Better Ally

After a lecture at a small university, a student raised his hand. He was not Native, he explained, but he was moved by the history of Indigenous people and wanted to do the right thing. And one thing in particular troubled him: he and his father liked to go salmon fishing and then cook the fish in the "Native way." Was he guilty of cultural appropriation? he asked, genuinely concerned. We assured the young man that cooking salmon over an open fire was not cultural appropriation. Now, dressing in a costume and pretending to be an Indian while cooking the salmon? Well, that would be something else. But the young man was also challenged to consider something else: what about if, after eating that fish, he and his father joined in partnership with local tribal communities to protect and preserve salmon? What if, inspired by that cookout, they turned their political and economic capital into supporting Indigenous fishing rights?

For non-Native people, this question of how to honor, listen to, and learn from Native North American religious traditions without being guilty of cultural appropriation is an important one. At its heart is a broader question: How ought one be a good neighbor? A good guest on tribal land? A good ally to Native people? This is an important question when studying about and learning from Indigenous cultures, particularly considering the long and destructive history of colonization, exploitation, and extraction of Native culture and knowledge by settler society. How do we respect, honor, and also learn from cultures other than our own?

Cultural appropriation is often defined as the inappropriate or unacknowledged adoption of and profiting from a nondominant culture's customs, practices, artistic work, or intellectual ideas by members of a dominant group. It's important to keep economic and political power in mind here: the detrimental impacts of cultural appropriation become evident when a *more powerful group borrows from the culture of a less powerful one.* And this is particularly apparent when it is members of a colonizing culture who are profiting from the appropriation of a colonized culture.

There are easily identifiable moments of cultural appropriation. One might envision the Plains-style headdress worn by a young white woman at an outdoor music festival. Or perhaps you've seen advertisements for a pay-as-you-go-spa-vision-quest-weekend promising enlightenment and a genuine Indian name for $9,995.

But there are far more gray areas. When are artists guilty of cultural appropriation, and when are they engaging in cultural exchange and inspiration? How does one learn from Native people and Indigenous traditions without being guilty of cultural theft? When does authentic listening become eavesdropping? When does inspiration become acquisition? For those seeking to be respectful allies of Native people and to avoid cultural appropriation, here are some helpful things to consider.

First, it is important to know that many stories, images, rituals, sacred objects, and songs are owned by individuals, families, or particular communities. They fall under traditional copyright and should never be borrowed without permission. There are other ideas, images, stories, or practices that exist within the public domain, as it were, and are not considered the particular property or responsibility of certain people. A good place to start is to consider if the action or object in question is surrounded by restrictions within its own culture: are only certain people allowed to go to this place, use this object, wear this item, or sing this song? Then a respectful ally will honor those restrictions as well.

Copying Native art, rituals, regalia, ceremonies, or songs is always problematic. Doing so contributes to a long history of colonization and cultural theft. But the line between inspiration and cultural theft can be tricky. At the simplest level, one ought to admire Indigenous creations but should never copy them or pass them off as your own creation. But of course admiring, listening to, and contemplating Native art and philosophy *ought* to lead to different ways of thinking, inspiring new ways of seeing and thinking about the world. Cultural exchange happens when we listen deeply to another culture and that listening finds its way into our own way of seeing the world, influencing the work we do. But as one's academic advisers will tell you: always cite your sources. Always acknowledge those influential individuals and traditions and whenever possible, give back.

Perhaps most important to this discussion of appropriation are questions of motivation and outcome. As others scholars have pointed out, New Age appropriation of Indigenous beliefs can be distinguished by its fundamentally self-centered focus. Its ultimate goal is self-fulfillment, fueled by a sense of personal entitlement within a spiritual marketplace. Thus, it casts a guise of spiritual altruism over what is essentially neocolonial manifest destiny. By contrast, Indigenous religious traditions are always ultimately about service to family and community. Individual spiritual growth and healing is vital—so that one can give back to and better care for one's extended family and tribal community. Indigenous spirituality is an expression of one's family and community, and ultimately belongs to that collective.

As this book makes clear, Indigenous communities *need* their cultures and traditions. It is, quite literally, a matter of life and death. Native ceremonies and sacred teachings are the peoples' best chance for healing from the devastation wrought upon them by colonialism. Non-Native people shopping in a spiritual marketplace can choose to go elsewhere. But for Native people, their ancestors' traditions are often their only and best prescription. As Arvol Looking Horse advised at the very outset of this book, non-Native allies can demonstrate their support for

Native people by staying *outside* the Sun Dance circle. Remain on the periphery. Be content to listen, to be supporting observers of those doing the hard work to recover their traditions and to heal from the wounds of what Gross has called "post-apocalyptic stress syndrome." Truly honoring Native traditions, cultures, and communities means not taking their traditions out of context, displacing them from the families and communities to whom they belong.

But perhaps a more effective discussion of cultural appropriation, instead, emphasizes what non-Native allies *should do*, rather than what they *should not do*. Those who want to honor, support, and ally with Indigenous communities should listen to their stories and teachings. They should work to apply the lessons learned in ways that are appropriate to their own cultural backgrounds. It is not a matter of cultural appropriation to honor a living earth, to acknowledge that it is inhabited by other-than-human persons who deserve our respect, care, and gratitude. It is not cultural appropriation to see the world as awash in gifts that ought to be cherished and that demand reciprocity in exchange for their generosity. It is not appropriation to consider the spiritual and cultural implications of climate change, the value of restoring ecosystems, or the sacred nature of water. It is not cultural appropriation to listen to Indigenous teachers, storytellers, theologians, and historians and to let the lessons they have to teach radically challenge the way we see the world, or the way we think about her Creator.

What non-Native allies *should do* is consider how they can put their good intentions into action, supporting Native communities as they fight to protect sacred places and safe drinking water, to access health care and traditional foods, or to ensure that Native women and children are safe from physical harm. This kind of support does not mean rushing in with answers and the promise of salvation. It means letting tribal communities take the lead and doing one's best to support their community-based efforts: because tribal communities know what their struggles are and how best to address them. Students and scholars can engage in true collaborative scholarship and learning by letting tribes set the agenda and determine parameters of research. Universities, churches, and communities can build real reciprocal relationships with local tribal communities. Future professionals can consider working with and for tribal communities that need committed biologists, nurses, teachers, and social workers who do not just stop in for an "outreach trip" but become part of the community and stay for the long haul.

Doing the Hard Work of Respect, Care, and Reciprocity

The thing about Native American religious traditions is that they're hard work. These are ways of life, and they encompass everything from running an errand for an elder to choosing how and what you eat and to how you live on the land. In the first chapter of this book, Larry Gross reflected on his experience teaching Native American religious traditions. He wrote, "By the end of the semester, I have dissuaded most of the students from their romantic notions about Indians being close to nature and instead have instilled them with a sense of the hard work and satisfaction that can come from maintaining healthy spiritual relationships with the Creator, spirits, other-than-humans, and human beings." Michael McNally comes to similar conclusions in his work with Anishinaabe people, and their traditions around honoring and caring for elders.

As McNally notes, one of the most striking things about Native communities is the respect and concern they show for their elders. In glaring contrast to the way the dominant North American culture regards its elders, becoming an elder in Native communities is something to look forward to, an honored position that comes with well-earned rewards. But McNally points out that this ethos is the result of great effort. He explains: "If Anishnaabe people do succeed in distinctly honoring elders, it is not because it is easy or natural to do so. Instead, honoring elders requires hard work, the disciplined labor of moral teaching and the ritualized decorum that constitute the authority of elders through practices of deference." The heart of this care lies with the notion of respect, which McNally defines as the ability to see someone as a *subject* and not simply as an object. Encountering another subject requires deference and care. But that sense of respect is not a human reaction by default. Rather, it is one of the primary foci of Indigenous religious traditions. This "discipline of learning" is reinforced through ritual actions, gifts, regulated speech, and behavior. As McNally writes, "One does not naturally honor or respect the other; one ritualizes the practice of it in order to make it so" (McNally, 1–2, 97, 103).

The teachings contained in this book challenge every reader—Native and non-Native—to enter into a discipline of listening; to find ways (ritual or otherwise) to honor and respect the other; to care for the elders in your life, to heed the *subject* within the natural world, and within those communities that history has too often reduced to objectified stereotypes. When we find ourselves as a person, surrounded by persons, we begin the work of entering into relationship. Being in relationship in turn requires that we consider our responsibilities to one another, and not merely to our own self-interest. This is hard to do.

Vine Deloria Jr. once asked: How long would it take for settlers to become indigenous to this place? It was probably a trick question. Indigenous cultures are born out of particular places and cannot be artificially replicated. These are lifeways and worldviews, languages, and spiritual traditions that emerged over millennia, co-evolving with their landscape. Perhaps settlers cannot become indigenous. But they can become *naturalized citizens*. How to do this? How to live in genuine relationship with our place? Kimmerer provides a compelling answer to this profoundly important question, inviting us to turn back to our first teachers, the plant people. Consider, she writes, the lessons offered by the humble plantain (*Plantago major*).

> It's a foreigner, an immigrant, but after five hundred years of living as a good neighbor, people forget that kind of thing. . . . Its strategy was to be useful, to fit into small places, to coexist with others around the dooryard, to heal wounds. Plantain is so prevalent, so well integrated, that we think of it as native. . . . Plantain is not indigenous but "naturalized."

Photo 9.2.   Broadleaf, or Greater Plantain (*Plantago major*). (Rasbak, Wikimedia Commons, Public Domain, https://en.wikipedia.org/wiki/Plantago_major#/media/ File:Grote_weegbree_bloeiwijze_Plantago_major_ subsp._major.jpg)

Being naturalized to place means to live as if this is the land that feeds you, as if these are the streams from which you drink, that build your body and fill your spirit. To become naturalized is to know that your ancestors lie in this ground. Here you will give your gifts and meet your responsibilities. To become naturalized is to live as if your children's future matters, to take care of the land as if our lives and the lives of all our relatives depend on it. Because they do. (Kimmerer, 215)

References and Recommendations

Atleo, Richard E. (Umeek). *Principles of Tsawalk: An Indigenous Approach to Global Crisis.* Vancouver: University of British Columbia Press, 2012.

Corntassel, Jeff. "Toward Sustainable Self-Determination: Rethinking the Contemporary Indigenous-Rights Discourse," *Alternatives: Global, Local, Political* Vol. 33 No. 1 (January–March 2008): 105–32.

Gross, Lawrence. "Cultural Sovereignty and Native American Hermeneutics in the Interpretation of the Sacred Stories of the Anishinaabe," *Wicazo Sa Review* Vol. 18 No. 2 (2003): 127–34.

Gross, Lawrence, "Silence as the Root of American Indian Humor: Further Meditations on the Comic Vision of Anishinaabe Culture and Religion." *American Indian Culture and Research Journal* Vol. 31 No. 2 (2007): 69–85.

Gross, Lawrence. "Some Elements of American Indian Pedagogy from an Anishinaabe Perspective," *American Indian Culture and Research Journal* Vol. 34 No. 2 (2010): 11–26.

Kimmerer, Robin Wall. *Braiding Sweetgrass: Indigenous Wisdom, Scientific Knowledge, and the Teachings of Plants*. Minneapolis: Milkweed Editions: 2015.

McNally, Michael. *Honoring Elders: Aging, Authority, and Ojibwe Religion*. New York: Columbia University Press, 2009.

Owen, Suzanne. *The Appropriation of Native American Spirituality*. London: Bloomsbury, 2008.

Rose, Wendy. "The Great Pretenders: Further Reflections on White Shamanism," in *The State of Native America: Genocide, Colonization, and Resistance*, edited by M. Annette Jaimes. South End Press, 1999.

Shanley, Kathryn W. "The Indians America Loves to Love and Read: American Indian Identity and Cultural Appropriation," *American Indian Quarterly* Vol. 21 No. 4 (1997): 675–702.

York, Michael. "New Age Commodification and Appropriation of Spirituality," *Journal of Contemporary Religion* Vol. 16 No. 3 (2001): 361–72.

Zogry, Michael. "Lost in Conflation: Visual Culture and Constructions of the Category of Religion," *American Indian Quarterly* Vol. 35 No. 1 (2011): 1–55.

Index

About the Authors

Suzanne Crawford O'Brien is professor of religion and culture and affiliated faculty in the Native American and Indigenous Studies program at Pacific Lutheran University. She received her BA from Willamette University, her MA from Vanderbilt University, and her PhD from the University of California, Santa Barbara. Her scholarship concerns health, healing, and ecological justice for Indigenous communities, with a focus on Native communities in the Pacific Northwest. Previous publications include *Coming Full Circle: Spirituality and Wellness among Native Communities in the Pacific Northwest* (2014) and *Religion and Healing in Native America: Pathways for Renewal* (2008). She lives in Seattle with her husband, Michael, and son, Declan.

Inés Talamantez was professor of religious studies at the University of California, Santa Barbara, where she created and directed the Religious Studies department's doctoral emphasis in Native American religious traditions. She received her BA, MA, and PhD from the University of California, San Diego. Her scholarship concerns the traditions of her Mescalero Apache community, with particular attention to *Isanaklesh Gotal*, the coming-of-age ceremony for young Apache women. Her tireless efforts helped to uplift the study of Native cultures, philosophies, epistemologies, and worldviews on their own terms. Having mentored dozens of students through the PhD, and influenced generations of scholars, her presence will be felt for many years to come. Notable publications include *Teaching Religion and Healing* (2006), "In the Space Between Earth and Sky: Contemporary Mescalero Apache Ceremonialism," in *Native Religions and Cultures of North America: Anthropology of the Sacred* (2000), and "The Presence of Isanaklesh: The Apache Female Deity and the Path of Pollen," updated and reprinted in *Unspoken Worlds: Women's Religious Lives*, third edition (2000). Her monograph on Mescalero Apache coming-of-age ceremonies is forthcoming from University of New Mexico Press.